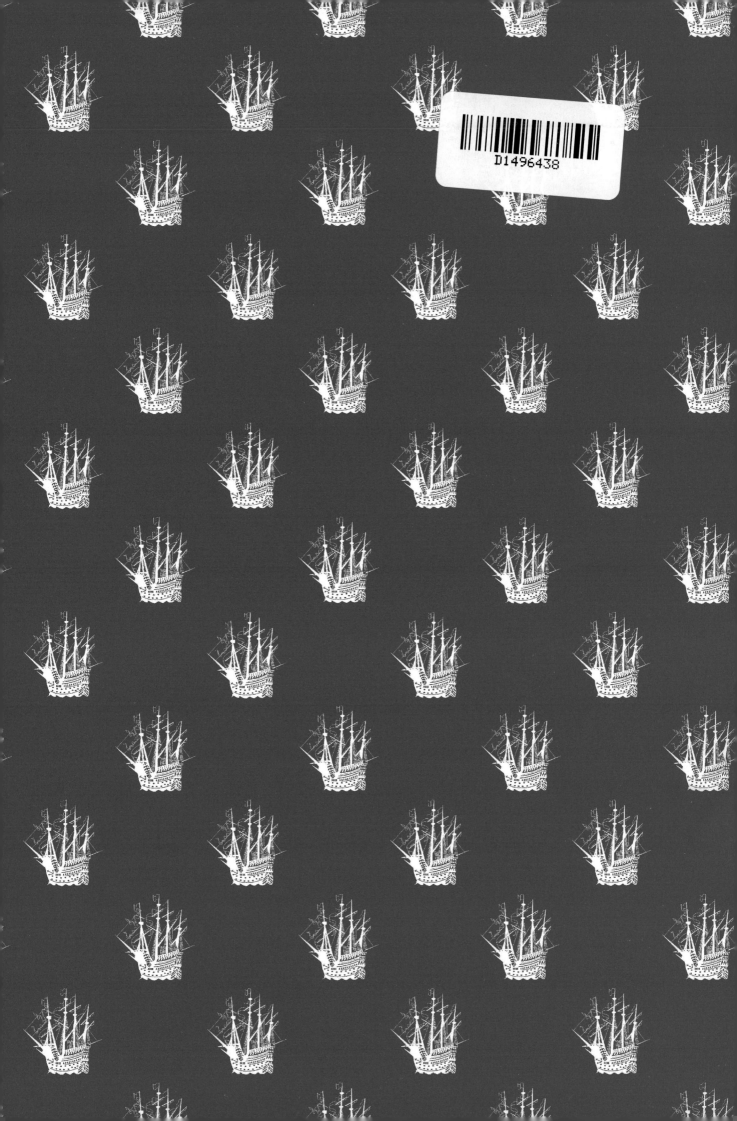

For Future Generations

Conservation of a Tudor Maritime Collection

edited by

Mark Jones

Dedicated to the conservators, research scientists
and students whose contributions have been
invaluable to the Mary Rose Project
over the last 20 years

For Future Generations

Conservation of a Tudor Maritime Collection

edited by

Mark Jones

with contributions from

Des Barker and Keith Watson

K. Collins, J. Gardiner, G. McConnachie, J. Mallinson, R. Mouzouras,

A.J. Pitman, S.B. Pointing and A. Pournou

The Archaeology of the *Mary Rose*
Volume 5

2003

Published 2003 by The Mary Rose Trust Ltd
College Road, HM Naval Base, Portsmouth, England PO1 3LX

British Library Cataloguing in Publication Data
A catalogue record for this book is available from the British Library

ISBN 0–9544029–5–2

Series Editor: Julie Gardiner
Series Editor (graphics): Peter Crossman

Designed by Julie Gardiner and Peter Crossman
Produced by Wessex Archaeology

Printed by Cromwell Press, Trowbridge, England

The publishers acknowledge with gratitude a grant from the Heritage Lottery Fund towards the cost of publishing this volume

The Mary Rose Trust is a Registered Charity No. 277503

Contents

List of Figures and Colour Plates

List of Tables

Acknowledgements

Many sections of this volume originated as internal reports produced for the Mary Rose Trust by a variety of individuals working directly for the Trust or for research organisations working with it. Grateful acknowledgement is made to the following colleagues: Dr B.D. Barker, Miss S. Bickerton, Dr R. Clarke, Dr L.R. Dean, Professor D. Cole-Hamilton, Dr K. Collins, Mr M. Corfield, Mr A. Falkner, Dr A. Firth, Mr C. Gregson, Dr D. Hamilton, Dr P. Hoffmann, Professor E.B.G. Jones, Dr B. Kaye, Glen McConnachie, Dr S.T. Moss, Dr R. Mouzouras, Mr. I. Panter, Dr A.J. Pitman, Dr S.B. Pointing, Dr A. Pournou, Professor C. Price, Miss W. Robinson, Dr M. Rule, Professor R. Thompson, Miss J. Watson, Dr. K. Watson. Keith Watson would like to thank Sue Bickerton and Simon Ware for their assistance.

I am grateful for the assistance and help provided by staff at Imperial College, University of London, the Universities of Nottingham, St Andrews, Southampton, and Portsmouth. Thanks are also due to the Leather Conservation Centre, Northampton, for their valuable help in describing current research in that specialised field.

Some of the scientific investigations I have reported on here were supported by grants from the Natural Environment Research Council (NERC), English Heritage, the Leverhulme Trust and the Heritage Lottery Fund. I am most grateful to the Heritage Lottery Fund for the generous support given to the publication of this volume and to Gill Andrews who has monitored proceedings on their behalf.

Finally I would express my thanks to Dr Julie Gardiner for her ready guidance and editorial skills and to the Mary Rose Trust's editorial board, their chairman David Price and members Professor Barry Cunliffe and Professor Seán McGrail; and to the Trust's successve former Chief Executives. At the Mary Rose Trust, much practical help accessing archive records, checking data, and providing illustrations was given by Peter Crossman, Christopher Dobbs, Andrew Elkerton and Simon Ware. Karen Nichols at Wessex Archaeology assisted with the production of the volume and Val Lamb of Oxbow Books designed the cover.

Mark Jones
August 2003

Summary

The conservation programme for the *Mary Rose* and her contents began even before the excavation commenced and turned into one of the largest and most complex programmes ever to have been undertaken on archaeological finds. Work to preserve the hull began as soon as she broke surface in 1982 and has continued ever since.

Very few of the 26,000 objects, timbers and samples recovered from the ship did not require some kind of scientific treatment to halt the effects of nearly 450 years of immersion in marine silts and prepare them for display and study. Such was the variety and immensity of the task that new methods and treatments had to be devised and tested.

This volume provides an introduction to the conservation programme devised for the *Mary Rose*. It addresses the complexities and problems facing marine archaeological conservationists. It describes the processes of decay and degradation and the results of bacterial and animal infestation that affect shipwrecks generally, and the *Mary Rose* specifically. Conservation of the hull required the application of tried and trusted techniques of wood conservation on a grand scale but the Mary Rose Trust has also been at the forefront of practical experimentation and testing of innovative methods that are described here.

A huge variety of materials was recovered: wood, textiles, leather, ceramics, glass, stone, metals, rope, pieces of sailcloth, and many hundreds of animal and human bones. This volume explains in simple but comprehensive terms the conservation methods used for treating and preserving each major category of material and evaluates the success of a variety of methods that were tried and tested.

Conservation does not stop with the stabilisation of objects. Museum display and the continuing storage of the vast reserve collection presented their own problems and requirements. The construction of specialised, environmentally-controlled cases was an essential part of the process of making the collection available for display and study. These had to be designed with provision for the control and continual monitoring of, among other things, temperature, light, atmospheric pollution and humidity as well as allowing access to the objects and maximum benefit to the viewing public. The volume discusses the requirements for display and how they have been achieved in the Mary Rose Museum.

Preface

At the time of her sinking in July 1545, the *Mary Rose* was a fully functional, fully laden, warship. She came to rest at an angle at the bottom of the Solent where she became partly buried in sediment. Her exposed parts gradually eroded away, leaving something less than half of the entire hull to be recovered so memorably in 1982, following years of painstaking excavation. It is the purpose of this series of volumes on the archaeology of the *Mary Rose* to attempt to understand and reconstruct (on paper at least) her form, construction, layout and contents and to provide an insight into how she was used and operated.

To that end, four of the five volumes are concerned with the thematic description and interpretation of specific component parts of the vessel and her astonishing assemblage of recovered objects, in order to try and piece together many aspects of the ship as a complete, 'living' entity.

This volume is rather different. Although the end result of much of the work it describes has indeed been, literally, the reassembly of many pieces, its theme is the conservation and care of all the many thousands of individual objects and ship's fittings that were excavated from the wreck – and, most impressively of all, of the hull itself. We believe that this is the first time that such a detailed discussion of the conservation of an archaeological assemblage has been presented in print. As a result, a word of explanation is needed about the ship herself as she does not appear in her complete guise in the pages that follow.

The *Mary Rose* was a carrack, a warship with four masts, two gun decks and high castles. The only surviving illustration of her is in an inventory known as the *Anthony Roll*, of 1546 (see Fig. 1.1), though the archaeological evidence shows that there is considerable artistic licence involved in this depiction. The two illustrations opposite indicate to the reader the main parts of the ship and the partially conjectured areas of stowage.

Internally, the lowest part of the ship was the Hold. Here was located the kitchen or galley, from where were recovered many objects associated with the cooking, serving and eating of food. Most of the remaining space was used for storage and for the many tons of gravel ballast that helped to stabilise the vessel.

Above the Hold was the Orlop deck, again mostly used for storage. This deck held stores of rigging and cables, spare gun carriage wheels, barrels of food and equipment and many of the personal chests of the crew.

The Main deck above was the principal gun deck, carrying a large compliment of heavy, carriage-mounted bronze and iron cannons of various types, as well as smaller guns and all the accompanying paraphenalia. The sides of the ship were fitted with gunports at Main deck level – their earliest known use. This deck also acted as a living space. There were at least four cabins: two for the Barber-surgeon, much of whose medical and shaving equipment was recovered; for the ship's carpenters, whose tools littered the cabin and filled at least eight wooden chests; and one possibly for the ship's navigators. Similar cabins were probably situated on the, now destroyed, port side of the ship.

The Upper deck was a fighting area. To fore and aft this deck was under cover, lying beneath the Fore and Sterncastles, with an open 'waist' between. Most of the forward part of the deck was destroyed in the sinking as was the Forecastle itself. The central, open, area was originally covered by horizontal 'anti-boarding' netting and it is here that some of the crew died, trapped beneath it as the ship sank.

The stern area of the Upper deck produced a great deal of archery and hand fighting equipment, including chests of longbows and arrows and staff weapons such as pikes and bills. The deck carried guns and many examples of stone and metal shot were recovered. The presence of personal and 'everyday' items such as flagons, pottery, fishing gear, musical instruments, jewellery, combs, coins, buckets, brooms and games, shows that this deck also provided cramped living accommodation for some of the crew. Examples of the latest in navigation equipment were also found together with the remains of decorative panelling.

Very little of the Sterncastle survived but at least one gun was found, on its carriage facing forwards.

Unfortunately none of the masts of the *Mary Rose* survives today, having probably been at least partly recovered in salvage operations during the sixteenth and nineteenth centuries. The positon of the base of the main mast is known, since the mast step survives in the Hold, but the position of the other three (the foremast, rising through the Forecastle, and the Main Mizzen and Bonaventure masts rising through the Sterncastle), can only be estimated from their possible fittings. The masts have not survived but many items of standing and running rigging have done and these are enabling experts to reconstruct the rigging pattern of the ship.

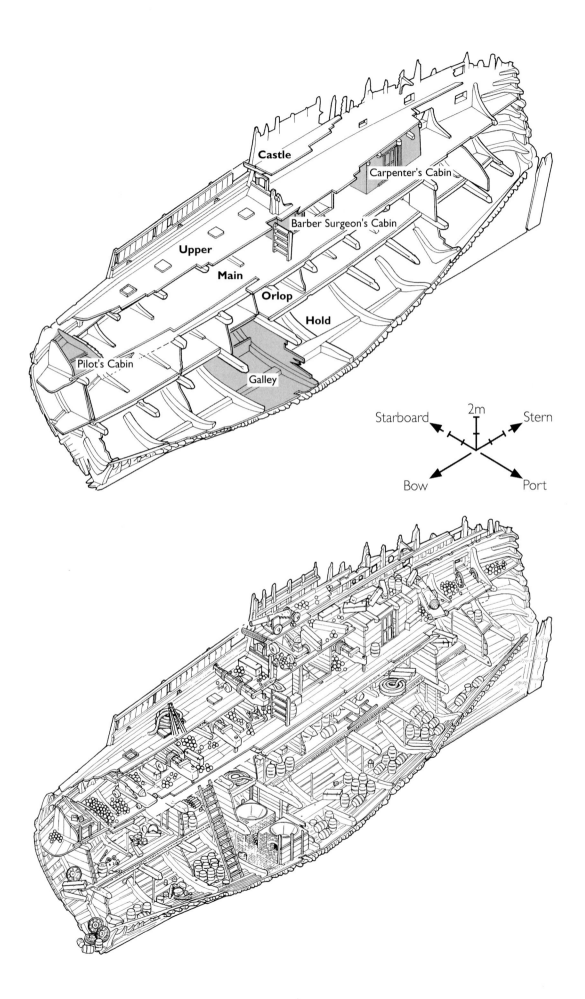

Castle

Carpenter's Cabin

Barber Surgeon's Cabin

Upper

Main

Orlop

Hold

Pilot's Cabin

Galley

Starboard

2m

Stern

Bow

Port

1. Introduction

Conservation and the *Mary Rose*

The *Mary Rose* was the pride of the Tudor navy for 34 years and flagship of Henry VIII's fleet, until she sank in the Solent during an engagement with the French in 1545. She lay buried in the seabed off Southsea, Hampshire, until her salvage by archaeologists in 1982 in what turned out to be a major media event – such was the excitement generated that her recovery was watched on television by millions, not just in Britain but throughout the world.

Excavation of the *Mary Rose* had continued for more than fifteen years from the first positive identification of the wreck site and the recovery of a fine bronze gun – that conclusively proved that this was indeed the wreck of the *Mary Rose* – to the final recovery of the excavated hull. She remains the only sixteenth century ship to have been excavated and her remains brought to the surface for conservation and display. Today the ship and collection form one of the most popular tourist attractions in southern England.

During those exciting years of painstaking work thousands of items were brought to the surface. Initially they were held in the reception areas on board *Sliepner*, the project's base vessel which was moored over the site during the dive season. There they were given immediate protective treatment to prevent deterioration while decisions were made on their future storage and conservation. From the outset it was clear that the *Mary Rose* would yield a wealth of information about Tudor life at sea from her own construction and sailing capabilities to the weapons in use during the first half of the sixteenth century. Added to that there were all the personal possessions of the men on board. These ranged from tiny paternoster beads to delicate items of clothing, plates and tankards in both wood and pewter, tools, games, and musical instruments; and even the Barber-surgeon's own chest with all its contents. Many of these finds were in an extremely fragile condition, some of them completely unrecognisable for what they were, presenting the conservators with hard but urgent decisions.

The concept of conservation is widely appreciated today, though often on the scale of landscape, buildings or the environment. Conservation of recovered archaeological remains is a specialised field essentially aimed at keeping objects from future harm, decay or loss. To recover thousands of waterlogged precious items from the bowels of a ship only to see them deteriorate because the processes needed to preserve them had not been fully understood would clearly not have been acceptable. We know that, in past times, valuable collections were lost when enthusiasm marched ahead of scientific knowledge in preservation techniques. Thankfully, those days are long gone. Since the first finds were brought to the surface in the mid 1970s the Mary Rose Trust has had the benefit of the services of specialist conservators. They have been backed up by the most advanced laboratories and scientific equipment available in the field of conservation, capable of dealing with both the immediate and long-term requirements for analysis and treatment of a huge range of items and materials. The international importance of the *Mary Rose* collection has attracted scientific expertise from around the world, sharing knowledge and experience in the conservation of unusual and challenging materials.

Everything from the minute insects that were living on the ship to the mightiest of the hull oak timbers were carefully registered and a specific conservation scheme devised. So far, some 12,000 items have completed their course of treatment but the scale of the task confronting the Trust can be gauged from the fact that there are still some 7000 objects held awaiting active conservation, of which perhaps 60% are individual ship fittings.

These objects had all been at the bottom of the sea for over 400 years and over that time anything immersed in salt water, or held in the silts and sediment of the seabed, had decayed to some extent, at a rate and in a manner dependent on the character of the materials from which they were made. Conservators working on the *Mary Rose* collection have never ceased to marvel at the state of preservation of some materials such as leather and fine silk threads, that had been able to withstand centuries buried in the silt. Once recovered, however, and exposed to the air, the decaying processes rapidly begin again, demanding immediate conservation action.

There is a story that the first object brought up from the Swedish warship *Vasa*, raised in 1961 (she sank in Stockholm harbour in 1628), was a slab of butter. After over 300 years it had become a hard, solid lump but it was not long before it began to melt. This may seem like a tall story but it is a useful reminder of the effect a changed environment can have on a prized artefact unless conservation measures are immediate and effective; it can literally vanish before your eyes. The key to successful preservation is to change the environmental conditions in such a way that decay and deterioration are halted. The task is to stabilise the material with as little loss of size or shape, colour or

Figure 1.1 The Mary Rose *as she appears in the* Anthony Roll *of 1546* (reproduced by courtesy of Magdalene College Cambridge)

texture as possible, so that the precious object can be reassembled if, as is often the case, it was recovered in a collapsed state. Only after this, which may take many years, is the object ready for study and display and, even then, the environmental conditions (such as light levels, temperature and relative humidity) must be strictly controlled if no further deterioration is to occur.

The development of conservation techniques leading to the preservation of many complex materials is an evolving science to which the Mary Rose Trust has been able to make an outstanding contribution over more than 20 years. At the Trust's Portsmouth base the largest freeze drying unit available for archaeological finds in Britain is just one example of today's technology making it possible to preserve large sections of ship's timbers as well as the myriad of smaller objects the *Mary Rose* gave up.

The treatment of waterlogged wood has been at the heart of the science and much has been learned through the programmes of research and experimentation undertaken in Portsmouth. Before World War II the most reliable method used for the preservation of archaeological wood recovered from wetlands and underwater excavations was immersion in a glycerine solution. Museums still display many examples of prehistoric wooden objects, particularly boat timbers, preserved by this means and they have stood the test of time. An improved method evolved in 1959, which replaced glycerine with polyethylene glycol (PEG), enabled large structures to be dealt with and it came into general use just in time for the biggest test that had faced the archaeological conservation specialists. The test was the preservation of the hull of the Swedish warship *Vasa*, lifted from the chilly waters of Stockholm harbour.

It was more than 20 years before the *Mary Rose* followed the Swedish ship to the surface. By then the process was firmly established and we were glad to have the experience gained by our Swedish colleagues in assisting with the conservation work on the timbers of the Tudor warship. Our professional relationship with the Swedish conservation team has been close and valuable. More recently we have been able to give them some technical help and advice when they were faced with unexpected problems affecting *Vasa*.

This volume, part of *The Archaeology of the Mary Rose*, seeks to present the knowledge and experience gained over the past 20 years conserving the incredibly fragile material recovered from the wreck after centuries buried at the bottom of the Solent. It is primarily focused at students and others concerned with the science of marine archaeological conservation. While some of the techniques used have now fallen into disuse it is hoped that the story of the 20 years since the ship was brought to the surface will help to guide others planning to recover major shipwrecks and, perhaps, caution them against setting out on what will be a long and expensive programme of work.

Advances in diving techniques and its growing popularity since World War II have led to a growth industry in underwater archaeology. Now, around the world, professional archaeologists and enthusiastic amateur divers are busy exploring the seabed and recovering valuable evidence of voyages since the dawn of history. Here in Britain we have also seen the tidal reaches of our rivers and ancient wetlands delivering exciting evidence of past human occupation and activity. It is little wonder that conservation laboratories are finding themselves facing an increasing task of dealing with the large numbers of fascinating relics being recovered. The Mary Rose Trust has recently established a specialist company, Mary Rose Archaeological Services, based at Portsmouth, set up to provide a service that is particularly directed to the world of maritime archaeological excavations. Expertise built up over the years preserving the delicate and weakened contents and the timbers of the Tudor warship is bringing an exceptional range of knowledge to the task of safeguarding other relics of our maritime history: to Iron Age boats from Fiskerton and Graveney, a 2000

Figure 1.2 The hull of the Mary Rose *on display in Portsmouth*

year old Bronze Age boat from Dover and a Gallo-Roman wreck from Guernsey, for instance. Material preservation techniques have been brought to bear on a prized relic of the Battle of Trafalgar – the fore-top sail of HMS *Victory*, found to be in a sad, dirty and somewhat frail condition, shot through by cannon balls, but now being stabilised and prepared for ultimate public display.

Recently an unexpected find has caused a ripple of excitement to flow through the archaeological world with the finding of the remains of a fifteenth century cargo vessel held fast in the mud on the banks of the River Usk, at Newport in South Wales. A rescue plan for the ship (in this case from a construction site) swung rapidly into operation. If all goes well, its recovery and conservation will closely mirror that of the *Mary Rose*, safeguarding this unique discovery too for future generations to better understand their maritime history. The Mary Rose Trust will be actively involved in the rescue plan, applying to it the Trust's long experience in the science of preserving ancient wet wood.

The aim of this book is to explain maritime archaeological conservation and those processes used and developed by the Mary Rose Trust. It is intended, in the main, for both professional archaeologists and conservators who will be engaged in the work of caring for those numerous relics brought up from the deep – the world's underwater heritage. But it will also appeal to the historian, researcher and student studying archaeological conservation. It will, we believe, also prove useful to the general reader enquiring into a

fascinating field that has been thrust more into the public eye in recent years as a result of numerous television documentary programmes featuring archaeological excavations – many covering underwater sites.

While greater emphasis has been placed on the material recovered from the wreck of the *Mary Rose*, an outline of the current state of marine archaeological conservation is also provided. The complex micro-biological underwater environment is considered, looking at the ways in which both organic and inorganic materials deteriorate over prolonged periods in sea water and marine sediments. The conditions found on the *Mary Rose* wreck site itself are examined, together with specific effects they have had on the timbers of the hull and the contents of the ship. There are chapters covering both the passive and active conservation regimes and the ongoing work treating the recovered wreck. The concentration on the treatment of waterlogged wood is particularly important given that the majority of finds are of wooden construction and the ship itself represents the largest timber structure recovered from the seabed now undergoing conservation since the *Vasa*.

But the final chapter on the preservation of the ship's timbers while she has been held in her cradle in Dry Dock No. 3 in Portsmouth's historic Naval Base must wait. We now enter the second phase of the active conservation process using a higher grade of PEG than has been used hitherto, and beyond that there will be a final phase – a period of drying out and the replacement of the remaining timbers back onto the deck structure. When that work is completed the *Mary Rose* will be made ready for display to the public in a way that we intend will excite the imagination and justify her recovery.

That is at least ten years down the line and it will not be before then that we will know for sure just how successful the carefully worked out conservation regime for the hull has been. But we have every confidence that the ship and all she contained have been preserved for future generations to study and enjoy and that through the experience they will gain a greater understanding of life in Tudor England.

Marine Archaeological Conservation

In many societies, past and present, seafaring activities have played an important role in the development of civilisation. From perhaps the the earliest days of modern man (*c.* 40,000 BC) to the nineteenth century AD, a boat or ship was the largest and most complex mode of transport taking explorers, colonisers and traders to new and distant lands.

Ever since ships first voyaged across the great oceans there have been shipwrecks and the very suddenness of such disasters has made marine wreck sites, in effect, accidental time capsules. As a result of these tragic incidents a mass of prehistoric and historic material has been deposited in the many oceans of our planet. Such a mass of material has provided underwater archaeologists and historians with a priceless collection of artefacts dating from earliest historic times (at least the Bronze Age *c.* 8000 BC in the Near East) to the present.

There is much more information in these historic time capsules than just collections of objects. The material recovered from the *Mary Rose* includes items relating to all aspects of life on board a sixteenth century warship. Their preservation is excellent and in many instances they represent the earliest extant examples of their types, providing unique sources of information for the study of human society in a specific context and time frame. Moreover, being precisely dated, they provide scholars with bench-mark examples which can be used to test and adjust chronologies and typologies. When the great Tudor warship *Mary Rose* set sail to engage the French fleet in 1545, we can assume that she was self-sufficient, self-contained segment of Henry VIII's fleet. On board were essential commodities needed to maintain a fighting ship of the realm. The hull was revolutionary in its design, one of the earliest carvel constructed warships, and the first known ship to carry gunports. She provides unrivalled evidence of ship building techniques from a period when ship plans and written evidence do not survive.

The crew and officers represented a cross-section of different social classes with class distinctive quarters and their personal possessions. Their distribution within the

Figure 1.3 Recovery of the Swedish warship Vasa, *now on display in Stockholm, Sweden*

ship may be represented even after wrecking. Information can be found about ship construction, ship life, armaments, navigation, monetary systems, nutrition, disease, trade, technology and societal and functional implications. This potential wealth of information makes this and other shipwrecks unique pieces of our maritime history.

Shipwrecks and their contents are sometimes found in a good state of preservation even though they may have remained undisturbed for many centuries. However, only rarely are ships found with masts still standing and cannons protruding through open gunports ready for action. More often all that remains are a few timbers and a small number of artefacts or, in some rare cases, the majority of the ship and its contents are found intact, such as is the case of the *Vasa* (Fig. 1.3).

The recovery of historic material from shipwreck sites will destroy the archaeological *context* of the site and relationships between parts of the ship and contents. Careful recording of all these relationships is an important pre-requisite, otherwise the operation is not considered an archaeological excavation, but a destructive salvage operation producing simply a list of objects (Hamilton 1996).

In contrast, many treasure hunters maintain that no artefact provenance other than site designation is necessary because such relationships are not important. Salvors assume that any patterned distribution of the ship's structure and her contents would have been destroyed over time by wave action and moving seabeds. This has certainly resulted in the destruction of considerable archaeological information. Permission for treasure hunting can be raised with only a limited amount of proven archaeological expertise and advice is available to the licensee. Such expeditions must be cost effective if they are to make a profit for their investors, and therefore they need to work quickly to complete excavations done by expensive equipment. This generally leads to the rapid removal of overlying debris and the destruction of non-saleable material in order to recover the more valuable objects.

Table 1.1 Recent excavations of marine sediments containing shipwreck material

Excavation/vessel	Reference
The *Vasa*	Barkman 1975
The *Batavia*	Green 1975
Zammerdam & Utrecht ships	De Jong 1977
The Bremen cog	Hoffmann 1981
The *Amsterdam*	van der Heide 1981
The Brown Ferry vessel	Singley 1982
The *Mary Rose*	Rule 1983; this series
The Gallo-Roman ships of Pommeroeul	Dewitte *et al.* 1984
The Viking ships of Haithabu Harbour	Nielson 1985
The *San Juan*	Waddell 1986
The Kinneret boat	Cohen 1991
The Dover boat	Corfield 1994
The *San Diego*	Goddio 1994

Such actions have raised questions as to the integrity of archaeologists working with treasure salvors. Some archaeologists, such as Robert Grenier, advocate the complete boycott of any group seeking to make money from the sale of marine finds recovered from the seabed. The sale of Ming porcelain recovered in 1985 from the *Geldernalsen,* which sunk in the China Sea in 1752, initiated a flurry of treasure hunting by individuals and organisations eager to locate similar wrecks (Hamilton 1996). The possibility of large revenue, either as a percentage of the artefacts or of the financial revenue from their sale, has lured many governments into granting licences (Hamilton 1996).

Marine archaeology evolved as a discipline primarily as a result of the development of the self-contained underwater breathing apparatus developed and promoted by Jacques Cousteau in 1945. This led to a rapid increase in underwater activities resulting in many shipwrecks being discovered. The first marine archaeological excavation was carried out in 1960 by George Bass and colleagues using this piece of equipment. Since then many shipwrecks and other marine archaeological sites have been located worldwide by both professional and leisure divers. As a result of underwater activity, many successful excavations of marine sediments have revealed quantities of wood materials in various states of preservation (Table 1.1).

The laws that frame the conduct of marine archaeology and the conservation of wreck material have recently undergone some important changes, both in England and internationally. At a global scale, the UNESCO *Convention on the Protection of the Underwater Cultural Heritage* was signed in November 2001. Its main effect is to give force to an international standard for carrying out marine archaeological projects. This standard is referred to as 'The Rules' (Rules concerning activities directed at underwater cultural heritage, which form an Annex to the Convention). The Rules require that proper provision is made for conservation and site management at the outset of each project. The UK Government has reservations about some provisions of the UNESCO Convention, but supports the provisions in the Annex. Meanwhile, the *National Heritage Act* 2002 removed some of the legal anomalies in England that had prevented the development of practices in marine archaeology that matched archaeology on land. Notably, English Heritage's land-based activities had to stop at the line of low tide until the 2002 *Act* explicitly added wrecks and other monuments in territorial waters to its responsibilities. The 2002 *Act* also gave English Heritage powers to support the survey, excavation, preservation and maintenance of wrecks – such as the *Mary Rose* – that are designated under the *Protection of Wrecks Act* 1973. These changes have allowed English Heritage to employ specialist marine archaeologists, as well as enabling its wide range of other specialists and professionals to address the full range of issues facing the long-term care of England's marine historic environment. Various projects are underway to develop methodologies for investigating and safeguarding archaeologically important wrecks sites, so that all those engaged in investigating our maritime past can look forward to higher standards and guidance in future.

Definitions

It is important to understand what is meant by various key terms used in their broadest sense and should read as such.

Artefact: a man made object which, over time, has become historically important.

Collection: all material remains excavated from a site and the associated records that are prepared or assembled in connection with the excavation.

Conservation: all actions aimed at the safeguarding of shipwreck material for the future, including interpretation.

Conservator: a person whose primary function is the conservation of cultural material, and who has the training, knowledge, ability and experience to carry out conservation activities. The term may also include some appropriately qualified and experienced conservation scientists, collections managers, educators and conservation technicians.

Documentation: all of the records, text, images, accumulated during the examination and treatment of marine finds; where applicable, it includes the examination record, treatment record, recommendations for future use, storage and display.

Examination: examination is concerned with establishing information on the composition and structure of an artefact, its condition and case history; identification, extent and nature of deterioration changes and loss;

Figure 1.4 Reconstruction of the Bremen Cog in Bremerhaven, Germany

evaluation of the cause of deterioration; determination of the type and extent of conservation treatment needed. Examination also includes the study of all relevant documentation.

Historic: here means 'of the past', including archaeological, palaeontological, geological history as well as more recent history.

Material remains: artefacts, object remains, specimens and other physical evidence that are excavated from a marine wreck site. Classes of material remains include components of structure (ships), intact or fragmentary artefacts of human manufacture (tools, weapons, pottery, textiles), intact or fragmentary natural substances (pigments), organic material (vegetable and animal remains), human remains (bone, teeth, flesh), environmental specimens (seeds, pollen, soil, sediment cores, bone, shell).

Preservation: all actions taken to retard deterioration of or prevent damage to marine finds and wreck sites. It involves controlling the environment and conditions of use and may include treatment in order to maintain an artefact.

Preservation in situ: all actions taken to retard deterioration of remains where they are found (*in situ*) and prevent damage to marine wreck sites through physical protection and reburial strategies.

Preventive conservation: actions taken to minimise deterioration of recovered material through the provision of optimum conditions of storage, exhibition, use, handling and transport.

Reconstruction: all actions taken to recreate, in whole or in part, the missing elements of an artefact, based on historical, graphic, pictorial, and scientific evidence. It aims to promote an understanding of an object with respect to remaining original material and clear evidence of the earlier state (Fig. 1.4).

Restoration: all actions taken to modify the existing materials and structure of marine finds to represent their earlier state. Its aim is to preserve and reveal the aesthetic and historic value of the object and it is based on respect for the remaining original material and clear evidence of the earlier state.

Treatments: consists mainly of direct action carried out on the artefact with the aim of retarding further deterioration or aiding physical interpretation.

Development of Marine Archaeological Conservation

The first complete and systematic excavation of a major shipwreck was undertaken to raise the great warship of King Gustavus Adolphus, the *Vasa*, which was found at the bottom of the sea in the harbour entrance to Stockholm and was recovered on 24 April 1961. She is the only wholly preserved ship from the seventeenth century. The decision to proceed with the lifting and recovery of this ship, with the thousands of contained artefacts, was made with the full realisation that there was little or no information available about changes that occur to materials that have been underwater for many centuries. The problems of conserving a 30m long waterlogged wooden hull or thousands of metal objects had never been encountered before (Pearson 1987).

Since the pioneering work of the *Vasa* conservators, considerable research has been carried out on the treatment and conservation of marine finds, including large wooden hulls, metals, textiles, leather, bone, rope, stone, glass and ceramics. A significant confirmation of professional progress in the field of marine archaeological conservation was the formation of a Waterlogged Woodworking Group, which was set up in 1979 to oversee and encourage research and collaboration in this area of conservation. This committee, under the auspices of the International Council of Museums, has taken a positive role in the conservation of materials recovered from shipwrecks. With the existence of this working group, the principles and practice of marine archaeological conservation have become internationalised. Over 450 references and reports have been published by workers from 30 countries in the field of wet wood conservation (Grattan 1987). There is still a long way to go before we fully understand and appreciate how materials found at wreck sites deteriorate in sea water and in the anaerobic sediments, and even longer still before we can confidently recommend a conservation treatment that will effectively stabilise the recovered material (Pearson 1987).

Marine Conservation in Practice

If a shipwreck site is to be excavated conservation must be fully integrated into the project plan. If the wreck is a designated site the applicants for licences to work the wreck must show that they have access to conservation advice. However, this is not enough, conservation cannot be seen as an optional extra, to be sorted out when the finds come ashore. Conservators must work closely with the excavation team so that facilities on shore are provided before materials are exposed on the seabed and the care of the materials begins at the point of recovery. The first stage of conservation begins before excavation commences. At this stage short term as well as long term storage and conservation facilities must be put in place to receive recently excavated material, and a conservation team appointed. The conservator should also ensure that adequate conservation material, mainly in the form of transportation and packaging, is available. An experienced diving conservator should be present on the support vessel at all times when marine finds are being recovered from the seabed. Having a conservator close by will ensure that the recovered artefacts are treated properly, and that, where necessary, the conservator can assist on the seabed. Because of the sensitive nature of marine finds to the atmosphere, all recovered artefacts should be under the direct control of a conservator until they are stabilised. It is important to keep in mind that an archaeological project does not stop in the field; it continues in the laboratory.

Many wreck site projects organise a field conservation laboratory on the support vessel or on land near the excavation site. However, field conservation facilities cannot be compared with a fully functional conservation laboratory. For this reason, field conservation facilities should be used only for essential cataloguing and documentation. Conservation begins when an artefact is first exposed on the seabed, continues through its preparation for display or storage and, from then on, as necessary to maintain it in an appropriate condition.

Artefacts need to be properly treated from the moment they become exposed to the aerobic conditions of the marine environment and steps taken to minimise both physical and biological deterioration of each find. If an artefact is going to be recovered, it must first be meticulously recorded *in situ*, securely packed and carefully brought to the surface. These are very specialist underwater techniques that require expert guidance and supervision. If the artefact is to be left *in situ*, reburial of the excavated site must be attempted otherwise the exposed find will deteriorate in a rapid and devastating manner (Robinson 1998).

Following excavation and recovery, it is important that the recovered artefact is quickly transferred to the conservation laboratory where it can be examined to appraise its condition and to identify the options for treatment first. Before any conservation treatment begins, consultation between archaeologist, conservator, finds assistants, finds specialists, and conservation scientists, corrosion experts and microbiologists is necessary in order to draw up a conservation strategy. The conservation strategy should incorporate an element of selectivity, which means that not all recovered finds will receive the same level of conservation. Finds from marine wreck sites may be divided into three categories. They are as follows:

Display conservation: work includes detailed analysis, recording, and conservation treatment (removal of accretions, stabilisation, and a certain amount of reconstruction, restoration and cosmetic treatment).

Full conservation: includes recording, analysis and conservation treatment, but with less cosmetic work.

Passive conservation: includes first aid, recording, photography, and storage under appropriate conditions.

Conservation Ethics

An ethical framework for conservators has been developed over the past couple of decades. The United Kingdom Institute for Conservation (UKIC) set out its *Guidance for Conservation Practice* in 1986 in which it promoted the concept that conservators should preserve the 'true nature of the artefact' which was defined as the evidence of the object's origins, original construction, the materials of which it is composed, and evidence as to the technology of its manufacture (Ashley Smith 1982). Ashley Smith also discussed the idea of reversibility becoming the prime objective, the idea being that it should be possible to undo everything that a conservator did to an object, however, it is now recognised that even the simplest act of conservation can only be undone to a limited extent, and conservators now use minimum intervention as their guiding principle. This does not mean that the conservator should limit the work done to an object, but that no more work is done than is necessary to secure its future and enable it to be used appropriately. The current UKIC *Ethics for Conservation* place emphasis on the conservator's aim to achieve the highest standards, including examination, treatment, preventive conservation, research, documentation, training and advice. The need to consider the relevance of preventive conservation is stressed, as is the maintenance of a balance between the preservation of objects and the need to understand them, and respect for their physical, historic, cultural, scientific, religious and aesthetic contents. Conservators are enjoined to recognise the limits of their own expertise, and that of those working for them when planning conservation work. (UKIC 1986; 1999).

Acknowledgement of the *Code of Ethics* has now been reinforced by the accreditation of conservators and the disciplinary procedures in place for those who transgress them. Outside of the UK, the International Council of Museums (ICOM) has defined the profession of conservation/restoration (a term used to recognise that in some countries the title of conservator is used by curators and restorers who do the work of conservation), and similar definitions of the profession are being developed in Europe by the European Confederation of Conservation Organisations. Robinson (Robinson 1981) set out the guidelines for conservators working on wreck sites, and has since elaborated these (Robinson 1998).

Since marine finds are the primary units of study in underwater archaeology, stabilisation treatment should not alter the natural appearance of the artefact nor alter any of its scientific characteristics (Hamilton 1996). When artefacts are conserved, the basic attitude and approach of the conservator should be cautionary. A preliminary examination of the artefact needs to be made to determine a conservation strategy that will preserve the integrity of the find and maintain any significant features relating its past history. In some cases the outer surface of a ships' timber may contain valuable archaeological data. In this instance it should be stabilised by preventing surface collapse resulting from poor consolidation. According to Plendeleith and Werner (1971), work carried out by conservators calls not only for knowledge, ingenuity, foresight and dexterity, but for infinite patience. It should never be hurried. Proper conservation of marine finds is therefore essential because it preserves the wonderful remains of our seafaring past.

Conservation of marine finds is not just a set of treatments; it goes far beyond that. Conservators are the caretakers of our cultural heritage – by preserving ancient objects for the education and benefit for all nations.

Conservation Management of Marine Archaeological Projects

In any underwater project, a team is appointed to carry out a number of linked tasks in order to achieve predetermined objectives. These tasks will be planned to take place in a specific order within time and cost constraints. Conservation management of a marine archaeological project seeks to ensure that the tasks undertaken are organised and monitored to preserve all materials removed from a wreck site. This is regardless of an artefact's condition or value, its aesthetic, historic, archaeological and physical condition (Hamilton 1996). To set up and run any conservation project effectively it is necessary to formulate and define clearly standards and objectives. It is important to establish soundly based estimates of the resources required to achieve the so-called objectives. Appointment of a conservation manager who can motivate and lead a team with appropriate knowledge and skills is vital. The manager must establish and maintain effective communication between all team members and any external consultants involved. The conservation team must operate a system of quality control and address any problems arising as soon as possible. These activities are fundamental to the success of any underwater archaeological project.

Rule (1983) identified four principal phases through which a large conservation programme would normally pass. These are as follows:

phase 1 – project planning
phase 2 – field conservation
phase 3 – laboratory conservation
phase 4 – display

Phase 1: project planning

The director of a planned underwater archaeological site should appoint a conservation manager who will, beforehand, set up suitable conservation facilities that will receive and treat recovered material. Alternatively, if funds are not available to set up these facilities, arrangements should be made with a conservation laboratory which specialises in the treatment of marine archaeological material.

At the project planning stage the following information should be discussed with the archaeological director of the underwater site (Cronyn 1996):

1. the type of materials likely to be excavated;
2. the size and volume of materials likely to be recovered;
3. the condition of materials likely to be excavated;
4. the type of field conservation facilities to be needed;
5. the type of long-term storage facilities to be made available;
6. the type of conservation laboratory to be made available;
7. requirements for display;
8. personnel requirements.

The end-product of the initial planning stage is the *project design*, a specification for conservation facilities and equipment which will be necessary to meet the conservation objectives of the project. In practice, the project design will provide a framework for the execution of the conservation programme through to completion. Even if the funding is agreed in a phase-related fashion it is necessary to have an overview of the aims and anticipated costs at the outset. Work on the conservation project design should also involve representatives of all relevant specialisms (eg, underwater archaeologists, environmentalists, engineers, scientists, artefact specialists, etc).

Once the composition of the conservation team has been established team members will wish to ensure that contact has been made with specialists who have an interest in the project. Consideration should also be given at this stage to seeking any additional academic guidance needed. At an early stage, these specialists need to be asked to identify any work which should be carried out on site, and their advice should be sought on how this should be done. While certain work can be more efficiently dealt with on site, the majority of information is best obtained under laboratory conditions.

The excavation of underwater wreck sites is costly and requires much specialist involvement. Without adequate financial and conservation resources such excavations should not be undertaken.

Phase 2: field conservation

When the conservation project design is complete, the archaeological director who is responsible for the care of the site will initiate the excavation programme. The fieldwork phase cannot commence until the proper conservation facilities are in place. At this stage, there must be a common understanding of the objectives of fieldwork between the underwater archaeologist and the conservator and of each individual's role in it. Individuals should be clear about their own role and their relationship to other team members. Recording and recovery policies and on site procedures must be fully explained, and any collective or individual training undertaken. It should be emphasised that careful records in the field are required and no amount of accuracy in the laboratory can compensate for inaccuracies, or inadequacies, in field information.

Materials, services and space requirements
All underwater projects should have a well organised field conservation laboratory near the excavation site. Depending on the size of the operation, the field laboratory should have the following capabilities:

1. simple lifting equipment;
2. labels and recording equipment;
3. a finds reception area with equipment to maintain wet condition of the recovered material;
4. large holding tanks, wrapping material, etc;
5. cleaning/washing equipment with a fresh water source;
6. a wet area for examining finds;
7. a dry area for updating records and documentation;
8. protected areas for the storage of packed artefacts and conservation chemicals;
9. packing materials such as barrier foils, polyethylene bags and sheeting and 'bubble pak'. Packing should provide a high degree of protection against desiccation and transport to the land based conservation laboratory. The system should be robust and long lasting which can continue to be used during long term passive storage;
10. cold storage in the form of a refrigerator is useful for the preservation of small, fragile organic finds;
11. suitable transport from the site to the conservation laboratory should be planned.

Equipment needed (after Robinson 1998)
Within the field conservation facility and depending on the quantity and nature of the recovered finds one should have available all of the following:

1. an assortment of clean containers of all sizes with well fitted lids. These should be watertight and resistant to a range of conservation chemicals;
2. absorbent materials, such as synthetic sponge or towelling to cover finds that will not fit into small

Figure 1.5 One of the great cauldrons from the ship's galley is lowered onto the deck of Sliepner

containers. These large finds should also be wrapped in polyethylene sheeting;
3. rolls of barrier foils, polyethylene bags and sheets to cover and protect large objects from drying out;
4. holding tanks for the storage of recovered finds which should be filled with water (fresh water if available or filtered pasteurised sea water if adequate supplies of fresh water are unavailable).
5. a supply of mesh bags to help carry containers to the seabed;
6. 'bubble pak' and foam to support fragile objects during their transport to the conservation laboratory;
7. a good supply of fade resistant, waterproof marker pens and waterproof labels;
8. lifting strops for the transfer of objects from the seabed to the recovery vessel;
9. conservation chemicals such as corrosion inhibitors for metals and biocides for organic material;
10. binocular microscope for the close examination of recovered finds.

The conservation supervisor should oversee the day to day retrieval, documentation, packing and the transport of the artefacts from the recovery vessel (field laboratory site) to the conservation laboratory. Careful attention should be paid to the health and safety warnings that accompany certain conservation

Table 1.2 Prioritising scheme developed for *Mary Rose* finds

Classification	Marine finds	Attention
Class A: highly unstable	Dye material, books or leather; skin & gut products; textiles; sailcloth	Deterioration can occur within minutes of exposure to light and air. Must undergo immediate active treatment
Class B: fairly unstable	Concretions; iron	Deterioration may occur within hours. Material must be kept wet at all times, in fresh water with a pH adjusted to a reading of 10–12 with sodium hydroxide
Class C: moderately stable	Wood; copper; bronze; brass; lead; pewter	Must be kept wet at all times. Prevent attack of wet wood by bacteria, fungi & insects during passive storage. Cold temperature (5°C) will reduce activity of these organisms
Class D: long-term stable	Bone; glass; silver; gold; stone; ceramics	Keep wet and desalinate. Some glass stable, others not

chemicals both when these are in store or in use. A risk assessment of fieldwork conservation should be undertaken before a site excavation commences.

All underwater personnel should be made aware of the requirements for *in situ* conservation – an extended delay between exposure of the material excavated to the aerobic conditions of the marine environment should be avoided. Marine finds should have a reasonable amount of deposit on them when retrieved. All marine finds should be recorded prior to lifting. Samples of marine deposits should be taken for use in sediment preservation studies. A simple lifting technique should be chosen for both complex and fragile objects. Before lifting, packing of marine finds is important otherwise fragile marine finds will be damaged during the transfer from the seabed to the recovery vessel. Robust small finds should be placed, with an identification label, into a polyethylene bag and then placed into a lidded container before being taken to the surface. A large number of individual containers can also be transferred to a crate ready to be raised to the surface by a winch or crane. Large items such as ships and guns present a additional problems and require extra support such as a lifting cradle (Fig. 1.5). Soft padding placed between the object and the supporting structure will cushion the find as it leaves the water. Lifting slings must not be in contact with the surface of the find otherwise they would damage it.

Prioritisation of recovered artefacts

As soon as marine finds arrive at the surface they must be taken immediately to the First Aid where they are formally logged, prioritised and placed in appropriate storage solutions or environments, bearing in mind that the passive storage method chosen must not interfere with future analysis and treatments. As each batch arrives the conservator at the First Aid should examine the find briefly and then determine what objects are at greatest risk during passive storage. It is essential that a prioritising scheme (Table 1.2) be operational before marine finds are recovered, identifying artefacts that require urgent treatment.

The marine finds at greatest risk are perishable items such as documents made from paper and card. These can be expected to deteriorate very quickly on exposure to light and atmospheric conditions (Robinson 1998). These finds should be stored at low temperature and kept in complete darkness. Other materials that require fairly urgent treatment are organic finds such as textiles, fibrous materials and leather (Fig. 1.6). Again, these finds need careful monitoring, and must be kept cool and in complete darkness. Other finds such as waterlogged wood and metals can be stored for long periods in solutions containing biocides and corrosion inhibitors respectively. Finds such as bone, glass and stone can remain stable for longer periods of time. They will, however, require weekly checking for signs of deterioration. Clean tap water should be used to replenish water levels. Once first-aid treatment has been carried out, the finds are then prepared for the transfer to the conservation laboratory. The finds must be packed to a high standard before the journey to the laboratory begins. Some journeys may involve different modes of transport such air freight, long sea and road transfers before reaching the laboratory. Security issues are part of this process and there are several threats that must be guarded against, such as theft. It is prudent to escort material on all transfer journeys.

Phase 3: laboratory conservation

There should be four functional zones within the conservation area: handling and wet storage facilities, treatment area, laboratories and post-treatment suites (environmentally controlled) (see also Appendix 1).

Handling and wet storage facilities

These form a key element in the conservation area and must be capable of storing large amounts of recently excavated materials.

Specification
- Convenient loading bay.
- Mechanical lifting equipment.
- High floor loading.
- Water and drainage points.
- Large floor space.

- Quarantine area.
- Large tanks.

Treatment area

This is where active conservation treatment takes place, capable of housing a range of equipment such as the Polyethylene glycol (PEG) treatment tanks and vacuum freeze-driers.

Specification
- Convenient loading bay.
- Mechanical lifting equipment.
- High Floor loading.
- Water and drainage points.
- Treatment tanks.
- Power supply.
- Daylight not essential but area needs to have good lighting.

Laboratories

These are where detailed analysis is carried out to determine the condition of the recently excavated archaeological artefacts.

Specification
- Microscopy room (light and electron microscopes).
- Chemical analysis room with fume cupboards.
- Conservation records office.
- Handling area.
- General store for materials.
- Spirits and corrosive stores.

Post-treatment suites

Following treatment, artefacts should be stored in environmentally controlled rooms.

Specifications
- Organic materials store (RH 55%, Temp. 18–20°C).
- Inorganic materials store (RH 40%, Temp. 18–20°C).

Passive storage

Generally speaking, all marine finds should, in the first instance, be kept immersed in sea water until a short- or long-term storage strategy can be formulated. Ideal passive storage systems for marine finds should:

1. maintain water saturation of the artefact at the same level as when recovered;
2. be compatible with future analysis requirements and conservation treatments;
3. prevent further corrosion of metals and decay of organic material, or at least not accelerate the existing rates of either corrosion or decay;
4. be safe, economical and energy efficient;
5. material should be accessible to conservators and specialists at all times;
6. be easy to maintain.

Figure 1.6 Leather bucket as recovered from the Mary Rose, *before conservation*

A more through discussion is provided in Chapter 3 which deals with passive storage of *Mary Rose* finds.

Conservation assessment: Before a marine find can be treated it is necessary to first identify and critically evaluate the condition of the artefact. Only after such careful evaluation can a course of action be planned. Information regarding an artefact's state of deterioration will influence the level of treatment needed to stabilise it. However, not all finds may receive the same level of conservation.

Cleaning: Cleaning should only be carried out by an experienced conservator. Over-aggressive cleaning not only causes damage to the surface of an object, but may inadvertently remove important archaeological or environmental evidence, such as identification marks of ownership or marks of wear or repair that testify to the find's use. Power tools and wire brushes should never be used. Corrosion products and concretions should first be analysed before their removal as they hold important archaeological information. Only a qualified conservator who will understand fully the risks of using such an aggressive form of cleaning must undertake chemical treatments.

Desalination: All marine finds require desalination to remove sea salts that have been absorbed by both organic and inorganic material. This is an essential process that takes place before the object undergoes active stabilisation. Desalination is another interventionist technique that should be carried out by conservators. It requires copious amounts of clean, filtered fresh water and can be a lengthy process, lasting many months to many years, where the end point must be carefully monitored and recorded scientifically (see discussion of the water cascade system in Chapter 8).

Stabilisation: The main objective of conservation is to stabilise the artefact without losing any of the archaeological evidence. Wherever possible all treatments undertaken should be reversible. Ideally a treatment used on a marine find should not cause any changes following a complete cycle of application, ageing and subsequent removal (Horie 1998). Reversibility of a treatment is determined by the properties of the polymer (conservation chemical), those of the object and how they interact.

Many treatments currently used to conserve marine finds are considered reversible which implies that, in most instances, an object can be taken back to a state that approximates to the pre-treatment state. The treatment, when reversed, should not affect subsequent treatments. For example, polyethylene glycol (PEG) is an example of a polymer which is considered reversible when used for the treatment of waterlogged wood. Epoxy resins, which have also been used in the treatment of wet ancient wood, are considered irreversible. It has been shown that only 50% of the epoxy resin can be removed by extracting in solvents (Horie 1983). In most cases where a stabilising treatment is necessary the object will be too weak to withstand the processes of removal.

The responsibility for choosing the correct treatment chemical and method of application lies with the conservator carrying out the treatment. The conservator must have sufficient understanding of the chemical processes involved to enable evaluation of possible irreversible effects.

Criteria used by *Mary Rose* conservators when making recommendations on the most suitable conservation method for the treatment of marine finds are:

1. ideally the treatment should be fully reversible and should not cause any changes to an object during application, ageing and removal;
2. previous successful use of the treatment;
3. be compatible with future treatment methods;
4. the treatment should give durability over time;
5. minimum intervention;
6. safety measures required;
7. accessibility of the object during treatment;
8. be economical and easy to maintain.

The best conservation treatment is that which interferes with or modifies the artefact to the least extent (Grattan 1987). Details of specific treatments involving *Mary Rose* objects will be presented in subsequent chapters of this volume.

Phase 4: display

Bringing a marine archaeological find to a conserved and dry state is only part of its stabilisation process. However well conserved, the artefact cannot be considered permanently stabilised, by the fact that it must be displayed to the public in an environment which has the potential to damage it further. Factors such as light, heat, relative humidity, pollution and biological organisms can affect all forms of artefacts, inorganic and organic, small or large. However, the organic materials such as textiles, paper, leather and wood are the ones which are most susceptible to deterioration by the environment (Jensen and Pearson 1987). Therefore, treated marine finds require a display or storage area which can provide the appropriate stable environment. In addition, conservators should regularly monitor the condition of treated artefacts in storage and on display. Without proper storage and display environments, the chances of long-term survival decrease over time.

2. The Seabed Environment

In the sea various micro-environments exist, each influencing the deterioration of shipwrecked material. Florian (1987) identifies five possible interfaces between shipwrecked material and the environment:

1. artefact/sea water/atmosphere;
2. artefact/sea water;
3. artefact/sea water/sediment;
4. artefact/sediment/interstitial water;
5. artefact/sediment/interstitial water below 0.50m.

It is the solid/liquid interface of the marine environment that is most closely associated with shipwreck material, since it is here that ancient wrecks lie. Therefore, the seabed environment will have the greatest effect on the degradation of shipwrecked material. To predict or interpret the changes that occur to a marine find at a shipwreck site requires an understanding of the nature of the marine environment and the chemical structure of an artefact.

The extent of material breakdown is dependent on many different and often inter-related factors (North and MacLeod 1987). Trying to predict what may happen to a specific material after wrecking is virtually impossible except in the broadest terms. Even on excavated shipwrecks where wood and its breakdown products have been thoroughly studied, it is still not often clear how certain wooden objects have become heavily degraded or why apparently similar objects are so differently attacked. From various studies of wreck sites, however, it is now possible to identify the factors that affect shipwrecked material. These factors are:

1. artefact composition,
2. sea water composition,
3. sea water temperature,
4. biological organisms,
5. seabed composition,
6. position of artefacts in relation to other ship-wrecked materials,
7. depth of burial beneath the seabed, and
8. the extent of water movement.

The combined effect of all these complex and inter-related factors means that each object should be considered individually when attempting to evaluate its recovered condition. It is the purpose of this chapter to describe the interaction of the chemical, physical and biological aspects of the marine environment with the *Mary Rose* hull and her contents. A discussion of the marine environment from the point of view of marine archaeologists and conservators need not be a summary of marine biogeochemistry. Rather, it should be a more specific description of the physical and chemical aspects of both sea water and bottom sediment. A classification of marine wreck sites according to Muckelroy (1976) is presented.

The Nature of Sea Water

Sea water is a physiologically balanced salt solution containing very high concentrations of solutes. It is a dilute solution of six main inorganic salt ions with some dissolved gases and traces of many organic compounds. In order of abundance, the major ions are Cl^-, Na^+, Mg^{2+}, SO_4^{2-}, Ca^{2+} and K^+. These ions are said to exhibit conservative behaviour because their distribution in the sea is largely controlled by physical processes such as precipitation, evaporation, freezing, thawing, molecular diffusion of ions between water masses, turbulent mixing between water masses and advection of water masses. Because the major ions are present in constant proportions, their concentrations are directly proportional to the total salt concentration, or salinity, which are reported in parts per thousand (‰). In the open ocean the salinity of sea water ranges from 33‰ to 37‰. The rest of the substances in sea water are not present in constant proportions because their concentrations are altered by the chemical processes that take place in the sea and sediment. Although most substances in sea water are non-conservative, they compose only a small fraction of the total mass of the ocean. The major classification and average concentrations of these substances are given in Table 2.1.

The salinity structure of the oceans in its broadest aspects resembles the temperature structure. Both show seasonal and diurnal fluctuations near the surface; sea currents modify both and cause mixing; both are highly variable at the surface where salinities are highest. However, salinity does not increase uniformly with depth. Temporal variations in salinity are largely found at the sea surface and coastal regions due to the influence of rainfall and river runoff (Florian 1987).

As a result of their abundance, the major ions (Table 2.1) cause sea water to have very high concentrations of positive and negative charges that results in chemical reactions which behave in a non-ideal fashion. Both major and some minor ions have been found to be important in the chemical changes that occur to both

Table 2.1 Chemical composition of sea water in order of abundance (after Libes 1992)

Category	Examples	Concentration rates
Major ions	Cl^-, Na^+, Mg^{2+}, SO_4^{2-}, Ca^{2+}, K^+	mM
Minor ions	HCO_3^-, Br^-, Sr^{2+}, F^-	μM
Gases	N_2, O_2, Ar, CO_2, N_2O, $(CH_3)_2S$, H_2O, H_2, CH_4	nM to mM
Nutrients	NO_3^-, NO_2^-, NH_4^+, PO_4^{3-}, H_2SiO_4	μM
Trace metals	Ni, Li, Fe, Mn, Zn, Pb, Cu, Co, Ur, Hg	<0.05μM
Dissolved organic compounds	Amino acids, humic acids	ng/L to mg/L
Colloids	Sea foam, flocs	< mg/L
Patriculate matter	Sand, clay, dead tissues, marine organisms, faeces	μg/L to mg/L

inorganic and organic material exposed to sea water. Increases in salinity can cause marked increases in galvanic corrosion of metals and can soften carbonate stones. Salinity will also affect the amount of dissolved gases (oxygen).

Dissolved gases

Gases are an important component of sea water. The most abundant atmospheric gases are introduced into the sea via molecular diffusion across the air–sea interface. Gases can also originate from biological activity and the decomposition of organic material. The most abundant gases present in the sea are oxygen and carbon dioxide. The solubility of these two gases decrease with increasing temperature and salinity and is dependent upon the external partial pressure and only slightly on the hydrostatic pressure of the water at different depths (Florian 1987).

In sea water, dissolved oxygen levels can vary considerably. The surface layer is well mixed by wind and water movement and oxygen concentrations are usually in equilibrium with atmospheric oxygen. At equilibrium, sea water is 100% saturated, if the saturation exceeds 100%, the sea water is supersaturated. At the sediment interface the dissolved oxygen may become depleted by the activity of aerobic biological decomposition of organic material. Oxygen is an oxidising agent (see below) and thus takes part in many reactions. Moreover, it is the absence or presence of dissolved oxygen in sea water which has the basic

control of organism activity and thus plays a key role in the deterioration of shipwrecked material.

The source of dissolved carbon is the atmosphere, and it is a by-product of respiration by marine animals and aerobic micro-organisms. Unlike oxygen, carbon dioxide reacts chemically with sea water as shown in (1) below:

$$CO_2 + H_2O \Leftrightarrow H_2CO_3 \Leftrightarrow H^+ + HCO_3^- \Leftrightarrow 2H^+ + CO_3^{2-} \quad (1)$$

This is called the carbon dioxide–carbonate equilibrium system and is the most important and complex system in the oceans. It controls the alkalinity of sea water, acts as a buffer system to maintain the pH of sea water, and controls the deposition of marine sediments, all of which will directly influence buried artefact material.

Alkalinity and pH of sea water

The precipitation and dissolution of calcium carbonate is governed by equilibrium reactions that stabilise the pH of sea water. These reactions are also responsible for controlling the solubility of atmospheric carbon dioxide gas within it. Sea water is a buffered, slightly alkaline solution and its pH ranges from 7.5 to 8.5. When in equilibrium with the carbon dioxide of the atmosphere, the pH increases slightly to 8.5. The removal of carbon dioxide by photosynthetic processes of marine algae can increases the pH to around 9.3. Should anything occur to increase the temperature or salinity or to raise the pH, carbonates will be precipitated, usually in the form of calcium, magnesium and/or strontium carbonate. It is important to note that sea water is supersaturated with respect to calcium carbonate.

Carbonate concretions often cover inorganic artefact material recovered from wreck sites. There are four ways in which these concretions may be formed:

1. by the growth of marine fouling animals on the surface of an artefact (physical process);
2. by the re-precipitation of carbonates (physio-chemical process);
3. by precipitation on the cathodic and anodic areas of metals undergoing corrosion (electrochemical process);
4. by bacterial precipitation of calcium carbonate on the surface (biochemical process).

The carbonate buffer system in the oceans results in the formation of concretions. Greater details of their formation are discussed in Chapter 5.

The stability of shipwrecked materials is greatly affected by pH: some materials are stable at neutral, some at acid and some at alkaline pH. For example, either a low (acid) or a high (alkaline) pH can accelerate the hydrolysis of organic material such as cellulose, which is affected by low pH and proteins being particularly susceptible at high pH. Metal such as iron dissolves away when the pH falls below 5.5.

Oxidation and reduction in sea water

In sea water, dissolved oxygen concentrations can vary widely. Oxygen-saturated sea water is strongly oxidising whereas sea water depleted in oxygen is a reducing environment. Reducing regions occur near the sediment interface. Oxidation and reduction reactions are considered as the transfer of electrons from one atom to another, reduction being the gain of electrons and oxidation being the loss of electrons. Thus many oxidation reactions do not involve molecular oxygen at all.

The energy involved in adding electrons (reduction) or in removing electrons (oxidation) is the oxidation-reduction (redox) potential. The redox potential (Eh), is a quantitative measure of reducing and oxidising strengths. This is usually measured with an Eh meter or a pH-Eh meter. The Eh range (given in millivolts) for marine environments can be categorised as follows:

Oxidising deposits: +700 to +400 millivolts
Moderately reducing deposits: +400 to +100 millivolts
Reducing deposits: +100 to -100 millivolts
Strongly reducing deposits: -300 to -100 millivolts

It should be noted that the redox potential of sea water is related to pH, since hydrogen ions can participate in oxidising reactions by accepting electrons. If the pH of a system rises, the redox falls. The interplay of pH and redox potential is important in predicting the stability of chemicals. Pourbaix diagrams are widely used in the study of corrosion of metals at wreck sites. This is discussed in Chapter 5.

The Nature of Sediments

Marine sediments are made up of unconsolidated particles that blanket the bedrock of the sea floor. They vary greatly in chemical composition, particle size, origin, sedimentation rate and geographical distribution. These characteristics are commonly used to classify marine sediments.

Sediments can also be categorised on the basis of grain diameter. Since grains are often irregularly shaped, the longest diameter is used to classify the particle as either clay, silt, sand, granule, pebble, cobble or rock (Pournou 1999). For the marine archaeologist whose wreck has come to lie on the bottom, it may be appropriate to modify this categorisation and refer to the seabed sedimentary particles as rock, sand, silt or clay. Note that this classification scheme conveys no information on the mineral composition of the particles.

Rock. A wreck that comes to rest in a rocky seabed area stands the greatest chance of physical break up. The movement of water around the rocks will carry off much of the shipwreck debris, while smaller artefacts may be washed into small crevices where some form of protection is provided.

Sand. A sandy bottom is often exposed to currents, which sweep across the site. This can lead to the rapid erosion of objects in or above the shifting sand. At these sites, mechanical damage and abrasion are the main causes of surface deterioration of both inorganic and organic material. Generally speaking, artefacts do not survive long under these conditions unless they remain buried. Exposed objects such as metal artefacts are subject to a form of sand blasting and this can be most pronounced with copper alloys (eg, bronze guns) where the formation of protective marine growths is limited due to the release of copper ions which are toxic to fouling organisms.

Silt. Slightly less extreme are those sites that comprise predominantly silts. Being of smaller grain size, silts do not settle where underwater currents are strong; hence objects found buried in silts will probably not have suffered surface erosion by water movement. If there is no chemical action on it, an object buried in the silt should be in a good state of preservation.

Clay. Clay minerals are crystalline, layered aluminosilicates. Because of its colloidal properties and small grain size, clay binds tightly any artefact buried in it, any movement being completely restricted. Generally, artefacts will rest on top of a clay bottom within an overlay of fine silt.

Diagenesis

Upon reaching the seabed, particulate matter is subject to physical, chemical and biological changes that are collectively referred to as diagenesis. The controlling factors in the diagenesis of marine sediments are the solid–liquid exchange phenomena, pH, redox potential and the various organic metabolic processes. These complex interactions can cause different chemical micro-environments, which change the nature of the sediment and the composition of interstitial water. The Eh and pH will control the nature of the mineral species in the sediments and, subsequently, will influence the degradation of artefact material. Where the redox potential is greater than +200 millivolts the stable form of iron is red-brown iron (III) oxides whereas, if the potential is less than + 200 millivolts, it is black iron (II) oxides. The reduction of iron (III) oxides to iron (II) oxides greatly increases its solubility. It will be released to the surface waters where the metal ions may be adsorbed in organic artefact material where they stain surfaces, especially pale porous material such as ceramics. The interstitial water found between sediment particles has a higher salinity than sea water. This is due to the upward movement of free water, compaction and the adsorption of hydrated ions on sediment particles. It is these changes that play an important role in the deterioration of buried artefact material. Deterioration of certain wreck material is often greater in sediments than in overlying water. Metal artefacts in particular show accelerated corrosion at the mud line due to oxygen gradients and the presence of reducing bacteria. Glass objects buried in recent sediments show greater deterioration than suspended or deeply buried glass (Florian 1987). Wood also undergoes chemical leaching in the sediment, the effects of which are presented in Chapter 4.

Biology of Marine Wreck Sites

All species of marine organisms inhabit the seas within preferred temperature and depth zones. Describing their habitats by their position or proximity to the coast may be a useful indicator of organisms that inhabit wrecks that are located in these zones. Species can be assigned to the following categories:

1. *Pelagic or oceanic species*: inhabit the open oceans and do not come near land, continental shelves or the seabed;
2. *Offshore species*: inhabit depths of water between 50m and 200m, these species seldom come near land but are not truly pelagic.
3. *Inshore or coastal species*: organisms found only near coastlines in depths of water less than 50m;
4. *Littoral species*: found close to the coastal fringe and therefore only occur in shallow depths. Many intertidal organisms fall into this category.

Plants and animals that float or swim in the seas are called 'pelagic'. Only those creatures that live in the open oceans well away from the coastlines, continental shelves and the seabed are said to be truly pelagic. Organisms, which inhabit the seafloor are called 'benthic'. Animals that live within the bottom substrates (including shipwreck material) are known as 'infauna' and animals that crawl over the bottom are the 'epifauna'.

It is thought there are only 16,000 species of plants and animals that live in the marine environment despite the large area of the surface of the earth that is covered by ocean. However, the large populations of some groups such as pelagic copepods (minute relatives of crabs and shrimps including plankton) and benthic molluscs compensate for this lack of species diversity. Within the marine environment only 3000 or so species live in the open oceans. The rest of the animals live on or close to the bottom.

In the context of marine wreck sites, the most significant bio-active organisms are, as a whole, anaerobic and aerobic bacteria, marine fungi, wood- and stone-boring animals and fouling organisms.

Fouling organisms

These organisms are the first colonisers of shipwreck material. A limited survey of wrecks by the Woods Hole Oceanographic Institute listed 300 species present (Anon 1952). A typical fouling community can include aerobic bacteria, protozoans, actinomycetes, diatoms, fungi, macro-algae, hydroids, bryozoans, ascidians, serpulids, isopods and molluscs. The diversity and quantity of organisms present on shipwrecked material is variable because of the seasonal sequence of growth and environmental parameters essential for growth. All fouling organisms require aerobic conditions to develop and grow and therefore do not survive in anoxic sediments (ie sediments devoid of any oxygen).

The growth of marine organisms on artefact surfaces is considered a very important factor in the protection of newly exposed wreck material. First, fouling organisms can provide a physical protective barrier between artefact and the sea water. This barrier can reduce considerably the erosion of artefact surfaces by seaborne sand and grit. A second effect of fouling is that the transfer of chemical species between the artefact and the open sea water is drastically reduced. Some fouling organisms such as bacteria and fungi can cause severe chemical and physical changes to artefact material. These reactions are discussed in detail in Chapter 3.

Marine bacteria

Bacteria are early colonisers of wreck material exposed to sea water. Their role as agents of decay is extremely important in the recycling of organic material that enters the sea. These organisms constitute a group of single celled entities only a few microns in size; the largest populations are found in the sea water/sediment interface. There may be as many as one million in a gram of oxygen-rich surface sediment (Fig. 2.1).

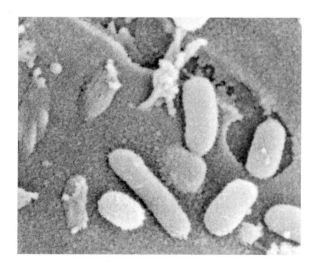

Figure 2.1 Scanning Electron Microscope (SEM) image showing attack of wood cell wall by bacteria (x7500)

In surface sediments with high concentrations of dissolved oxygen, aerobic bacteria are dominant. As oxygen becomes depleted by aerobic oxidation of organic material, facultative bacteria (ie ones which are normally anaerobic but which can tolerate oxygen) become dominant and finally, under anoxic conditions, anaerobic bacteria are dominant. Aerobic bacterial populations are greatest in the first 25mm of sediment and decrease at the 100mm level. Anaerobic bacteria at the *Mary Rose* site have been recorded at depths of 3m beneath the seabed surface. It seems likely that these micro-organisms could lie active at greater depths within the seabed sediments. In terms of deterioration, breakdown of organic material occurs over a shorter time-span than inorganic (abiotic) degradation. Bacterial presence may not be visible to the naked eye, but they can often be smelt in sediments as they give off distinctive odours (rotten egg smell). Bacteria secrete enzymes which are capable of breaking down a number of organic substrates such as wood.

The role of bacteria in the deterioration or change of artefact material is extensive. The following is a list of only a few specific examples involving wood and metal artefact material.

1. Bacterial infauna are the major agents of wood decay in anaerobic marine sediments. The nature of such degradation may vary with the water chemistry of the burial environment and the anatomy and chemistry of the wood. Degradation features are most pronounced at the cellular level. The first stage in the abiotic degradation of hardwoods is the swelling of the secondary wall, this loosens the wall structure and exposes hemicellose to degradation (Hoffmann and Jones 1990). This swelling has not been observed on abiotically degraded softwoods. Degradation of the S_2 and S_3 layers leads to a loss of crystalline cellulose structure, complete cellulose breakdown results in a lignin skeleton remaining.

2. In sea water and aerobic sediments, bacteria are minor agents of wood decay. The nature of such degradation results in a loss of polysaccharides and an increase in lignin as a percentage of dry weight is typical. The breakdown of lignin in oxygenated sea water has not been demonstrated and is thought possible only after chemical modification or de-polymerisation.

3. Sulphate reducing bacteria such as *Desulphovibrio* spp. are involved in the corrosion of metal artefacts. In anaerobic sediments, they reduce sulphates to sulphides, their activity often being detected by the smell of hydrogen sulphide ('bad eggs'). Hydrogen sulphide accelerates the corrosion of copper base alloys by the substitution with sulphide for the more protective oxidised corrosion products that form on copper alloys in oxygenated sea water.

Marine fungi

The importance of marine fungi as recyclers of lignocellulose or as potential bio-deteriogens of wooden structures is well documented (Mouzouras *et al.* 1986). Generally, it is accepted that wood decay falls into three taxonomically unrelated categories; brown rot, white rot and soft rot. The former two types are caused by species of the Basidiomycotina, whereas the latter is caused by members of the Ascomycotina and Deuteromycotina.

Brown rot
Hyphae of brown rot fungi penetrate into the wood cell lumina through pits and then lie in the lumen of the cell (Bravery 1971). They are only capable of degrading cellulose and hemicelluloses of the wood cell wall, leaving lignin relatively unaltered (Kirk 1973) and maintaining the shape of the wood cell. The wood rapidly becomes brittle, later becoming discoloured and finally brown and soft. On drying, extensive checking occurs across the grain giving a cubical pattern and finally the wood crumbles. Brown rot has not been reported in the marine environment.

White rot
Hyphae of white rot fungi (Fig. 2.2) also penetrate cell walls through pits and bore hole formation and eventually lie in the lumen of the cell (Bravery 1971; 1976). In contrast to brown rot fungi, where the degrading agents completely penetrate the ligno-cellulose matrix, activity of white rot fungi results in the progressive thinning of the wood cell wall from the lumen inwards. Later in the decay process, the troughs may coalesce and lysis proceeds inwards from the S_3 to the S_2 (for explanation see Fig. 4.5, etc). Lignin is degraded extensively by white rot fungi (Kirk 1973).

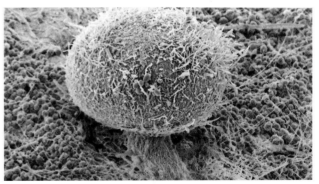

Figure 2.2 Basidiocarp (fruiting structure) of the white rot fungus Nia vibrissa *found growing on oak staves (SEM) (x18)*

Soft rot
Soft rot fungi grow within the S_2 layer of the wood cell wall forming distinct cavities (Fig. 2.3). The term 'soft rot' was first suggested by Savory (1954) on account of the softening produced in the surface layers of wood by the activity of these fungi. Soft rot cavity formation

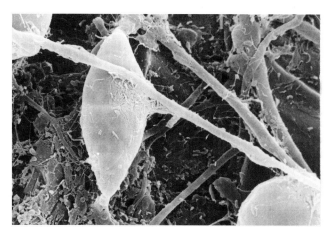

Figure 2.3 Ascospore (fruiting structure) of Nereiospora cristata *(soft rot fungus) attached to the surface of oak (ship's timber) (SEM)*

commences when a hypha lying in the wood cell lumen sends a fine hyphal branch through the S_3 into the S_2 layer. In this layer the penetration hyphae branches bi-directionally, with each branch growing parallel to the cellulose microfibrils, and enzymatic dissolution of the S2 layer ensues. This produces a cavity with conical ends; further cavities may occur to produce chains of discrete cavities (Corbett 1965). Lignin remains unaffected by the activities of soft rot marine fungi. This group plays an important role in the decay of wooden artefacts in the marine environment.

Fungal colonisation of wood in the sea has been more extensively studied than it has, for instance, in textiles (Kohlmeyer and Kohlmeyer 1970). The number of lignicolous species described total around 150. So far, 84 species have been tested and 63 have the ability to decay wood. The work of Mouzouras (1990) has shown that the most successful group of lignicolous fungi are those which cause soft rot decay of wood. To date, 58 marine fungi have been shown to cause type I (cavity) soft rot attack of wood, while three basidiomycetes have been shown to cause white rot decay. As stated above, brown rot of wood in the marine environment has yet to be reported. In the case of large dimension timbers, only marine fungi can penetrate deeply into the wood, for bacteria do not possess this capability. Marine fungi growing within the wood cell wall are better adapted for the aquatic environment since their enzymes are not susceptible to dilution. Also, the morphology of fruiting structures such as ascopores and conidia of many species are small and more persistent. They are not affected by low oxygen tensions, since they preferentially degrade cellulose through a non-oxygen demanding process (Levi and Preston 1965).

All marine fungi grow in aerobic environments and require dissolved oxygen levels greater than 0.3ml/L. In general, fungi can grow in more acidic conditions than other micro-organisms, but they flourish at near neutral pH. A more detailed account of their role in the decay of wooden material such as the *Mary Rose* hull is discussed in Chapter 4.

Marine borers

Several marine organisms are responsible for heavy losses of wood exposed in sea water. These organisms may cause severe damage to wooden artefacts in a relatively short period of time. Intensity of wood attack by borers varies in different regions, but is generally more severe in tropical than in temperate waters: even the naturally resistant wood species, such as greenheart, may have a very short service life in some tropical areas. The damage done usually takes the form of tunnelling, either vertically or horizontally, into wooden artefacts, and this may be so extensive as to destroy the object completely. Two main groups of marine borers are the agents of deterioration, the crustaceans and the molluscs. They do not live in anaerobic conditions and require oxygen for all bodily functions.

Crustaceans
The majority of the wood boring and wood inhabiting crustaceans are members of the Isopoda and include the Limnoriidae (gribble; Fig. 2.4) and the Sphaeromatidae (pill bugs). The remaining group, the Cheluridae, are members of the Amphipoda and include the genus *Chelura* which is commonly associated with limnoriid attack of wooden archaeological material.

In terms of decay of wooden artefacts, isopods are more destructive and the most important group genera are the *Limnoria*. There are around 19 species of *Limnoria* with many of them occurring in cool, temperate and warm waters. Of these, three species are considered to be the most destructive in wood: *L. lignorum* which occurs in colder waters; *L. quadripunctata* which is found in temperate waters; and *L. tripunctata* which has been recorded in both temperate and tropical waters. The most destructive *Limnoria* is *L. tripunctata*. Limnoriids are small animals, generally 2–4mm in length and greyish white in colour. They excavate long narrow tunnels 1–2mm in diameter, with regularly spaced respiration holes to the artefact surface. In softwoods, *Limnoria* spp. preferentially bore into earlywood leaving the latewood irregularly perforated,

Figure 2.4 The marine crustacean Limnoria *sp. inhabiting exposed* Mary Rose *timbers (SEM) (x10)*

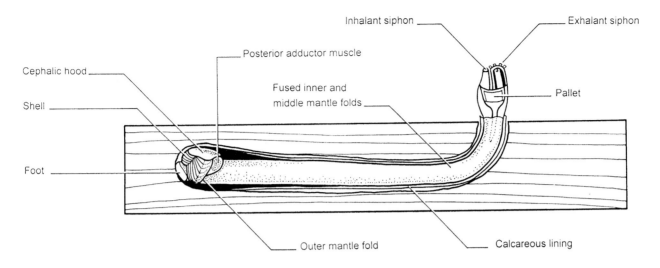

*Figure 2.5 Diagram of an entire organism (*Teredo *sp.) showing relative physical position of shell, pallet and siphons (after Turner 1966)*

resulting in characteristic concentric zones of deterioration. Underwater currents on *Limnoria* infested artefacts remove the superficial degraded surface layers allowing borers to penetrate even deeper into the wood.

Temperature affects the reproductive and boring activity quite considerably. The cold water species *L. lignorum* does not develop at temperatures above 20°C and reproduction only begins when temperatures reach 10°C. In contrast, *L. tripunctata*, which is found predominantly in warmer waters, has an optimal activity at 22–26°C. However, the tunnelling activity of *Limnoria* species declines markedly when temperatures fall below 10°C. Changes in salinity also affect *Limnoria* spp. but they will normally grow to tolerate sea water concentrations of 14–18‰ for short periods only (Eaton and Hale 1993).

Members of the Sphaeromatidae produce a distinct honeycombed pattern in wood. They are more important in tropical regions, especially in brackish waters. Animals such as *Sphaeroma* spp. can reach a length of 10mm and, when fully matured, the diameter of channels found in wood can reach up to 6mm (Becker 1971).

The amphipod family Cheluridae is the smallest group of important wood boring crustaceans. There are three *Chelura* spp. and in natural situations they are associated with *Limnoria*, usually enlarging their tunnels (Kuhne 1966; 1971). Their tunnels are longer and wider than those of *Limnoria* and when both crustaceans are present, *Chelura* occupies the outer zone while *Limnoria* migrates deeper into the wood (Becker 1971).

Molluscs

There are only two groups of bivalve molluscan wood borer: the Teredinidae (ship-worm) and the Pholadidae. The Teredinidae is by far the larger of the groups and include members which have a world-wide distribution within a given climatic range. The best known ship-worm *Teredo* (Fig. 2.5), is of great importance in many

seas of the world as a destroyer of wooden hulled ships and harbours (Hickin 1968). The free swimming larvae are produced in hugh quantities and actively swim in search of wood. On contact with wood, the larvae attach and then start to burrow. The animal remains in the same tunnel throughout its life and a calcareous deposit is laid down lining the tunnel. The animal can attain a length of 450mm or so, and its burrows can be up to 40mm in diameter. The only signs of external damage are the small openings in the wood made by the larval stage when they first bored in.

The pholads and piddocks are bivalve molluscs, which also bore into wood, but also include genera more commonly found boring into soft carbonate rocks by the rasping action of their shell. The Pholadidae are more restricted in their occurrence than the Teredinidae and are found mainly in warm temperate and tropical waters. Piddocks have been found at depths of up to 2000m. The tunnels produced by these animals are approximately 5–10mm in diameter and range in depth from three to eight times the length of the shell.

Archaeology of Marine Wreck Sites

A shipwreck is an event by which a highly organised and dynamic assemblage of artefacts is transformed into a disorganised and static state with varying lengths of stability (Muckelroy 1978). An organised assemblage such as a ship and its contents will have passed through numerous processes to produce the collection of items excavated on the seabed. Both ship and its contents will have undergone a series of transformations through time, emerging as the results of an excavation.

Although underwater wreck sites may be located in different geographical parts of the sea, several factors influencing the survival of archaeological material at any particular site may be similar. Just as the nature of a ship involves basic common concepts, so the phenomenon of

Table 2.2 The five main classes of wreck sites
(after Muckelroy 1976)

Class	Hull preser-vation	Organic artefact survival	Inorganic artefact survival	Assemblage distribution
I	Extensive	Many	Many	Coherent
II	Elements	Some	Many	Scattered, ordered
III	Fragments	Some	Many	Scattered, ordered
IV	None	Few	Some	Scattered, disordered
V	None	None	Few	Scattered, disordered

the shipwreck process must involve regular features common to all instances (Muckelroy 1978). The following is a list of the most important factors involved in the transformation of a ship and her contents over time:

1. The nature of the seabed deposit is the main determining factor in the survival of archaeological material. Factors which are considered important in the process of wrecking include the slope of the seabed, particle size of seabed sediments, sedimentation rates, the degree of compaction, composition of interstitial water and sediment diagenesis. Ancient remains are more likely to be preserved within soft substrates than within rocky ones (see above). A wreck that lands in a rocky area stands the greatest chance of physical break-up.

2. The strength of tidal currents over a wreck site. At sites in high surge areas, the current and wave action is so strong that the ship and its contents are physically rolled and bumped back and forth across the seabed. Ships and artefacts will not survive long under these conditions. Slightly less extreme are sites where underwater currents are not strong

enough to lift the ship or artefacts but are fast enough to pick and carry sand, grit, shells, etc. Under these conditions a ship and its content are subject to a form of sand blasting and this can cause very rapid erosion of surfaces.

3. Weather conditions can also have an impact on the survival of materials which lie in sheltered areas. Artefact survival is good in sheltered areas where the disturbance of protective sediments is low. Wreck material exposed to very frequent stormy conditions will have a low chance of survival. In these areas, seabed sediments are unlikely to be built up over wreck material lying on the seabed.

4. Many wrecks occur in shallow waters (0–100m) but some archaeological material is occasionally recovered from vessels at much greater depths. At deep water wreck sites, where underwater forces are less aggressive than those encountered in shallow waters, organic artefact material is usually found in a good state of preservation (temperature and dissolved oxygen levels are low). The presence of high pressures will also prevent the formation of protective corrosion product films.

5. Biological activity at the wreck site is also an important criterion in the survival of archaeological remains. In the marine environment biological organisms are restricted in their distribution by environmental parameters such as dissolved oxygen, salinity, temperature, depth, pressure, currents, nutrients and sediment characteristics. In general terms, sites which exhibit high aerobic biological activity are more likely to have less preserved archaeological material than the anoxic sediments of the seabed. Within these sediments, deterioration of both organic and inorganic artefacts is far less than in the overlying water.

As a result of numerous studies investigating the process of artefact preservation at wreck sites, certain general conclusions can be reached (Muckelroy 1976). Underwater wreck sites in the marine environment can

Table 2.3 Physical, chemical and biological characteristics of the five classes of wreck sites described in Table 2.2

Class	Seafloor type	Slope	Underwater currents	Biozone	Dissolved oxygen	Redox potential	pH	Organisms
I	gravel–clay	minimal	weak	sediment/below 1.0m	zero	-0.4	7.0–7.5	anaerobes
II	boulders–silt	<2°	weak–moderate	sediment/below 0.5m	zero–1cc/L	-0.3–0.1	7.0–7.5	anaerobes
III	boulders–silt	<4°	moderate	sediment/open circulation	zero–6cc/L	-0.3–0.3	7.0–8.2	anaerobes/aerobes
IV	boulders–sand	<6°	moderate–strong	open circulation	6cc/L	0.1–0.3	7.0–8.2	aerobes
V	boulders–gravel	>6°	strong	open circulation	6cc/L	0.1–0.3	7.5–8.2	aerobes

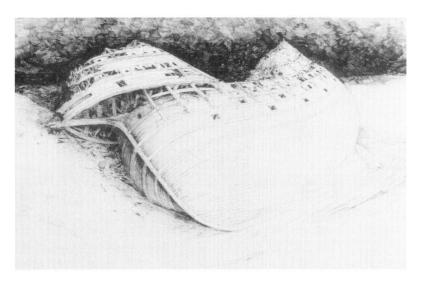

Figure 2.6 Artist's impression of the Mary Rose *on the seabed (Courtesy of Jon Adams)*

be divided into five classes and this classification has proved useful in a number of contexts (Table 2.2).

Arising from, and making use of, this classification, a series of general statements regarding the environmental characteristics appropriate to each class is proposed and given in Table 2.3. The classification has been compiled in such a way that every site can be accommodated within specifications for the appropriate class under a number of headings. This table can be used in a predictive sense, in assessing the preserving potential of a newly discovered and as yet undiscovered site.

The Sinking of the *Mary Rose*

Between 1509 and 1512 the new king, Henry VIII, ordered at least seven ships to be built, as part of a major programme of re-armament. One of these ships was the *Mary Rose*, which was named after the King's favourite sister, Mary. The *Mary Rose* was built between 1510 and April 1512. In July 1511 the 600 ton carrack made her maiden voyage to the River Thames where she was completely fitted out and made ready for war (see *AMR* vol. 1). The ship was built almost entirely of oak with a tripartite elm and oak keel and she was strengthened many times between 1511 and 1545. She is variously described as having been armed with 78, 91 and 96 guns (*AMR* vol. 1, 9). She was a successful fighting platform, far superior to the ill-equipped under-gunned merchant vessels from the previous century.

In 1544, Henry VIII and Charles V of Spain joined forces and invaded France. This campaign reached a climax with the capture of Boulogne, and four days later Charles V terminated the alliance with Henry VIII. England was left to defend the town and the King withdrew his fleet for winter.

In the spring of 1545, Henry stood alone and Francis I of France began to assemble a fleet for the invasion of England. By July, the French fleet was fully equipped and loaded with 30,000 men, ready to attack Portsmouth with the aim of destroying the King's ships in their own anchorage. The action commenced on 18

July 1545, with no notable losses. The following day, 19 July, was calm and still, and the English ships were immobilised with scarcely a breadth of wind to fill a sail. This suited the French galleys that began to advance upon the English carracks. As the morning wore on, an offshore breeze sprung up and the carracks began to hoist sail.

As the English fleet was sailing out to engage the French invasion fleet the *Mary Rose* sank in the Solent in approximately 10m of water. The loss was certainly sudden and unexpected. English accounts claim that while the *Mary Rose* was hoisting sail and getting underway to assist the *Henry Grace à Dieu*, which was under attack from the mobile French galleys, she suddenly heeled while going about. Her gunports were open, her guns run forward and ready for action. As soon as this happened water entered over the gunport sills and the resulting loss of stability with the additional weight of the insurging water caused the heel to become a capsize (Rule 1983; Fig. 2.6). The archaeological evidence casts considerable doubt on this explanation (*AMR* vol. 1, chapter 13) but certainly the ship must have sunk rapidly to result in the loss of so many lives. This tragedy was a great loss to King Henry VIII, but the battle was inconclusive. Further details of the history of the *Mary Rose* are described by Rule (1983) and in *AMR* Vol. 1.

In terms of the wrecking of the *Mary Rose*, three main processes can lead to the loss of material at a wreck site. These are as follows:

The process of wrecking

The *Mary Rose* sinking involved the ingress of water resulting in a capsizing. This is considered the most common wrecking situation in which a ship sinks to the bottom intact and, in this case, the vessel probably remained reasonably undamaged for many decades. In the case of the *Mary Rose*, artefacts trapped between the decks had a chance to become waterlogged and/or buried. Sinking of a ship without considerable structural damage onto the seafloor is rare and this situation bears little relationship to the majority of shipwrecks.

Salvage operations

Salvage attempts to raise shipwrecks from the seafloor can result in damage to hull integrity. In some instances partial break up of the hull can result in the loss of material which simply floats away. The other extreme is when the vessel disintegrates during a salvage operation, totally spilling all heavy and light objects onto the seabed. Attempts were made by Venetian salvors shortly after the sinking to drag the *Mary Rose* into shallower waters. During these operations, damage to the hull occurred resulting in the loss of fore and mainmast. After abortive attempts to raise the hull in the sixteenth century, the wreck lay abandoned until 1836 when John and Charles Deane rediscovered the wreck and recovered a number of important objects including several guns (*AMR* vol. 1, chapter 2).

Loss of perishable materials

The extent of deterioration of shipwrecked material is dependent on many different and often independent factors. Trying to establish what may have happened to the *Mary Rose* or, indeed, to any specific object after sinking is virtually impossible, except in the broadest of terms. Indeed, even on the *Mary Rose* site where artefacts have been thoroughly investigated, it is still often not clear how certain objects have deteriorated or why similar objects are so well preserved by comparison. Over the years there have been numerous studies involving the deterioration of shipwrecked material in sea water. Unfortunately the majority of these investigations have been carried out under idealised laboratory conditions, which are so different from actual wreck site conditions. Of somewhat more relevance are several studies carried out on a number of important marine archaeological sites. From these studies it is possible to identify the major factors, which may have influenced the condition of the *Mary Rose* and her contents prior to burial beneath the seabed sediments of the Solent.

Knowledge about the interaction of the biological, chemical and physical aspects of the marine environment with shipwreck material is central to our understanding of the way in which large and small artefacts can survive in good conditions for many centuries. The ocean environment is not only our source of fresh water, distilled many times through evaporation and precipitation from the sea surface, but also a larder of our maritime heritage, preserving thousands of ships that were lost at sea. These shipwrecks are invaluable time capsules, which provide a wonderful insight into our past.

Ships and their contents are occasionally found in a surprisingly good state of preservation even though they have remained underwater, buried within the sediments of a seabed, for long periods of time. The excavation of the *Mary Rose* site has revealed fragile organic and inorganic based objects in good condition with a large proportion of the hull still intact suggesting that the ship and her contents had come to an equilibrium with the burial environment.

Site Conditions and Factors Influencing the Preservation of the *Mary Rose*

The *Mary Rose* sank without breaking up too much, thus providing protection of her contents prior to burial. After the ship sank, she lay on her starboard side at about 60° from the vertical with the bow of the ship pointing north towards Portsmouth Harbour. Over a short period of time current-laden silt, which compacted into a light grey clay, was deposited within the hull. The ship lay broadside to the strongest currents, which ran from east to west, interspersed by lesser currents from the north-east and south-west. A large proportion of the starboard side lay buried and protected within the soft sediments of the seabed. The portside and upper structures of the ship remained exposed for longer periods of time. The combined weight of the *Mary Rose* and her contents, plus the partial sinking of the starboard side into the soft sediments, meant that the underwater currents were not strong enough to shift the hull back and forth across the seabed. Exposed portions of the hull were, however, subject to a form of sand blasting by the abrasive action of the silt-laden currents of the Solent waters (Fig. 2.7). This resulted in the planks and frames of the *Mary Rose* becoming thinned and weakened. The erosion of the uncovered super-structure continued with many timbers falling into an adjacent scour pit. This resulted in an increase in sedimentation with a corresponding decrease in the size of the ship. Continued erosion finally resulted in the collapse of the ship's bow leaving only a few deck beams exposed to the water column.

Weakening of the *Mary Rose* timbers can also be attributed to the activities of biological organisms such as bacteria, soft rot fungi, actinomycetes and wood boring animals (for further details see Chapter 4). Soon after being wrecked, the timbers of the *Mary Rose* absorbed sea water and were soon colonised by micro-organisms in probably the following sequence: bacteria, soft rot fungi, actinomycetes. The predominant bacterial types would have been rod- and oval-like in appearance and some of these organisms would have caused severe degradation to the outer surface of timbers during their early stages of exposure. Their long-term effect on *Mary Rose* timbers would have been a pronounced increase in the permeability of the wood structure due to the degradation of the pit membranes (see Chapter 4). This

A second type of bacterial attack found in the timbers of the *Mary Rose* is tunnelling, which takes place within the wood cell wall. A characteristic feature of this attack is the concentric wall-like structures, probably composed of polysaccharides, secreted by the tunnelling bacteria. A single bacterium can be seen in the front of each tunnel. Division of the bacteria leads to an increase in the number of these micro-organisms, some of which will initiate new tunnels in different directions. This results in a branched pattern of tunnels. The third type of bacterial attack of ships' timbers, called cavitation, has not been seen within timbers of the *Mary Rose*. Like tunnelling bacteria, cavitation also takes place within the wood cell wall. Cavities which are usually angular in shape are produced within the S_2 layer. A cavity will enlarge due to an increase in the number of bacteria present within the cavity.

Finally the difference in susceptibility of hardwood and softwood ships' timbers is worthy of comment. Identical decay patterns were produced in both hardwood and softwood types examined. However, softwoods, such as pine, would have been more resistant because they contained toxic substances which inhibit bacterial decay. Once these toxins had leached out of the timbers, softwood timbers were then rapidly colonised and degraded by bacteria. Bacteria would then have been superseded by marine fungi in their role as a major decay species.

The first wood-rotting marine fungi to colonise exposed ships' timbers are the soft rot fungi (Levy 1982), as described above. An additional type of attack by soft rot fungi was described by Corbett (1965). He demonstrated that some soft rot fungi can cause erosion of the wood cell wall. This form of attack has not been seen in *Mary Rose* timbers. Soft rot attack by members of the Ascomycotina and Deuteromycotina has contributed significantly to the softening of outer surface layers of *Mary Rose* timbers (Jones *et al.* 1984; Mouzouras *et al.* 1992; Mouzouras 1991). As a result of bacterial and fungal decay, the softened outer surface of exposed ships' timbers were then attacked by marine boring animals, as outlined above.

The majority of wood-destroying crustaceans are members of the family Isopoda and Amphipoda. The adults have segmented bodies and legs and are able to crawl over timber surfaces allowing adults to move from one timber to another. This contrasts with the wood boring molluscs which remain in their burrows for life. The most commonly recorded wood boring crustacean at the underwater site are the genus *Limnoria* which are members of the Isopoda. Evidence of attack of *Mary Rose* timbers soon after wrecking by limnoriids is supported by the presence of an extensive network of galleries within recently excavated ships' timbers and wooden artefacts from Tudor sediments. Attack by limnoriids is superficial and results in the formation of a network of galleries beneath the timber surface. Deck beams, carlings and planks all show signs of attack by

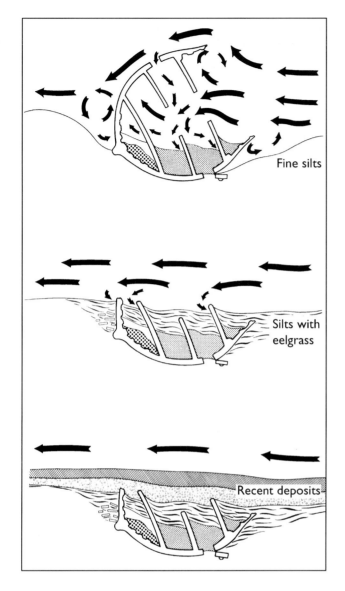

Figure 2.7 Sequence of erosion and burial of the wreck

phenomenon would have occurred within a few months of sinking.

Examination of ancient attack of ships' timbers reveals decay patterns of the wood cells that are suspected of being caused by marine bacteria. The most common type of degradation is caused by erosion bacteria and can be distinguished by the appearance of lysis zones which are produced by the organisms themselves (Fig. 2.1). Bacteria can be seen lying in an erosion trough which conforms closely to the shape of the micro-organism. This form of attack in *Mary Rose* timbers is very common and can occur in both aerobic and anaerobic conditions. Erosion troughs are probably the result of cell wall-bound cellulases or extracellular activity attacking the cellulose component of the S_3 and S_2 layers of the wood cell wall. This results in partial or total conversion of these layers into an amorphous mass of residual cell wall and bacteria. The middle lamella is not degraded. Severe attack by erosion bacteria extends deeply into the ships' timber (see Chapter 4).

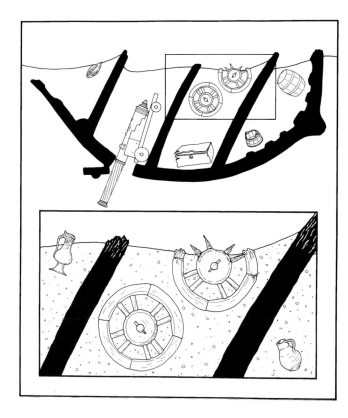

Figure 2.8 The effects of erosion on archaeological material exposed at the surface of the seabed sediments

these crustaceans. In the pine half-beams of the Upper deck, the earlywood appears to be attacked first leaving thin plates of latewood. A large number of softwood and hardwood timbers of the *Mary Rose* had been infested with these organisms, resulting in long narrow tunnels 1–3mm in diameter with respiration holes present throughout the infested timber. Three species, *L. lignorum*, *L. quadripunctata* and *L. tripunctata* are common to the Solent waters and were isolated from exposed *Mary Rose* ships' timbers. These species are considered to be extremely aggressive degraders of timbers and played a significant role in the destruction of the port side timbers.

After a period of time, the port side and upper structure of the ship became so weak that it collapsed downwards. A hard layer of clay and crushed shells was then deposited over the site, sealing the ship and her contents. A mobile seabed of soft silt was formed above these layers. This was wholly or partially removed from time to time by the action of underwater currents. It was probably as a result of such exposures that the *Mary Rose* was rediscovered in 1836 and 1971 (Rule 1983).

The Nature of the Tudor Sediments

For a full appreciation of the wreck site environment it is useful to have some understanding of the physical, chemical and biological processes that influence the preservation of exposed and buried archaeological material (Fig. 2.8). Chemical variables, which are known to affect organic and inorganic material include salinity, dissolved gases and pH, as described above. Other environmental features that affect shipwreck material include water and silt movement, temperature and the activities of living organisms. Scientists associated with the study of the *Mary Rose* site environment investigated all these factors and many more.

Sediments were sampled by inserting corers. Corers measured 500mm in length with an internal diameter of 75mm. After retrieval from the site environment, sediment cores were removed immediately from the corers and profiles of temperature, pH, redox potential, and dissolved oxygen with depth determined. Physicochemical and microbial analyses were carried out in the conservation laboratory. Cores obtained appeared grey/black in colour with a very distinctive sulphurous odour (see below).

Particle size analysis

Marine sediments are made up of unconsolidated particles that cover the bedrock of the seafloor. In compositional terms they vary greatly in their origin, chemistry, particle size and sedimentation rates. All these characters are used to classify sediments. Sediments from the wreck site have been categorised on the basis of grain diameter, as described above, as either clay, silt, sand, granule, pebble, cobble, or boulder using

Table 2.4 Wentworth scale of grain size for sediments

Particle	Minimum size (mm)
Boulder	256
Cobble	64
Pebble	4
Granule	2
Sand	
Very coarse sand	1
Coarse sand	1/2
Medium sand	1/4
Fine sand	1/8
Very fine sand	1/16
Silt	
Coarse silt	1/32
Medium silt	1/64
Fine silt	1/128
Very fine silt	1/256
Clay	
Coarse clay	1/640
Medium clay	1/1024
Fine clay	1/2360
Very fine clay	1/4096
Colloid	1/4096

Table 2.5 Particle size of Tudor sediment

Fraction size (microns)	% of total 0–50mm	% of total 150–200mm	% of total 300–350m
clay (<3.9)	17.8	14.4	22.2
fine silt (3.9)	17.6	22.5	24.2
coarse silt (15.6)	38.2	24.5	35.0
fine sand (125)	13.9	14.0	14.4
medium sand (500)	1.5	2.6	0.9
coarse sand (1000)	0.8	2.0	0.7
granule (1000)	0.4	5.1	0.9
pebble (2000)	2.4	8.3	1.6
other	5.2 (8000 microns)	6.6 8000 microns)	none

Table 2.6. Physico-chemical data for recent sediments (after Pointing *et al.* 1997)

Fraction size (microns)	% of total 0–50mm	% of total 150–200mm	% of total 300–350m
clay (<3.9)	17.8	16.8	17.1
fine silt (3.9)	17.8	13.0	16.4
coarse silt (15.6)	23.9	26.8	24.0
fine sand (125)	35.2	41.4	40.4
medium sand (500)	2.1	0.6	0.4
coarse sand (1000)	1.1	0.8	0.1
gravel (2000)	1.2	0.6	0.2
coarse gravel (4000)	none	none	none
Other	0.8 (shell)	none	1.36 (shell)

the criteria shown in Table 2.4. The types of particles fall into each of these size classes are shown in Table 2.5 (after Griffiths 1967; Pointing 1995).

No clear variations in particle size within the depth of the samples were recorded. The sediments at the site are poorly sorted deposits formed by processes that move many particles quickly. The thickness of the sedimentary deposits depends on the rate of particle supply to the site and the degree to which particles are preserved following sedimentation.

Sedimentary characteristics have been determined and consist largely of clay, silt, and sand (Table 2.5) with coarse silt forming the largest single fraction. Fine sands constituted less than 15% of sediment at each depth, larger particle sizes recorded consisted of pebble and shell fragments.

Clay minerals are a ubiquitous component of the site sediments. They are crystalline, layered alumininosilicates and covered all ships timbers and artefacts. Above this deposit, lenses of seaweed appeared within the silt and enclosed a significant portion of the hull and her contents. The average thickness of this sedimentary deposit is 2.5m. A hard shelly layer, which was, on average, 0.3m thick was found to cover the whole site area and effectively sealed the remains of the ship and her contents from further deterioration. Above this layer, modern soft marine sediments continued to be deposited up until the commencement of the excavation. The average depth of this layer was 1.0m and consisted largely of clay, sand and silt (Table 2.6), with fine sand accounting for the largest single fraction at each depth. Larger particle sizes accounted for less than 5% of the total sample. Recent and new sediment displayed a slightly lower percentage of smaller (silt) particles than Tudor sediments.

Organic and moisture content

Organic content of sediments at all depths sampled was low, ranging from 7.055–7.882% (Table 2.7). The highest organic content was observed in the upper regions of the core sample with this component decreasing with depth. Moisture content of sediments ranged from 43%–92%. Sediments also demonstrated a decrease in water content with depth.

Table 2.7 Organic and moisture content of Tudor sediments (after Pointing *et al.* 1997)

%	0–50mm	150–200mm	300–350mm
organic content	7.882	7.801	7.055
moisture content	92.325	60.653	42.731

Chemical components

Analyses of sediment by X-ray fluorescence (XRF) show that silicate (62–64%) is the dominant inorganic component. The major elements detected are shown in Table 2.8. Trace elements are given in Table 2.9.

Physico-chemical data

A negative redox potential of –34 to –52mv was recorded for cores immediately after sampling. As expected for such low Eh values dissolved oxygen was absent from all samples, pH was slightly above neutral in all cases (Table 2.10). Redox results are interpreted in terms of degrees of oxidation or reduction according to the ranges applicable to soils (Gambrell and Patrick 1978) as shown in Table 2.11.

Table 2.8 XRF major element analysis (% weight)

Type	SiO_2	Al_2O_3	MgO	CaO	Na_2O	K_2O	TiO_2	MnO	Fe_2O_3	P_2O_5	Total
coarse	64.31	9.04	1.21	9.67	0.32	1.66	0.39	0.03	6.72	0.02	93.37
fine	62.06	8.46	1.08	8.50	0.25	1.55	0.36	0.05	8.17	0.01	90.49

Table 2.9 XRF trace element analysis (ppm)

Type	Cu	Ni	Zn	La	Zr	Y	Sr	Rb	Ce	Nd	Cr	V
coarse	23	193	219	31	278	10	360	68	64	28	62	87
fine	24	2057	823	23	229	13	178	52	63	28	65	79

Type	Ba	Sc	Nb	U	Th	Pb	Hg	Sn	Cd	Mo	As	Sb
coarse	262	4	10	2	8	61	2	9	1	9	12	1
fine	197	<1	10	<1	6	1044	<1	8	<1	8	7	<1

Table 2.10 Physico-chemical data for sediments analysed immediately after recovery
(after Pointing *et al.* 1997)

	0–50mm	150–200mm	300–350mm
pH	7.6	7.9	7.6
Eh (mV)	-34	-46	-110
dO_2 (mg/L)	0	0	0
Temp (°C)	17	17	18

Table 2.11 Categories of redox potential

Oxidation/reduction status	Range of redox potential
Oxidised	>+400 mV
Moderately reduced	+100 to +400 mV
Reduced	-100 to +100 mV
Highly reduced	-300 to -100 mV

Sediments were anoxic, as evidenced by the absence of dissolved oxygen and measurements of redox potential that revealed negative values ranging from –34 to –110 mV, although values for a fine sand sediment may decrease to –250mV at depths below 50mm (Gray 1981). Nonetheless, redox values recorded indicated a reducing to highly reducing environment within the sediments of the *Mary Rose* site.

Microbiological analyses of sediments

Anaerobic heterotrophic bacteria were numerically dominant, but all sediments supported significant sulphate-reducing bacterial populations (Table 2.12). Battersby and Brown (1982) recorded a similar pattern in the study of estuarine sediments. The method chosen to assess sulphate reduction in this study counted total sulphate reducing numbers of both *Desulfovibrio* and *Desulfomaculatum* species (Macfarlane and Gibson 1991). Numbers of sulphate-reducing bacteria increased with depth.

In terms of deterioration of artefact material, the sulphate-reducing bacteria are one of the most important components of sediment biota. These bacteria require anoxic conditions, sulphate and other essential nutrients essential for growth. Sulphate-reducing bacteria produce hydrogen sulphide which can accelerate corrosion of copper-based alloys and reacts with iron oxide found in sea water to form black iron sulphide often observed in buried shipwreck timbers, glass and glazed pottery.

All analysed samples of Tudor sediments possessed cellulolytic bacterial activity. Identified anaerobic bacteria include obligate anaerobes such as *Clostridium* species and facultative anaerobes such as *Bacillus* species. Despite the low organic content of Tudor sediments, cellulolytic bacterial numbers observed compare well with results obtained for these bacteria in sediments enriched with organic matter (Battersby and Brown 1982). The presence of cellulolytic bacteria within wreck site sediments is due to the presence of large quantities of organic artefact material.

The presence of detectable numbers of cellulolytic anaerobes can be related to the presence of high numbers of sulphate-reducing bacteria. Madden *et al.* (1980) suggested that rates of cellulose decomposition in anaerobic marine sediments depend upon a close relationship between sulphate-reducing bacteria and cellulose degraders in the bacterial community. Lactate and acetate fermentation products of cellulose degradation are often utilised by sulphate-reducing bacteria.

Table 2.12 Bacterial numbers in sediments (after Pointing *et al.* 1997)

Sediment depth	Heterotrophic bacteria	Sulphate-reducing bacteria	Cellulose degrading bacteria	Cellulose degraders (presence/absence)
0–50mm	6×10^2	1.5×10^3	zero	+++
150–200mm	2×10^3	1.6×10^2	9×10^2	+++
300–350mm	2×10^4	5×10^3	1.6×10^3	+++

+ = present

Characteristics of the open circulation environment (excavation period)

The overall range of parameters for the *Mary Rose* wreck site is shown in Table 2.13. The English mainland to the north and the Isle of Wight to the south provided shelter to the site. Tidal currents of up to 1.02m/s, flowed across the site, principally from east and west alternately. The seabed was flat, soft, organically rich recent sediment, which is typical for this part of the Solent. The remains of the Tudor warship *Mary Rose* were found buried in mud, 10m below sea level.

The wreck of the *Mary Rose* can be accommodated within class I according to the classification of five main wreck sites described in Table 2.3. Environmental characteristics at the *Mary Rose* site compliment the majority of specifications listed for this class. Artefacts found buried at a Class I wreck site will be found in a surprisingly good condition even though they may have been underwater for several centuries. The environment at Class 1 sites is usually stable in that it has a buffered pH range of 7.0–7.5. At Class I sites, artefact material may be re-exposed for short periods of time by a mobile seabed. At the *Mary Rose* site a semi-mobile upper layer was identified during the excavation. From time to time ships timbers and artefacts would have been exposed, covered and re-exposed.

The Raising and Recovery of Large Amounts of Waterlogged Remains

The ethical and moral decisions concerning whether to salvage a wreck will always be difficult. During the 1978 season, it became clear that there was a coherent structure with personal possessions and ship's stores well preserved. As a result of these important discoveries the Mary Rose 1967 Committee convened two important meetings in Portsmouth. Archaeologists, ship historians, naval architects and museologists, who were asked to consider the archaeological evidence and the importance of the ship and her contents in social, military and cultural terms, attended the first meeting. There were many possible courses of action to be considered. Should the *Mary Rose* and her contents be left undisturbed or partially excavated to salvage a representative sample of artefacts? A third proposal looked at the possibility of a full excavation and that all the artefacts and hull be recovered. Salvage consultants, structural engineers and naval architects and the Mary Rose 1967 Committee attended the second meeting, and all agreed that on the evidence available it should be feasible to recover the hull safely. A decision was then made to excavate and salvage in entirety (*AMR*, Vol. 1, chapter 5).

In museological terms, it was an advantage to raise the *Mary Rose* and her contents: this would enable a total archive to be made available to the public and to scholars for their educational needs and interests. On archaeological and conservation grounds, once the wreck site had been disturbed, the hull and her artefacts would no longer be protected by the preserving silts and deterioration would recommence, often in a rapid and devastating fashion. In fact, excavation of large underwater wreck sites without retrieval is vandalism, the hull and artefacts are much safer being left buried in the preserving sediments of the seabed (Pearson 1987).

Like land archaeologists, we are aware that the single most destructive force to threaten our underwater heritage is man. Searching for and locating new sites imposes a threat, as does excavation. Should a project fail due to lack of funds midway through an excavation, it is possible that the site will be destroyed. Some archaeologists are asking the question 'must we excavate, must we discover'? In many instances the decision to excavate is directly related to the fact that a site is threatened, either by economic pressures, such as the medieval wreck recovered from St Peterport Harbour, Guernsey in 1985 (threatened by dredging operations) or by changing environmental conditions, making a site unstable, as evidenced by a Roman wreck being uncovered by propeller wash when deeper-keeled ferries were brought into the same harbour. Unfortunately, underwater wreck sites are not yet subject to the same protective legislation as land sites.

A major problem in underwater archaeology has always been the lack of funding, both for excavation and for conservation. The decision to proceed with the recovery of the *Mary Rose* and her contents was made with the full realisation of the implications involved in the handling and storage of such large numbers of marine finds.

The excavation

The main excavation of the site was carried out in the four main diving seasons of 1979 to 1982 (see also *AMR*

Table 2.13 Characteristics of the *Mary Rose* open circulation environment (excavation period)

Item	Mean value	Remarks
Temperature	7.19–19.28	varies with time of year
Pressure	2 atms	pressure increases 1 atm for every 9m of depth
Salinity	33–35‰	normal value for the Solent
Dissolved oxygen %	70	65–77
Hydrogen in concentration (pH)	8.30	range 8.17–8.68
Conductivity	44100μs	

Figure 2.9 Divers using airlifts accompanied by an inquisitive cuttlefish

timbers are uncovered, they are once more exposed to the open circulation environment. Within this aerobic (oxygen rich) environment, shipwreck material will undergo further deterioration. This often occurs in a rapid and devastating fashion, so recovery of exposed material should proceed at full speed. Before removing any artefact, however, it must be meticulously recorded, securely supported, packed, and then carefully raised.

Biological colonisation of excavated material at the Mary Rose site

Excavation of an underwater site is slower and more dangerous than an archaeological dig on dry land. The work on the *Mary Rose* was painstakingly slow, with problems with weather on the surface and appalling visibility underwater. It took from 1971 to 1979 to uncover the upper part of the surviving hull. In 1979 the excavation of the interior began in earnest. Hundreds of artefacts were handled for the first time since the ship sank in 1545. As soon as the ship and her contents were exposed to aerobic conditions, colonisation and deterioration of excavated material by microbes and marine animals began.

During this period, a variety of hard substrates such as steel grid poles, concrete blocks and plastic sheeting were introduced to the site, providing additional habitats for colonisation. It was generally observed that freshly exposed archaeological material was not colonised as quickly as adjacent steel, concrete and plastic surfaces. This may be due to biocide action of unknown substances being present or released from the newly excavated material.

Colonisation of ships' timbers
The nature of events occurring immediately after re-exposure of ships' timbers to sea water was assessed by a combination of photography, microscopy and chemical analysis, including light and electron microscopy, x-ray microanalysis and XRF. Survey dives were generally of one hour duration which was sufficient to examine exposed timbers. The timbers were surveyed approximately monthly in 1980 and 1981 and every two weeks during the excavation season of 1982. Additional valuable information was obtained from the observations of the diving archaeologists working on the site.

Vol. 1, chapter 4). In the majority of cases the artefacts that were found were in a good state of preservation with a large proportion of the hull still intact. It is beyond the scope of this book to discuss all the excavation methods used in detail. Site excavation was carried out by divers suspended from a grid of steel pipes supported around the ship. A grid, 3m square, was used to divide the site into a series of 'trenches'. Using hand held tools, site sediments were taken away layer by layer and unwanted spoils fed to a 0.1m diameter airlift supported some 0.45m above the bottom of each trench (Fig. 2.9). All artefacts were surveyed in relation to the hull rather than the grid which was not used for survey. The success of the underwater excavation depended on the pre-dive briefing session. When the briefing sessions went well the operation progressed ahead with few difficulties.

During these operations, steps were taken to minimise deterioration when the finds became exposed. On any wreck site, as soon as artefacts and ships'

Table 2.14. Sequence of colonisation of re-exposed ships' timbers (1980–1982)

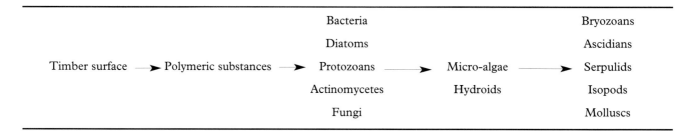

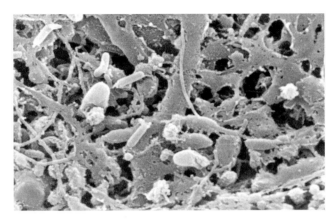

Figure 2.10 Bacterial attack of exposed ship timber (SEM) (x3500)

The build up of a biological community followed a fairly distinct pattern and a representative model of the sequence of events is shown in Table 2.14.

The process of timber colonisation began with the formation of a macro-molecular layer which serves as a conditioning layer for a variety of organisms. The absorption of non-living material was then followed by the attachment of bacteria, and then diatoms, and eventually macro-algae and marine animals.

Marine Bacteria: Bacteria settled on re-exposed timbers within a day and, after three days, cellulolytic bacilli and pseudomonads were present. Some of these organisms were associated with timber degradation as shown in Figures 2.10 and 2.11. During the first week of exposure, rod- and ovoid-shaped bacteria were present on the timber surface. Most bacteria were restricted to the surface layers of the timbers and only rods were found at greater depths. After one month's exposure, and for the remaining exposure times, the population was more diverse in morphological type but the ships timbers were never completely covered by bacteria. The extent of bacterial growth and cover on timbers surfaces appeared to be governed by water movement. Table 2.15 lists some of the bacterial species isolated from re-exposed ships' timbers. Any activities that are considered important to timber degradation are also noted.

The data in Table 2.15 indicate that five genera of bacteria were found colonising ships' timbers. These bacteria differ morphologically from one another and

Table 2.15 Bacteria isolated from re-exposed ships' timbers

Species	Activity
Alcaligenes spp.	produce cellulases
Bacillus spp.	attack pectin, xylan, a cellulose & holocellulose
Eschrichia coli	—
Pseuomonas spp.	cellulolytic
Vibrio spp.	—

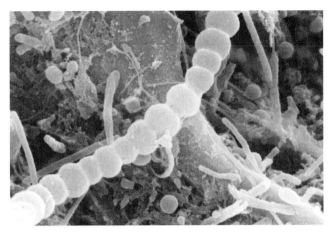

Figure 2.11 An array of microbes present on the surface of an exposed hull timber (SEM) (x3500)

each particular organism will exhibit characteristic enzymatic activities which contribute to the process of timber decay.

Actinomycetes: Actinomycetes colonised the timber surface in low numbers after one months exposure. They consisted of thin elongated rod-shaped organisms which are capable of degrading both lignin and cellulose (Crawford and Sutherland 1980). No decay patterns were observed.

Marine Fungi: Fungal activity was extremely low until the sixth week and, although spores were occasionally found on the surface of exposed ships' timber (Fig. 2.12). The amount of fungal attack occurring after re-exposure is hard to ascertain because the outer surface layers of *Mary Rose* ships' timbers were heavily degraded. Soft rot cavities observed were probably formed before timbers were re-exposed during the 1980–1982 site excavation period.

Diatoms: Diatoms are one-celled marine organisms with skeletons based on silicon. These were superficial colonisers throughout the period of exposure.

Marine animals: Collins and Mallinson (1983) determined the sequence of animal colonisation of

Figure 2.12 Fungal spores on the surface of an exposed ship timber (SEM) (x3500)

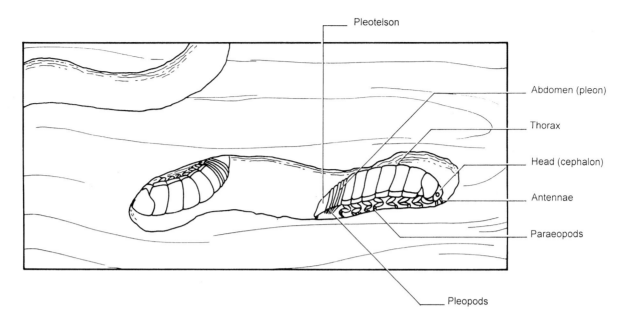

Pleotelson

Abdomen (pleon)

Thorax

Head (cephalon)

Antennae

Paraeopods

Pleopods

Figure 2.13 Limnoria *attacking wood (after Pournou 1999)*

ships' timbers exposed during a three year period. During early stages of exposure hydroids (*Kirchenpauria pinnata* and *Obelia* spp.) and bryozoans (*Bugla turbinata* and *Bicellariella ciliata*) were the main colonisers forming discrete patches of growth. As these developed, a variety of other animal species became established such as ascidians (*Botrylloides leachi* and *Ascidiella aspersa*), and anemones (*Metridium senile* and *Sagartiogeten laceratus*). The density of cover of marine animals increased proportionally with the length of timber exposure. In general terms, the under-surface of both structural and deck timbers was most densely colonised.

After a period of three months, the wood boring isopod *Limnoria* were found inhabiting the surface layers of ships' timbers (Fig. 2.13). The three *Limnoria* species (*L. lignorum*, *L. quadripunctata* and *L. tripunctata*), all in breeding condition, were found in the surface layers of all exposed timbers. Numerous old calcified tubes of the mollusc *Teredo navalis* were seen in the surfaces of newly exposed timbers. These were attributed to previous exposure during changes to seabed level. However, one live specimen was found. Both *Teredo* and *Limnoria* spp. have been previously recorded in the waters of the Solent.

The numerous crevices in the wreck structure provided a habitat for a range of benthic organisms. Large crabs (*Cancer pagurus*) and lobsters (*Homarus gammarus*) were found living amongst the exposed timbers. These thick shelled organisms were not found in any great numbers and damage to timbers and artefacts was not observed.

The most numerous crevice inhabitants were velvet swimming crabs (*Liocarcinus puber*) and the squat lobster (*Galathea squamifera*). Certain species of fish were also found in these timber crevices; the butterfish (*Pholis gunnellus*), the common eel (*Anguilla anguilla*),

scorpion fish (*Taurulus bubalis*), the black goby (*Gobius niger*) and the tompot blenny (*Parablennius gattorugine*). At night, corkwing wrasse (*Crenilabrus melops*) and the ballan wrasse (*Labrus bergylta*) were seen sleeping in crevices.

Colonisation of material associated with the excavation, by K. Collins and J. Mallinson (1983)
Steel poles, concrete sinkers, plastic sheeting and labels were rapidly colonised by marine fouling organisms. Like the colonisation of exposed ships' timbers, hydroids, bryozoans and ascidians were important. Certain species appeared to settle preferentially on these hard surfaces, in particular barnacles (*Elinius modestus* and *Balanus improvisus*) and the bryozoan (*Electra pilosa*).

Throughout the excavation period, large quantities of driftweed accumulated in the site. This was apparently linked with spring tides and stormy weather. The bulk of the material was Kelp (*Laminaria saccharina*). There was a continuous influx of the red alga *Ceramium rubrum* and a recently introduced Japanese seaweed *Sargassum muticum*. Associated with this driftweed were a number of amphipods, eg, *Gammarus locusta* and molluscs (*Rissova parva* and *Mytilus edulis*).

Pelagic species

Exposed wrecks are known for attracting large numbers of fish. As the excavation of the site increased there was a corresponding increase in mid-water fish activity. Theses were attracted to the site by the shelter afforded from tidal currents. The most frequently recorded species was the pout (*Trisopterus luscus*). This fish was often seen swimming around throughout the year in shoals of 20–25.

The other common fish was the pollack (*Pollachius pollachius*), often seen stationary above the wreck in groups of 5–10. Occasionally larger shoals (50–100 fish) were observed feeding on the spoil from the airlift. Another notable mid-water fish was the bass (*Dicentrarchus labrax*), which appeared either in small shoals or as large solitary individuals. Most fish species were not disturbed by the presence of divers excavating the wreck site. Regular visitors to the excavated site during the period of May to late July were the cuttlefish (*Sepia officinalis*; Fig. 2.9).

The diversity and density of marine organisms at the wreck site was greatly increased by the activity of the underwater excavation, which provided a number of new habitats; ships' timbers, hard surfaces such as steel poles and shelter from tidal currents. Exposed organic archaeological material also provided a source of food for a number of micro-organisms and boring animals. A total of 13 marine fungi, 130 animal species and 23 drift algae species was recorded. All of these have been previously recorded locally. The colonisation of timber surfaces was almost entirely faunal.

The significance of marine organisms identified at the wreck site during the excavation period 1980–1982 is immense. From Table 2.14 it can be seen that the main destructive organisms were the bacteria, soft rot fungi and the boring isopods such as gribble (*Limnoria* spp.). The presence of marine fungi in the surface of wooden artefacts enhances the feeding and reproductive activity of *Limnoria* spp. As stated above, this organism creates shallow tunnels in the surface layers of exposed wooden timbers and objects. In combination with fungal attack, deterioration can be rapid. The problem is that if any wooden finds are not raised relatively soon after being exposed to aerobic condition, colonisation by marine fungi and wood boring animals will occur. If left unprotected, exposed wooden finds are likely to deteriorate rapidly. For small wooden objects, recovery from the seabed may occur soon after the finds become exposed. For intact structures such as ships' hulls, however, the excavation period may take 2–5 years to complete. During this period attack by wood boring animals can be totally devastating, leaving ships' timbers drastically weakened. The numerous large bore-holes through the wood, however, may leave it amenable to treatment.

Throughout the excavation period, marine borer attack greatly increased with time. Intensity of attack became very evident towards the end of the 1981 excavation season. All exposed timbers (softwoods and hardwoods) were susceptible to attack. Recent gribble damage was more commonly found on the surface of large structural timbers such as deck beams and port-side hull planking. As a consequence of marine borer attack, the infested timbers became more susceptible to erosion by underwater currents. Water movement

removed existing tunnels exposing new layers to further woode-boring attack.

In situ *protection of exposed hull timbers*

Steps were taken to minimise wood-borer attack of the *Mary Rose* hull as timbers were re-exposed during the excavation period. Short-term experiments involved exposing ships' timbers to formaldehyde. Results suggest that this method had little effect on controlling borer infestation. Attempts were then made to cover excavated individual timbers with recently excavated sediments. Structural timbers such as deck planks and half-beams were removed from the hull and carefully placed into seabed depressions. The aim was to try to re-create anaerobic conditions until the timbers could be carefully removed from the site. This method also failed because tidal currents took away the sediment cover. However, recent experiments regarding *in situ* protection of timbers within marine sediments are proving successful and indicate a means of avoiding the financial burden of recovery, storage and conservation.

Although it was not possible during the excavation of the *Mary Rose* to cover large areas of the re-exposed hull with a physical barrier, plastic material such as polyvinyl chloride (PVC) and polypropylene covered small areas around the ends of deck beams and frames. This type of protection prevented further attack to these areas by wood boring organisms. Even the small wood borer larvae were unable to penetrate these materials. However, when this barrier system was damaged, the larvae were able to enter the underlying wood. Plans to cover the whole site with a physical barrier at the end of each excavation season were not considered practical by the team of underwater archaeologists, although the feasibility was proved by covering the entire length of the exposed port side planking in the Hold with terram at the end of one season.

More recent excavations have, however, physically protected underwater archaeological sites by covering the entire site with a physical barrier (Pournou 1999). At the Zakynthos wreck site (a fifteenth–sixteenth century Spanish trading ship; Delaporta and Bound 1993) where marine borer activity was high, the site was covered by a geo-textile (Terram 4000) at the close of each excavation season. The geo-textile used is ideally suited to this application because it possesses good physical and mechanical properties. This material is resistant to the abrasive action of tidal currents. One other important property is the ability to trap sediments. This resulted in rapid covering of the fabric with sediments and marine plants and animals. It also quickly returned the site to preserving conditions (anaerobic). Further research in this area is needed in view of the rapid increase in underwater archaeological activities in recent years, which has resulted in large volumes of waterlogged wood being excavated. Since recovery is not always feasible, *in situ* protection appears to be an attractive solution to a very serious problem.

Retrieval of Mary Rose *finds*

Between 1979 and the middle of the 1980s the register of finds included 18,778 artefacts, 1175 human remains and 3533 samples. It was an enormous task to record, securely pack and carefully raise these finds. The 18,778 artefacts recovered have rightly earned the title 'a time capsule of Tudor life at sea' (Rule 1983). It would be beyond the scope of this book to discuss the retrieval of all the artefacts in detail, but the following examples give an idea of the range of lifting techniques used.

Techniques to retrieve artefacts from the seabed can be simple or complex. The most satisfactory methods of lifting are those which protect the artefact from damage without prejudicing future conservation techniques and which interfere least with the surrounding archaeological features and ongoing excavation activities. Methods chosen by the Mary Rose Trust to assist lifting were designed with the purpose of retrieving material quickly, cost effectively and safely. Archaeologists experienced in the lifting of delicate archaeological finds trained underwater divers. It need hardly be mentioned that working underwater is much more complicated than on land, not only because of the obvious difficulties involved but because thought processes become dimmed when the diver comes tired and, perhaps, cold.

The usual practice of recovering small artefacts was to use mesh baskets and, for larger ones, plastic trays (Fig. 2.14) or crates which could be winch lifted carefully to the surface. Finds that were considered delicate or flimsy were packed in sediment for protection and placed either in polythene bags or into boxes and then sealed before lifting. Individual boxes were then transferred with labels to a crate ready to be raised by winch or carried to the surface. In the case of some of the chests, a wooden box was constructed, just large enough for the chest to be placed into it on the seabed so that it could be raised intact without disturbing the contents. The box was lined with polythene sheeting to prevent the water draining out.

Figure 2.15 Recovery of a bronze gun by a simple lifting method involving strops

Large items, such as the wheels from a carriage of a wrought iron gun, presented additional problems. Such artefacts needed extra support in the form of a wooden tray. Plastic containers with plenty of soft padding were used to support and cushion the wheels on the wooden tray during the lifting process. Straps were used to secure them to the lifting structure; these were never in direct contact with the surface of the artefact. Precautions were also taken to prevent the lifting cables from cutting into the softened surfaces. On reaching the surface, they were then carefully shrouded in water-saturated synthetic foam and sealed within polyethylene sheeting to protect the object from drying.

Recovery of heavy objects such as the large wrought iron guns on their timber beds took place whenever tidal conditions were favourable, and sometimes the work continued after dark. These objects were always encapsulated with a thick concretion (see Chapter 5) which provided the metal object with a strong protective barrier. The iron corrosion products interact with biological organisms that settle and grow on iron objects to form concretion. These organisms build up a layer of skeletal material, predominantly calcium carbonate (see Chapter 5). Padded lifting strops were wrapped around the heavily concreted bronze guns and winched slowly through the water to the recovery vessel (Fig. 2.15). On reaching the surface large metal objects were carefully wrapped in polyethylene sheeting before being transferred to the conservation laboratory.

Recovery of the Mary Rose hull

The decision on what method should be used to raise the *Mary Rose* evolved over many years resulting in a number of schemes presented to the Mary Rose 1967 Committee (see *AMR* Vol. 1 for further details). Some involved moving her complete with contents to a wet dock ashore for excavation, whilst others favoured removing all the artefacts and then lifting the hull with her deck timbers in place. As the excavation of the hull progressed it became clear that it would not be possible

Figure 2.14 Plastic trays were used by divers to safely lift excavated objects to the surface

Figure 2.16 *Twenty to forty timbers were placed into truck bodies on the seabed. The truck body was then raised to the surface and placed into a waiting barge to be shipped ashore*

Figure 2.17 *A local pond was used to store large timbers for a limited period of time*

to lift the hull with the deck timbers in place. Although the hull was securely fastened with oak treenails, the internal structures were found to have lost all their metal fastenings that had previously secured them firmly in position. These metal (iron) fastenings had corroded away leaving a concretion of iron corrosion products with no structural strength. The deck planks for example, which had once been fastened to the underlying deck beams with iron nails, were now held in place by the weight of the covering sediments and, once cleared, the planks were found to move. The whole internal structure was considered unstable and inherently dangerous (Rule 1983). Based upon these findings, a decision was made in 1981 to record and dismantle all the internal structure before attempting to salvage the empty hull. Hence, most elements of the internal structure were removed.

At the end of the 1981 season the timbers were dismantled and placed into large steel containers, which were placed close to the site. Twenty to 40 hull timbers were placed carefully into these containers and then lifted through the water by crane onto a floating barge (Fig. 2.16) and towed into Portsmouth Naval Base. On reaching the surface exposed timber surfaces were covered by water saturated foam and several sheets of polyethylene. The timbers were transferred from this lifting structure and placed into a large fresh water pond for periods of 12–24 months (Fig. 2.17). Following this period the timbers were stored in Dry Dock No. 3 alongside the ship.

The key to the successful raising of the *Mary Rose* hull involved many years of careful and meticulous preparation. A scheme was approved in principle and it was agreed to transfer the hull into a lifting cradle whilst still underwater. A giant crane would then lift the hull into the air supported by the cradle. Both hull and cradle would then be placed onto a barge for transport ashore. In order to achieve this, the recovery programme for the hull was broken down into six phases (see also *AMR* Vol. 1, chapter 5):

Phase 1: After excavation within the hull was completed, a steel framework was placed in position directly above the hull. It was towed to the site in June 1982 and gently lowered to the seafloor. The four legs of this underwater lifting frame stood firmly supported in the firm clay deposits of the seafloor.

Phase 2: Holes were carefully drilled through the hull at pre-determined positions and steel bolts and backing plates firmly secured to the timbers. Eyes were fastened to the internal ends of the bolts and, from these points, wire cables connect the hull with the underwater lifting frame. As each wire was secured in position, tunnelling by the under-water engineering team could proceed in safety.

Phase 3: A prefabricated steel cradle was designed to conform with the lines of the *Mary Rose* hull and was placed in position on the seabed close to the wreck site.

Phase 4: The hull of the *Mary Rose* suspended by steel cables was lifted from the seafloor using the hydraulic jacks in the legs of the underwater lifting frame. This was done slowly and when the hull broke free from the seabed, the frame was lifted into position directly above the support cradle. At this

Figure 2.18 *The giant crane* Tog Mor *lifting the* Mary Rose *from the sea*

Figure 2.19 The Mary Rose *on the lifting cradle just after she emerged from the sea*

stage the hull was extremely vulnerable to tidal conditions.

Phase 5: The underwater lifting frame was lowered slowly into the steel cradle and the legs of the frame were securely locked into the steel cradle. The cradle was lined with water bags to cushion the hull during its transfer from the sea onto a barge (Figs 2.18, 2.19).

Phase 6: The *Mary Rose,* secured between the supporting water cushions, the cradle and the underwater lifting frame, was slowly and carefully lifted from the sea onto a barge for transport ashore.

On the wet cold morning of 11 October 1982, with the right tidal conditions, the raising of the *Mary Rose* in her support cradle began. At 9.03 am the *Mary Rose* began to break the surface of the water. At that point the sea became flat and the strong winds fell away and the *Mary Rose* was eventually taken into the safe haven of the Royal Naval Base, Portsmouth. During its journey ashore, a large surface area of the hull was covered with water-saturated foam which prevented the hull timbers from drying. Intermittent spraying of the hull with sea water allowed the hull timbers to maintain maximum water saturation.

Recovering the hull and bringing it ashore to a temporary location in Dry Dock No. 3 in the Royal Naval Base, Portsmouth was in every sense a homecoming and it is appropriate that the initial work to restore the hull of the *Mary Rose* and prepare for a long-term programme of active conservation took place only a few yards away from where she was originally built. The recovery of the hull and artefacts is a shared triumph for all those involved in the Mary Rose Project.

The methods used to passively store and conserve the recovered artefacts and hull are the subject of the remainder of this book.

3. Passive Storage of Marine Archaeological Objects

Passive storage may be defined as a safe storage method for recovered archaeological objects that must prevent further deterioration to the object until the commencement of active conservation treatment. The period spent in passive storage can vary from a few hours to several years.

The decision to proceed with the recovery of material from a wreck site must be made with the full realisation of the implications involved in the storage of waterlogged material (Grattan and Clarke 1987). Many problems and loss of potential archaeological information have occurred to recovered waterlogged material as a result of inadequate and unsuitable storage conditions.

The storage of archaeological material should be discussed at the planning stage with input from a range of specialists including conservators, wood technologists, materials scientists, corrosion experts and chemists. Advice from these people may prove useful for determining whether a storage method chosen prevents or minimises further deterioration.

Ideally, storage facilities must be established and ready for use before the excavation begins. As previously discussed, waterlogged archaeological material will deteriorate immediately on exposure to air. Therefore safe and immediate transfer into ideal storage environments is essential. Material recovered from the *Mary Rose* site was placed into temporary storage soon after reaching the surface.

Storage methods must fulfil a number of requirements and six main criteria were identified by conservators at the Mary Rose Trust. Any storage method used had to:

1. prevent or minimise any further deterioration to either organic or inorganic material;
2. be compatible with future examination and conservation treatments methods;
3. be safe and inexpensive;
4. be easy to maintain;
5. provide accessibility of all artefacts to conservators during treatment; and
6. provide accessibility of the hull to public and specialists during passive storage.

Once in storage, it is essential that ideal conditions are maintained. During a passive storage phase of variable duration, post-excavation recording, cleaning and reconstruction work can be carried out with relative ease. In addition, information regarding the physical and

chemical properties of recovered archaeological material is usually determined during the passive holding phase. Ideally, any conservation method adopted to treat an artefact should be determined by the condition and nature of the material to be treated (Christensen 1970; van der Heide 1972; Florian *et al.* 1978). It is essential, therefore, that archaeological material be maintained in ideal storage environments until such determinations can be made.

Equally important to bear in mind is the possibility that financial support for active conservation may not be available during the excavation and recovery periods. Long or extended storage is inevitable in cases where large wrecks and their contents are recovered (Rule 1983). If suitable storage facilities are not adequately supported, then the recovery of wreck material is difficult to justify. For the Mary Rose project, suitable storage facilities were set up prior to the recovery of archaeological material.

The passive holding regimes adopted by the Mary Rose Trust are considered in this chapter, together with an assessment of what they achieved and what their advantages and disadvantages have proved to be.

Waterlogged Wood

Cleaning of waterlogged archaeological wood

Washing is a very important first step prior to the passive storage of waterlogged wood and should not be rushed. The main point to remember is that waterlogged archaeological wood does not have the same strength properties as fresh wood. Microscopic analysis of *Mary Rose* wooden artefacts and ship's timbers revealed that the outer surface was heavily degraded. All wood species, with the exception of yew (longbows; Fig. 3.1), were found to have little inherent strength in the outer surface cells. The surfaces of waterlogged archaeological objects may appear sound but will easily damage on cleaning.

Removal of marine sediments

Before placing *Mary Rose* waterlogged wooden artefacts and timbers into passive holding, burial deposits such as marine sediments were removed carefully from the object surface. Each object was immersed in a tank of clean fresh water and the surrounding sediments gently washed away. This procedure usually removed the bulk of settled deposits without harming the very degraded

Figure 3.1 The first yew longbow recovered by diver Adrian Barak (seen here)

outer surfaces. For more resistant surface sediment deposits, outer surfaces were gently brushed with fine hair brushes under a gentle stream of running water. When this did not work, the temperature of the water was raised to 30°C, which resulted in the removal of the most resistant sediment deposits.

Large structures, such as the hull of the *Mary Rose*, took many years to clean. Sediments trapped between the frames were often removed by hand. Water hoses of small diameter (10mm) were also used to clean areas of the hull which contained compacted marine sediments. These areas were very anaerobic in nature with high levels of sulphate-reducing bacteria.

Removal of surface stains
A feature most frequently encountered with wooden artefacts and timbers recovered from the *Mary Rose* wreck site was the presence of iron compounds on the surface. Such deposits were present on approximately

50% of recovered wooden artefacts and timbers and often appeared as rusty orange to red brown deposits.

To dissolve these iron compounds, artefacts and timbers were soaked in water tanks containing a 5% solution of the disodium salt of ethylene diamine tetra acetic acid (EDTA). The length of treatment varied from 1 day to 3 months; longer immersion periods were found to soften the wood surface. To remove the more resistant iron compounds (iron sulphide), 5% oxalic acid was used for periods of 24–36 hours. An important point about the removal of iron compounds is that the chances of removal can be made easier if the wood is temporarily maintained in an anaerobic condition (Grattan 1987). This can prevent the formation of highly insoluble iron hydroxides and oxides. Wrapping waterlogged wood in a barrier foil containing an oxygen scavenger ('Ageless') is a simple way of creating and maintaining an anaerobic environment for recently excavated timbers.

Although investigated by Trust conservators, the bleaching of hull timbers with 2% hydrogen peroxide (pH 9) in a buffer solution was not recommended for general use because it attacks the lignin matrix of wood cell walls. The black appearance of hull timbers was due to the presence of iron tannates.

Storage of waterlogged archaeological wood

The fundamental problem encountered if waterlogged archaeological wood is allowed to dry in an uncontrolled manner is that it may collapse, shrink, distort, split and even, in severe cases, disintegrate completely (Grattan 1987). The situation becomes a particular problem if the wood is stored under unfavourable conditions. This post-excavation damage will continue unless suitable storage environments are maintained. In an ideal world, it is probably worth aiming for a holding period of less than a year (English Heritage 1995). This is not always possible when dealing with a well preserved marine wreck site which can produce many tons of waterlogged wood. In such cases, passive holding periods of up to 20 years are not uncommon.

A number of methods were adopted for the storage of the *Mary Rose* hull and her wooden artefacts. Four basic requirements for the ideal storage of waterlogged wood were suggested by a panel of experts and proved useful as a guide to good practice. The requirements were:

1. the ability to keep the wood at maximum moisture content;
2. the exclusion of light to reduce algal growth;
3. the prevention or minimisation of the activity of bacteria, fungi and insects; and
4. that storage be safe and economical.

These requirements were met in a number of ways.

Figure 3.2 (left) A newly recovered wooden chest wrapped in polythene sheeting to prevent drying before being transferred to controlled storage facilities in Portsmouth Naval Base

Wrapping artefacts and individual timbers in polyethylene bags

The majority of *Mary Rose* artefacts and ship's timbers were carefully packaged in polyethylene bags of various sizes. 500 gauge polyethylene sheeting was used to create suitable bags and all edges were hermetically sealed (Fig. 3.2). Timbers and artefacts were often kept within buildings which had no temperature control. To control bacterial and fungal activity, both were pre-treated with biocides and then wrapped in the polyethylene bags. All artefacts and timbers were kept in the dark. Random sampling of polyethylene wrapped objects was undertaken on a three-monthly basis to determine any problems. Polyethylene acts as a good barrier to water movement, provided that the bags are well sealed. Temperature values within the wet storage sites were more dependent on the external environments. Temperatures ranged from 5°C (winter months) to 21°C (summer months). The polyethylene wrapping did not act as a temperature barrier, thus the temperature within the wrapping was very close to that of the storage site.

Maintaining the waterlogged state of artefacts and timbers is an important criterion and should not be underestimated. Desiccation of wood leads to collapse and distortion, which is normally an irreversible process. If the wood is maintained in a waterlogged condition, the growth of wood-rotting fungi may be restricted since water saturation will limit the amount of available oxygen which is required by the fungi (Scheffer 1973). However, low oxygen tensions may not totally prevent the growth of certain fungi, especially soft rot fungi (Cartwright and Findley 1958; Duncan 1961; Scheffer 1973). These fungi are better adapted to decay wood in conditions of low oxygen tensions, since they preferentially degrade cellulose through a non-oxygen process (Levi and Preston 1965).

Examination of stored *Mary Rose* timbers for fungal activity has been demonstrated by Mouzouras (1991). Fruiting structures of seventeen fungi were found on the surface of timbers. Three of these were terrestrial and fourteen were marine fungi (Table 3.1). The most frequent species recorded was *Monodictys pelagica*, recorded on 23% of timbers examined.

Despite the large number of wood-decaying fungi found fruiting on the surface of timbers, few signs of recent attack were observed by Mouzouras (1991) (Fig. 3.3). Soft rot cavities were observed, but were not numerous. Such decay patterns were only observed after

Table 3.1 Fungal species observed on the surface of stored timbers (Mouzouras 1991)

Species	Decay type
Ascomycotina	
Ceriospora halima	soft rot (type 1)
Corollospora maritima	soft rot (type 1)
Lulworthia sp.	soft rot (type 1)
Neriospora cristata	soft rot (type 1)
Zopfiella sp.	unknown
Deuteromycotina	
Cirrenalia macrocephala	soft rot (type 1)
Dictyosporium toruloides	unknown
Gliomastix murorum	unknown
Humicola alopallonella	soft rot (type 1)
Monodictys pelagica	soft rot (type 1)
Penicillium sp.*	staining
Stachybotrys atra*	staining
Trichocladium achrasporum*	soft rot (type 1)
Zalerion maritimum	soft rot (type 1)
Zalerion varium	soft rot (type 1)
Basidiomycotina	
Digitatispora maritima	white rot
Nia vibrissa	white rot

* = terrestrial species

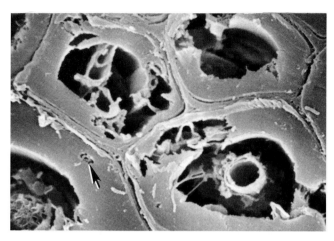

Figure 3.3 Conidium (fruiting structure) of the fungus Monodictys pelagica (SEM)

Figure 3.4 Soft rot fungal attack (arrowed) of the secondary wall layer of a wood cell fibre (oak) (SEM)

extensive examination of a large sample, indicating that fungal attack of stored polyethylene wrapped timbers was very localised. The absence of brown rot fungi and the isolation of two white rot fungi is not surprising (Fig. 3.4). This can be attributed to the vulnerability of their enzymes to dilution in the marine environment. As a result, brown rot fungi were not found in stored *Mary Rose* artefacts and timbers. The marine rot fungi *Digitatispora marina* and *Nia vibrissa* (Fig. 3.5) were found to be inefficient degraders of stored timbers (for

effects of the organisms on the wreck as she lay on the seabed, see Chapter 2).

Bacterial decay was more frequently observed. Once again this form of decay was also very localised. Erosion and tunnelling decay patterns were observed in a number of timbers. The erosion troughs were observed below the decayed layers of timbers whilst tunnelling or burrowing bacteria were observed closer to the outer cell layers. Tunnelling was restricted to aerobic bacteria and is usually a characteristic of an advanced stage of decay.

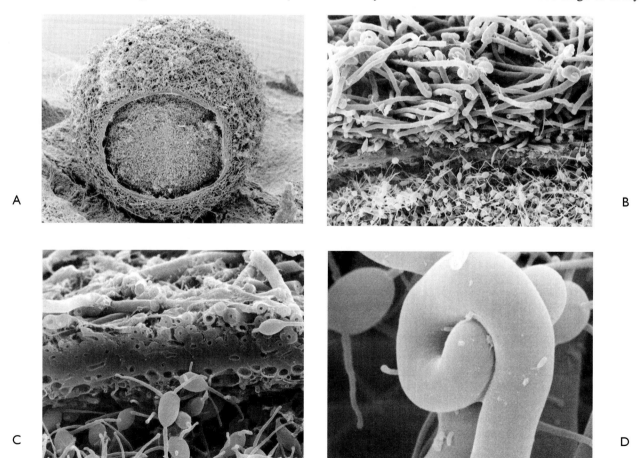

Figure 3.5 The fruiting structure (basidiocarp) of Nia vibrissa *(white rot) which has been freeze fractured (A) to show wall layer (B and D) and spores (C) (SEM) (x18, x50, x50, x150)*

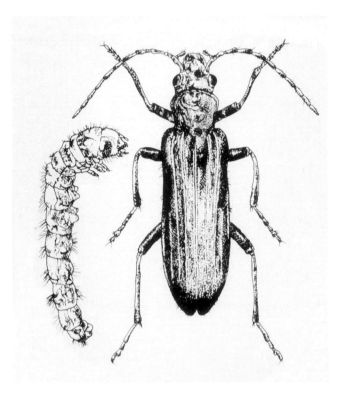

Figure 3.6 Wharf-borer beetle larva and adult (after Hickin 1968). Adult length 13–15mm

If, as suggested by Mouzouras (1987), anaerobic bacteria can only cause erosion of the wood cell wall, this indicates that the core of waterlogged archaeological timbers may be anaerobic. A low oxygen tension, which exists in the core of *Mary Rose* timbers, may also explain the absence of fungi deeper in the wood.

The possible explanation for the lack of active decay in polyethylene wrapped stored wood may be simply that unfavourable conditions exist in timbers which are encapsulated in polyethylene. Oxygen levels within the bags are very low, with little gaseous exchange across the polyethylene barrier. Also, with little or no water vapour exchange between the polyethylene barrier system and the external environment, a build up of toxic substances and secondary metabolites takes place, thereby inhibiting the growth of fungi and aerobic bacteria. The combined action of low oxygen and presence of these substances may explain the lack of recent decay by aerobic micro-organisms in stored timbers.

Biocides have been employed in attempts to control microbial growth (Jones *et al.* 1986). However, their limited efficacy over time makes re-treatment necessary. This is often time-consuming and creates future problems for conservators both in handling the wood and in the safe disposal of biocide solution. It must also be noted that biocides may interfere with radiocarbon dating and future active conservation treatment processes.

Cold storage of polyethylene wrapped *Mary Rose* wood revealed that the activity of wood degrading micro-organisms is arrested. However, viability of the mixed microbial flora (bacteria and fungi) supported by a range of wrapped timbers was not affected by cold storage. The threat of renewed bio-deterioration under more favourable conditions therefore exists. Cold storage and biocide treatments are therefore only suitable for the short-term storage of wrapped timbers where the risk of bio-deterioration is considered low.

The fruiting structures of fungi present on the wood surface can also be a health hazard to the handlers of stored timbers. The fungus *Stachybotrys atra* was found to be present on a number of stored timbers. This fungus causes a mycotoxicosis known as stachybotryotoxicosis, which can be fatal in humans. It must be stressed that archaeological timbers in storage should be carefully monitored for microbial growths and that control of these organisms be undertaken.

A number of *Mary Rose* timbers have also been stored in a carbon dioxide atmosphere. This method was ineffective in preventing either microbial wood decay activity or the viability of the mixed microbial flora found growing on them. During a study to evaluate the efficacy of this method, the anaerobic environment created was found to support the growth of anaerobic human pathogens, presenting a serious health risk.

In short, during the study of stored polyethylene wrapped wet wood it became apparent that this method was efficient in preventing desiccation but ineffective in preventing microbial decay activity or the viability of the mixed microflora identified. Cold storage and biocide treatments did, however, help reduce microbial activity.

More recently, another type of decay organism was found living in stored timbers wrapped in polyethylene. A survey of 1568 stored timbers revealed that the larvae of the wharf-borer beetle (Fig. 3.6), *Nacerdes melanura*, infested 2% of these timbers. Attack is not always apparent from examination of the outer surfaces. The presence of flight holes or small piles of fras (insect droppings) was often the only visible indication that the timbers were infested.

Damage caused by the wharf-borer larvae is often extensive. They produce tunnels throughout the softer

Figure 3.7 Wharf borer damage to surface of timber

Figure 3.8 Larva of wharf-borer attacking surface of oak timber

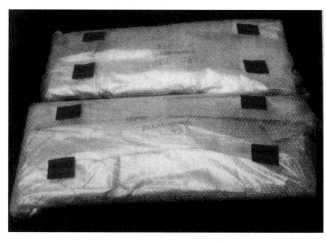

Figure 3.9 Stored timber wrapped in a metallised polyester barrier, hermetically sealed and covered with 'bubble pak'

decayed regions of timbers. The tunnels vary in dimensions depending on the size of the larva and were found on both upper and lower surfaces of stored timbers (Fig. 3.7). The extent of damage within stored timbers varied and depended upon the degree of larval infestation. Timbers with high larval numbers (18–20) showed extensive attack and destruction. This attack was restricted to the outer surfaces of the timbers to a depth of 10mm (Fig. 3.8). Timbers attacked included oak, poplar, and pine, indicating that the larvae of *Nacerdes melanura* was capable of infesting both softwoods and hardwoods. The infested timbers surveyed had a moisture content ranging between 131–670%.

The survey of stored timbers also indicated that the polyethylene sheeting could be penetrated by emerging adults and that seals on some packaging were poor. Studies involving different types of packaging materials indicated a need to replace polyethylene with a more suitable material. Technical data presented in Table 3.2 show the barrier properties of a number of wrapping materials tested. Data show that all materials tested were more impermeable to oxygen and moisture than the polyethylene originally used to wrap stored *Mary Rose* timbers.

The material chosen to replace polyethylene was a barrier foil T1-19v (Fig. 3.9). This material possesses

Table 3.2 Physical properties of wrapping materials tested (after Pitman 1994)

Wrapping material	Oxygen transmission rate	Water vapour transmission rate
60 Surlyn/1001 Surlyn	9.5	1.1
70 Nylon/1251 Surlyn	9.5	0.9
Tl-19V	<0.01	<0.05
Tl-25x	<0.01	<0.05
Polyethylene (500 gauge)	4.0	1500

OTR = cm^3 m^2 $24hr^{-1}$ WVTR = g m^2 $24hr^{-1}$

low oxygen and water transmission properties making it a suitable candidate for the storage of archaeological timbers. Lower oxygen tensions that existed within T1–19V wrapped timbers reduced microbial activity and prevented further infestation by wharf-borer beetle. T1–19v is now used to wrap all stored archaeological material from the *Mary Rose*.

Cold water spraying of the Mary Rose *hull*

Problems arise when complete or partially complete large wooden structures have to be held passively without suffering serious drying. Tanking large ships is expensive and often impractical. In such instances, direct spraying is employed. The spraying of ships and other large structures with fresh water has an added advantage in that the mud, silt and salt deposits are washed out. The purpose of passive holding of the *Mary Rose* hull, as with any waterlogged or decayed wooden artefact, was to maintain water saturation and prevent further deterioration. It also provided an opportunity to study the condition of the hull in order to determine a suitable treatment.

A major problem with the passive storage of the *Mary Rose* hull was one of size. Many of the storage methods described in the literature (van der Heide 1972; Barkman 1975; Dawson *et al.* 1982) have been developed for the storage of small finds and most are not capable of expansion to a larger scale. The only suitable method to passively hold the hull of the *Mary Rose* was by water spraying (Fig. 3.10). A research programme was then set up to compare a warm (20°C) and cold water (5°C) spraying regime using original ship's timbers. The results were predictable, showing significant differences in bacterial activity between warm water and cold water spraying regimes. Maintaining a water spray temperature of below 5°C substantially reduced the degree of microbial activity within hull timbers.

Figure 3.10 The ship under spray during the passive holding phase

Figure 3.11 The ship during a non-spraying period

Based upon these findings, a low temperature water spraying regime was chosen to passively store the hull of the *Mary Rose*. The reasons for this were as follows:

- water saturation of the hull timbers would be maintained by the constant flow of water;
- temperature of the spray water maintained between 2 and 5°C. At these temperatures, microbial activity is well below the optimum growth temperature of many marine and terrestrial fungi and bacteria which cause wood decay;
- the method was safe and non-toxic;
- the method was compatible with future conservation treatment processes.

Following its recovery in October 1982, the entire hull of the *Mary Rose* was sprayed with cold water. Using this method, the hull was passively held for a period of 12 years during which post-excavation recording, cleaning and reconstruction work were completed. In addition to these important tasks, the passive holding period provided the Trust's conservators with an opportunity to investigate the nature and condition of the hull timbers.

Throughout the period of passive holding, the hull was displayed to the public in a specially constructed building within Dry Dock No. 3 at HM Naval Base, Portsmouth. The building itself protects the hull from the external environment by providing appropriate thermal and vapour insulation properties. The fabric of the building consists of a double layer of Treveira (polyester cloth covered with PVC). Inside this building, a spray system ensured that the entire hull was saturated with recycled, refrigerated, filtered fresh water.

The spray system operated continuously during non-working hours, only being turned off for a maximum of four 1 hour periods each week day to allow staff to reconstruct the various decks (Fig. 3.11). The water spray system consisted of an interconnecting system of variously sized PVC pipes with full jet spray nozzles positioned at 1 metre intervals. Filtered, chilled fresh water was furnished to each nozzle where it was atomised into small droplets (250 micron diameters). In total, 567 nozzles were positioned around the hull ensuring complete coverage.

Reducing the temperature of the spray water was achieved by passing filtered water through four industrial-sized refrigeration units. These units reduced the temperature of the water to between 2 and 5°C. Two submersible pumps situated in the water reservoir pumped cold water to the spray nozzles. Returning spray water was collected in a catchment tank situated beneath the hull. The water then passed into the settlement tank where it was filtered and pumped into the spray water reservoir (Fig. 3.12). Re-chilling occurred and the filtered, cold water was once again furnished to the spray system.

Data of the passive holding system
- One catchment tray (35m long, 15m wide, 0.5m deep);
- One GRP settlement tank (4x3x1m);
- One spraywater reservoir (4x2x1m);
- 162 metres of 3.5 inch (*c.* 90mm) PVC piping;
- 115 metres of 1.5 inch (*c.* 40mm) plastic connecting hose;
- 30 metres of 1 inch (*c.* 25mm) PVC piping;
- 567 full jet Dela-Fit nozzles (0.25 inch (6mm) BSPT). 431 l/min, spray angle 115° at 2 bar;

42

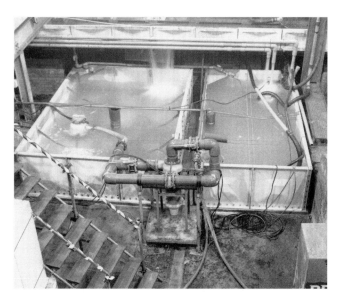

Figure 3.12 Water tanks containing large submersible pumps used to pump cold water to the spray nozzles

- One Dorr-clone filter (RP) 12 inch (*c.* 305mm) filter;
- One Flygt BS 2151 submersible filter pump (1136l/min);
- Two Flygt BS 2125 submersible spray pump (590l/min);
- One Flygt BS 2125 chilling unit pump (590l/min);
- One Flygt BS chilling unit pump (100l/min);
- Four chilling units.

Experimental work

After preliminary studies, a standard monitoring procedure was adopted by Trust scientists and subsequently used throughout the passive holding period. These are summarised below.

Environmental data

The shiphall environment and spray water temperature were monitored continuously using a multi–channel data logger. External temperatures were also recorded.

Chemical analysis of spray water

Total chemical analysis (Table 3.3) of spray water and raw mains water was carried out on a monthly basis to monitor diffusion of sea salts from the ship's timbers.

Monitoring of bacterial populations in the spray water

Weekly measurements were taken to quantify the number of colony-forming units per ml (cfu/ml) of spray water. This was achieved by the use of Tillomed nutrient agar dipslides to measure total aerobic bacteria. The dipslide tongue, which is coated with a layer of nutrient agar, was removed from its bottle and immersed into the spray water for about 10 seconds so that the agar surfaces were covered. The slide was then removed and allowed to drain for 2 seconds and replaced into its bottle. Dipslides were then incubated at 20°C for 2–7

Table 3.3. Analysis of spray water

pH value	Silica (mg/l)
Conductivity at 25°C	Total phosphate (mg/l)
Total hardness (mg/l)	Ortho-phosphate (mg/l)
Magenesium hardness (mg/l)	Meta-phosphate (mg/l)
Alkalinity (mg/l)	Copper in solution (mg/l)
Chloride (mg/l)	Boron (mg/l)
Nitrate (mg/l)	Titanium (mg/l)
Sulphate (mg/l)	Iron (mg/l)

days. Growth of bacterial colonies was compared with charts provided to estimate level of contamination (cfu, 10^3: very slight growth; 10^4: slight growth; 10^5: moderate growth; 10^6: heavy growth; 10^7: very heavy growth).

Macroscopic examination of hull timbers

The hull timbers were examined macroscopically for the following features:

- Presence of slime.
- Presence of fungal sporulating structures.

This was achieved by direct examination of the timber surfaces with the aid of an illuminated magnifier. In addition, slivers of wood bearing fungal sporulating structures were removed with a razor blade and examined under a light microscope. To isolate fungi that did not sporulate on the ship's timbers, core samples taken with an increment borer were inoculated onto antibiotic containing sea water cornmeal agar and sea water agar plates. These plates were then incubated at 20°C and examined regularly for fungal growth. Techniques and procedures for the examination and identification of marine fungi were those described by Kohlmeyer and Kohlmeyer (1979).

Monitoring microbial activity within hull timbers

Catalase is an enzyme common to all microbes and can be used to determine a microbial activity through timbers from surface layers to the inner sound core. Catalase activity (Line 1983) expressed as dissolved oxygen in parts per million was recorded every 10 seconds over a period of 1 minute. The amount of dissolved oxygen after 1 minute was then used as a measure of catalase (microbial) activity within hull timbers.

General observations

Throughout the 12 years of passive holding the water temperature was maintained between 2 and 5°C. During this period the system functioned well although some localised biocide (polybor) treatment of hull timbers was necessary to control microbial slimes (bacteria, cyanobacteria, diatoms and green algae) and fungal fruiting structures. Build-up of slime was a

Table 3.4. Microbial isolates recorded during the passive holding period

Bacteria	Fungi
Aeromonas sp.	*Neriospora cristata*
Alcaligenes sp.	*Lulworthis* sp.
Pseudomonas sp.	*Humicola alopallonella*
Vibrio sp.	*Monodictys pelagica*
	Cirrenalia macrocephala
	Trichocladium sp.

Figure 3.13 Ultrasonic tank used for cleaning and storage of large wooden objects

symptom of poor water flow over certain regions of the hull. Accelerating flow rate of the spray water prevented surface fouling by micro-organisms. However, over-excessive flow could result in the removal of the decayed outer surface of timbers to a depth of a few millimetres. Such destruction of important surface layers is unacceptable since they contain unique information, such as details of fabrication marks, etc. Further evidence that suggested the success of the cold water system relates to data obtained from micro-biological analysis of the spray water. Maintaining spray water temperature below 5°C substantially reduced the degree of microbial growth. Although micro-organisms can survive low temperatures (Atlas and Bartha 1987), their metabolic activities and growth rates decline below the optimal temperature. Differences in the number of viable aerobic bacteria for spray water temperatures of below 5°C and 20°C are 10^3 and 10^8 respectively. This reduction in viable bacterial numbers was clear evidence that a cold water spraying regime was an effective passive holding system. The optimal growth for bacterial and fungal isolates found inhabiting hull timbers was found to occur between 20 and 30°C (Table 3.4). This supports the view that suppression of microbial activity is temperature dependent.

Although bacteria and marine fungi were found to grow superficially on hull timbers, little active decay of the wood was observed by microscopy of wood samples. Bacterial and fungal attack of the wood cell walls was only observed in a few cases.

Throughout the passive holding period, there was a real risk of bacterial infection to staff working in the shiphall. Many common aquatic bacteria are able to colonise man-made water systems. Poorly maintained water systems provide ideal sites for their growth. *Legionella pneumophila*, a common aquatic bacteria, was considered a threat. The risk of Legionnaire's disease from the *Mary Rose* spray system was controlled by maintaining low water temperatures, maintaining a clean spray system, carefully monitoring of micro-biological populations and selective use of biocides to reduce the growth of biofilms (slime). Adhering to these simple guidelines removed the risk of infection to both public and staff.

Storage of large individual timbers and artefacts

Large individual waterlogged wood objects (gun carriages) and individual ship's timbers were stored in large tanks containing water (Fig. 3.13). The size of individual objects dictated the type of water tanks used. Plastic tanks with lids to exclude light were often used for the storage of smaller items. The advantage of this type of container is that it is stackable and can be used where space is an issue.

For the many large wooden objects and timbers recovered from the *Mary Rose*, purpose built tanks were constructed from a variety of materials, such as polypropylene and polyethylene, supported by a framework of steel tubing. These tanks were covered with black polyethylene to prevent light penetration. Tank water was changed on a regular basis to prevent heavy build up of slime.

All storage tanks, apart from one extremely large tank, were kept inside a building to prevent the occurrence of temperature extremes. Freezing of waterlogged wood will cause damage and high temperatures will accelerate the decay process. Although this method proved successful in preventing moisture loss from the timbers, growth of slime and wood-degrading organisms was not arrested. From time to time it was necessary to control the growth of micro-organisms within storage tanks. Bio-control using snails (*Physa* sp.) proved most effective in controlling bacterial numbers whilst ampholytic surfactants and ultraviolet light performed relatively poorly.

For a limited time after recovery the Trust stored a large number of individual ship's timbers in a local pond (Fig. 2.17, above). This pond was ideally suited for this purpose because of it was tolerant of various local environmental conditions. It was also found to support large numbers of the common pond snail (*Physa* sp), which was well suited for the removal of organisms on the timber surface. No grazing damage to the timber surface was observed and there was little evidence of surface fouling.

Table 3.5 Radiosensitivity of wood decay organisms (after Pointing 1995)

Organism	Data source	Minimum lethal dose (KGy)
Aerobic bacteria	*Mary Rose* timbers	2.4
Anaerobic bacteria	National collection of bacteria	2.5
Invertebrates	*Mary Rose* timbers	3.2
Marine fungi	*Mary Rose* timbers	12.0
Terrestrial fungi	*Mary Rose* timbers	13.0

Gamma irradiation sterilisation

In many projects, the temporary storage of wood after excavation all too frequently turns into longer-term storage while conservation issues, such as funding, are debated or deferred. Extending passive storage indefinitely may lead to the degradation of the wood over a period of several years until it is in too poor a condition for conservation. To prevent this situation from developing, Trust scientists have been involved in the search for an improved passive holding method which fulfils all the criteria laid down by Dawson *et al.* (1982). The bio-deterioration of irreplaceable wooden artefacts has been demonstrated in the various methods employed by the Mary Rose Trust and the need for a passive conservation method that will prevent bio-deteriogenic organisms has resulted in the use of gamma irradiation to control bacteria, fungi and insects living in stored ancient wet wood. Research by Pointing (1995) has shown that gamma irradiation is a superior alternative to cold and wet storage and it has been adopted by the Trust since 1998.

Screening a representative range of organisms (Table 3.5) revealed that a dose of 15 KGy is required for inactivation of most organisms. Gamma irradiation may also be desirable as a treatment for wood excavated from polluted archaeological sites. Applying UK medical sterilisation standards of 25 KGy (Anon 1994) ensures inactivation of any human pathogens in addition to wood decay organisms.

A dose level of 15–25 KGy had no adverse effects on the chemical and physical properties of waterlogged archaeological wood (Table 3.6). However, at dose levels in excess of 100KGy radiolytic damage was observed resulting in increased hygroscopicity, warping and splitting during drying, loss of surface texture, reductions in compressive and bending strength, and chemical alteration and degradation of wood cell wall components (Pointing 1995; Pointing *et al.* 1997). At very high dose levels, losses in cellulose crystallinity were observed with alkane and cycloalkane breakdown products formed.

Advice to conservators

A range of wrapped waterlogged timbers from the *Mary Rose* supporting a mixed bio-deteriogenic population have been successfully treated using gamma irradiation.

Table 3.6 Physical and chemical properties of *Mary Rose* wood after gamma irradiation effects on the (after Pointing 1995)

Wood	Appearance	Hygroscopicity	Shrinkage	MOR (bending)	MOE (stiffness)	Polyose chemistry	Lignin chemistry
Maximum dose does not affect wood quality (KGy)							
Recent oak heartwood	5000	500	NT	500	500	1500	1500
Mary Rose oak (class III)	1500	100	1500	NT	100	1500	1500
Mary Rose oak (class I)	1500	100	1500	NT	NT	1500	1500
Recent oak sapwood	5000	100	NT	100	100	1500	1500
Mary Rose oak sapwood (class I)	500	100	NT	NT	NT	1500	1500
Recent pine sapwood	5000	500	100	100	100	1500	1500
Mary Rose pine sapwood	1500	100	NT	NT	100	1500	1500

MOR = modulus of rupture; MOE = modulus of elasticity; NT = not tested; wood classification based on de Jong (1997)

More than ten years since their treatment, the timbers have remained sterile, with no evidence of microbial or insect activity. This level of efficacy cannot be achieved by other passive holding techniques (wrapping, cold storage, use of biocides, UV sterilisation, and water storage at low temperature).

Gamma irradiation, is suitable for the treatment of both slightly and heavily degraded waterlogged wood. An absorbed dose of 100KGy is acceptable for any one timber, and this dose level should not be exceeded in a single or repeated treatments, since higher irradiation doses may adversely affect the physical and chemical nature of the wood. An additional drawback to this process is that gamma-irradiated timbers are unsuitable for radiocarbon dating and any analytical process invalidated by exposure to radiation.

Gamma irradiation treatment involves wrapping timbers and transporting them to an irradiation facility. Exceptionally large objects that cannot be transported easily by hand will be unsuitable for this treatment. Smaller artefacts and individual ship's timbers were sterilised by this technique. For *Mary Rose* timbers inactivation of wood bio-deteriogens was achieved by a single dose of 20KGy for slightly degraded timbers not exceeding 75mm in thickness and for heavily degraded timbers up to 150mm in thickness. For much larger timbers the dose must be recalculated based on size and density of the timber but must not exceed 100KGy.

Timbers and artefacts selected for gamma irradiation must be heat-sealed in a radiation-stable wrapping material (volumetric barrier foil T1–19v). Further wrapping with a protective material such as 'bubble pak' is advised to avoid damage during transport. The wrapped object should be clearly labelled. A conservator should always supervise the wrapping, transportation and treatment in order to minimise the risk of accidental damage.

Following irradiation treatment it is important to maintain the integrity of the wrapping material surrounding the sterile object. Any breach will allow contamination of the sterile environment within the wrapping. Conservators at the Trust periodically check wrapping material for damage. No specialised storage environment (cold storage) is required. Once the timber is unwrapped, timber sterility will no longer be maintained. The gamma irradiation of timbers and artefacts helps reduce biological activity during active conservation.

One of the advantages of gamma irradiation treatment is that there is no residual radioactivity in the treated object which is, therefore, completely safe for handling by conservators and other specialists. This presents a clear advantage over biocide treated objects which often present toxicity problems. Gamma irradiation is also a low cost alternative to cold storage, with far greater efficacy in preventing on-going wood decay. Finally, gamma irradiation may be compared favourably to the criteria for an ideal passive holding method as laid out by Dawson *et al.* (1982) (Table 3.7).

Examination of wooden artefacts and timbers during passive holding

To ensure that the maximum information could be obtained from the assemblage of wooden material recovered from the wreck of the *Mary Rose* it was essential that all artefacts and ship's timbers were examined in detail. A great deal of this work took place during the passive holding period prior to active conservation. The examination of wooden material was designed to answer specific questions about the site, such as the preserving nature of the burial environment, type of timbers utilised, method of conversion of timber, manufacturing techniques, dating, deterioration information, etc.

Recording of the *Mary Rose* hull and her wooden artefacts was done on artefact and conservation recording cards. Archaeologists and conservators designed these when the excavation began. The wood recording work cards were tailor-made to suit all recovered wooden material. With the exception of artefact and timber dimensions, the recording on the conservation recording sheets was always carried out by a conservator specialising in wood technology or staff suitably trained and experienced. It should be noted that drawings and sketches were found to be more helpful than written descriptions. Information recorded on the cards in the winter of 1979–80 included the following:

Wood species identification
Woods are ordinarily known by their common, rather than their botanical, names. The species and varieties of wood are many, differing in colour, odour, weight and

Table 3.7 An evaluation of gamma irradiation as an ideal passive holding method
(after Pointing 1995)

Criteria for ideal storage*	Evaluation of gamma irradiation
Prevent or minimise further decay	Complete sterility of artefacts and ships timbers
Compatibility with future conservation treatments	At recommended dose levels (below 100KGy), effects unlikely but require further evaluation
Ease of maintenance	No specialised environment needed but wrapping material must remain intact
Cost effectiveness	Initial cost involved in wrapping and irradiation, but low storage and maintenance costs
Health and Safety issues	Does not result in any residual activity in the exposed wood

*after Dawson *et al.* (1982)

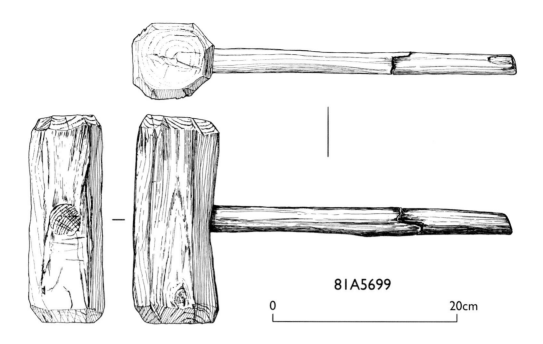

81A5699

0   20cm

Figure 3.14 Illustrating wooden objects: a mallet (scale 1:4)

physical properties. Identification of an unknown wood proves very useful in determining the uses of different woods during the sixteenth century. Attempts to identify the wood used in artefacts and ship's timbers was always made before conservation, as it is much easier at this stage and may have implications for the selection of a conservation treatment to be adopted.

Identification was achieved using microscopic characters and keys described by Schweingruber (1978). Free-hand sections from both artefacts and ship's timbers were cut with a stainless steel razor, mounted in distilled water or lactophenol and examined with a light microscope (x10 mag). The sample location was then marked on the archive drawing. Wood structure was examined on the three principal axes.

Functional interpretation
For convenience of recording, an excavated wooden object was given a simple name which often described its everyday use and function. Examples of simple names include plates, bowls, tankards, beams, planks, etc.

Technological evidence
The aim of recording archaeological wood is to allow detailed and accurate interpretation of the whole woodworking process from the selection of the tree to its final use as an artefact or structure. The choice of wood falls naturally into two categories; first, where the inherent characteristics are more important than availability; secondly, where availability is the primary factor, the properties of the wood being secondary. Species identifications of wooden artefacts and timbers were made to establish whether the natural

characteristics of a wood were being exploited to the full.

The conversion of a tree by the various methods of splitting, hewing or sawing was usually determined by examination of the ring patterns in cross-section. The study and recording of surviving tool marks also provided valuable information on the types of tools used to finish a timber. These features are a means of identifying the tool employed where surface preservation is very good. The variety of joints and treenails used during the building of a large wooden ship was also an important source of information on early ship building and woodworking techniques.

Technical examinations
Specific procedures for analysing waterlogged wood should distinguish between pre- and post-immersion damage. Of principal concern are the physical, chemical and biological forms of degradation that can range from total destruction by wave action (physical) to alterations at the ultrastructural level (chemical and biological). All artefacts and timbers intended for conservation were analysed to determine condition. There were three main aspects that needed to be considered:

- Physical state of the wood: size, weight, fragmentation, strength properties.
- Materials losses: loss of cell wall material due to the dissolution of lignin, cellulose, hemicellulose, degree of waterlogging, biological degradation, contact with corrosive material (copper, iron, marine concretions).
- Natural features: presence of bark or sapwood, grain orientation.

Photographs and illustrations

Artefacts and a selective sample of ship's timbers were photographed prior to active conservation. In addition to general shots, photographs of surface features, toolmarks, joints and areas of staining and wear were taken. During photographic sessions timbers were regularly sprayed with water to prevent surface desiccation. Slightly damp surfaces were found to be ideal for recording toolmarks. Both natural and artificial light was used in photography. Artefacts were always photographed on a light, but not white, background.

In addition to basic photography, x-rays were used to detect Tereinid (ship-worm) attack in ship's timbers. X-rays are able to penetrate wood and were used to recognise regions of damage and decay. X-ray facilities at HM Naval Base, Portsmouth were used to examine the internal conditions of ship-worm damaged timbers. Regions of attack were recognised by increased density on X-ray films.

Wooden artefacts and timbers were illustrated prior to active conservation. A measured pencil drawing was made on cartridge paper using standard techniques. Drafting film was then laid over the pencilwork and the final illustration drawn in ink using a standard range of drafting pens (Fig. 3.14), usually at scale 1:1, and provided with the unique identification number of the object and a bar scale. Illustrations show the following features: size, shape, direction of grain and position of branches or knots; areas of bark or sapwood and exposed heartwood; areas of decay, damage, staining and concretions, wear and compression; position and character of joints, holes nails and toolmarks. At least one cross-section showing relationship to other drawn faces was undertaken. Cross-sections showed the pith, sapwood, ray and ring patterns and, for ship's timbers, drawings were made of both ends. All illustrations were checked by a timber specialist.

Leather and Skin Products

Wet archaeological leather and other skin products from the *Mary Rose* site had been in equilibrium with their

Figure 3. 15 Unconserved leather shoe, as recovered

underwater environment for over 400 years. At the Trust, conservators were encouraged to recreate these conditions in passive storage (Fig. 3.15). Data required for such an approach include temperature, pH, dissolved oxygen, salinity and microbial activity. Armed with this information, the storage condition was designed to discourage biological activity and to remove inorganic salts from the leather objects.

First, adhering soils were removed by gentle brushing in de-ionised water, thus avoiding abrasion to the friable surface. The flesh side of the wet leather artefact was found to be weaker and cleaning of this surface was only carried out when the object was completely submerged. Accretions were then removed, either by special wooden hand tools or within an ultrasonic bath. Ultrasonic cleaning was not used for fragile material which might break up under the influence of the frequencies used. Following accretion removal all artefacts were rinsed out in tanks with gently running or agitated water.

Following cleaning, all wet leather artefacts and skin products were stored at low temperatures until active conservation methods commenced. This holding period was necessary for post-excavation recording, further cleaning to remove salts and stains, and reconstruction work. For the storage of leather artefacts, a continuous cold temperature environment was recommended. The reasons for this were threefold:

1. the artefact would be kept wet by wrapping in hermetically sealed polyethylene sheeting;
2. the low temperature (2–5°C) helped reduce biological growths;
3. the method was non-toxic.

On rare occasions quaternary ammonium salts (broad spectrum biocides) were used to control heavy bacterial and fungal growths. Following treatment with a biocide, all wet leather artefacts were rinsed thoroughly in de-ionised water. The passive holding phase for wet leather and skin artefacts varied from weeks to several months duration prior to the commencement of active conservation.

Textiles

Textile fragments of cotton, wools, hemp and silk were all found preserved by the anoxic silts of the Solent. While some finds such as wools and silks were found in a good state of preservation, cellulosic fragments were physically weak and required careful handling at all times.

All textile artefacts were stored in complete darkness and under low temperature (2–5°C) for periods of 1–2 weeks prior to the commencement of active conservation. Passive storage methods involved storage in sealed polyethylene bags and water baths containing chilled fresh water (pH 7–7.5). Water within the storage containers was changed on a regular basis to prevent a build up of biological growths. Biocides were not required.

Cordage

Rope from the *Mary Rose* wreck site was found in a well-preserved condition. All examples of rope, particularly the anchor cable, were heavily impregnated with tar. All cordage finds were placed in chilled fresh water to remove surface sediments and inorganic salts for periods of 1 week for non-tar impregnated finds and up to 12 weeks for tar impregnated objects prior to the commencement of active conservation.

Bone and Ivory

Artefacts made from these materials were stored in fresh water to prevent the crystallisation of salts, which often cause physical damage. Following desalination, little more was generally required unless the artefact was heavily stained with metal ions. Ivory finds were stored at low temperature (2–5°C).

Metal Artefacts and Concretions

Metal finds recovered from the *Mary Rose* site were found in what appeared to be a good state of preservation. However, some, in particular cast iron objects, were found to be in a very unstable state and required immediate storage in a stable storage environment to prevent active corrosion.

Iron artefacts

In both cast and wrought iron artefacts, the presence of chlorides accelerates the corrosion process (Fig. 3.16). During passive storage, iron finds must never be allowed

Figure 3.16 Unconserved iron gun with concretions

to dry out. When raised to the surface, the main factors that can accelerate corrosion are oxygen, water and chloride ions. Trust conservators undertook the elimination or control of these agents of deterioration by creating an ideal storage environment. Storage in a 5% w/w, solution of sodium sesquicarbonate in fresh water was used to store iron finds for periods of up to six months prior to the commencement of desalination and active conservation. This alkaline environment keeps out oxygen, neutralises any acidity resulting from the presence of chlorides and also forms a passivating film on the surface of the metal.

Copper and alloys

The major problem with copper and its alloys was again exposure to the atmosphere. The chlorides which penetrated the metal object often set up the cyclic corrosion process known as bronze disease (see Chapter 5). Deterioration of these finds is again caused by the presence of oxygen, humidity and chloride ions, which must be controlled.

Passive storage of copper and copper alloy finds was in a 5% w/w solution of sodium sesquicarbonate for periods of 3–6 months prior to desalination and active conservation.

Silver

Although silver finds were corroded and eroded at the *Mary Rose* site, once excavated and exposed to the atmosphere, they were not prone to further deterioration. These artefacts were stored dry until commencement of active conservation.

Gold

Gold coins associated with the wreck of the *Mary Rose* were not subject to corrosion and no problems were encountered on exposure to the atmosphere. As with silver objects they were washed and dried.

Lead, pewter and alloys

These metals and their alloys are stable when exposed to the atmosphere. Concretions were removed prior to dry storage. Lead artefacts, which are prone to gaseous pollutants, were wrapped in acid free tissue and sealed in polyethylene bags.

Glass, Ceramics and Stone

Upon recovery, glass, ceramic and stone objects were stored in an aqueous environment (Fig. 3.17). These

Figure 3.17 A wicker covered ceramic bottle

objects were immediately immersed in sea water, ensuring that all parts remained submerged, otherwise sea salts crystallisation would occur upon exposure to the atmosphere. The storage solution (sea water) was filtered and replenished every three days to prevent build up of biological growths. To prevent osmotic shock to glass and ceramic finds, replacement of sea water with fresh water was achieved slowly in a water cascade system (Chapter 8) over a period of two weeks. Ceramic and glass finds were never immediately stored in either tap water or de-ionised water.

4. Conservation of Waterlogged Archaeological Wood

The extent of deterioration of shipwrecked wood is dependent upon many factors that are often inter-related. Over the years, scientists have studied how different materials deteriorate within the marine environment. Research has focused not only on the physical, chemical and biological aspects of sea water but, more importantly, on the bottom sediments. From these studies scientists have attempted to predict how archaeological wood is affected by the many different factors that influence the rate and mechanisms of deterioration. However, even on wreck sites that have been thoroughly studied, it is still not clear why certain artefacts may have deteriorated while similar artefacts are well preserved.

Over the years there have been numerous scientific studies involving the deterioration of archaeological wood at the *Mary Rose* wreck site (in archive and see bibliography). From these important studies it is now possible to identify the major factors which affect archaeological wood at this site. These factors are:

- artefact composition, seabed composition
- seabed and tidal movements
- oxygen levels
- temperature
- pH, and
- marine organisms.

These factors are obviously inter-related and can affect the extent of deterioration in a number of different ways.

The combined effect of these complex factors is that an archaeological object made from wood must be considered individually when attempting to evaluate its decay history. In this chapter, the structure and general changes to archaeological wood within the marine environment will be discussed before describing in greater detail conservation treatments used for a number of individual artefacts.

Structure and Chemistry of Archaeological Wood

Throughout the course of history wood has always been, and still is, one of the most valued materials put to a variety of purposes. The unique physical properties that are associated with different timber species confirmed its suitability as a material for a wide range of uses. Even

to early civilisations, it supplied fuel, building material for shelter, weapons, a means of transport on both land and sea, and material for fabricating tools, utensils and furniture (Eaton and Hale 1993).

Many factors have contributed to the popularity of wood as a raw material, among the more important of which might be mentioned are the following: its availability in great quantities, often as a renewable resource in managed forests; its ease of working with tools to any desired size or shape; the ease by which it may be bent or twisted to special shapes; the readiness by which wooden components can be fastened together by treenails and iron nails; the natural durability of certain timber species against agents of decay; the ease by which it can be salvaged and re-used; its ability to float; its beauty of figure, and many other factors of greater or lesser importance.

Examining the artefacts recovered from the wreck site of the *Mary Rose* and looking at the diversity in the uses to which wood was put illustrates its importance. It was used for fabricating the hull, decks, masts, etc. and, in addition to the ship's structure, a wide range of wooden artefacts were found: rigging components, ship's furniture such as officers chests and tables, personal items such as wooden tankards and many kinds of weapons (longbows, arrows etc) and tools (planes, adzes, etc). These wooden artefacts had survived in varying states of preservation for an incredibly long period of time. Basically, the variability in the states of preservation of wooden artefacts recovered from the *Mary Rose* wreck site is due to the sum total of the length of time of burial, the depth of burial, different agents of decay, and the inherent characteristics of different wood species (Dinwoodie 1981). General statements about these aspects are presented below. If ancient wood is to be successfully treated then it is necessary to understand the decay process that occurs in the marine environment.

Cell types

This section, which describes the structure and chemistry of cells in some detail, is not intended as a complete dissertation on the subject, but is included simply for the purpose of considering the changes that occur in wooden shipwrecked material. From this view point we may begin picturing as a structure a natural organic product composed of tiny cells packed so tightly

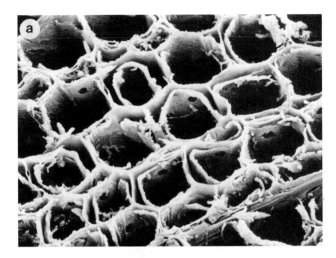

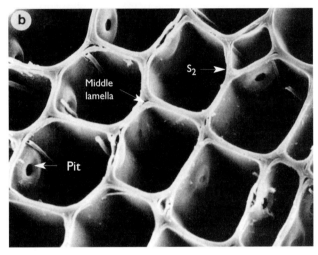

Figure 4.1 Transverse section of a sample of pine (after Mouzouras 1991); a) decayed region with S₂ layer of the cell wall totally degraded; b) sound early wood with the cell walls still intact (SEM) (x250, x300)

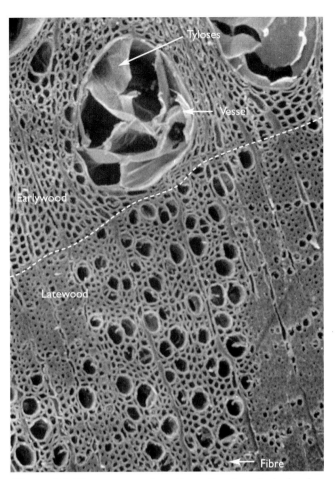

Figure 4.2 Transverse section of sound archaeological oak. Cell wall layers perfectly preserved. The transition between early and late wood is marked by a dotted line(SEM) (x100)

together that they form a 'honeycomb'. This structure can be seen, with the aid of a microscope, on a thin-section cut across the grain of the trunk or branch of a tree. The thickness of the walls of the cells determines the density of the wood, so that woods characterised by thick-walled cells are heavy and those with thin-walls are of a relatively light weight.

These cells vary also in size, shape and chemical composition and these differences are used to group wood into two general classes, commonly called 'softwoods' and 'hardwoods'. These terms are not entirely accurate, since some softwoods are actually harder than some of the hardwoods. Botanically speaking, the so-called softwoods are conifers, classified in a group called Gymnosperms, a term which broadly signifies a tree that bears exposed seeds (cones). The yew and pine trees are well known examples of this group. The other botanical group, comprising the various orders of hardwoods, consists of the angiosperms, which have true flowers and seeds enclosed in a fruit. The oaks and the elms are well known examples of this group. The various cell types

(collectively called the xylem) are organised into the axial and ray systems of the tree and the structure of individual cells and the arrangement of these cells into different zones reflect their function within the living tree by providing mechanical support, acting as water and nutrient conducting elements and as storage cells.

At the microscopic level, the difference between softwoods and hardwoods is determined by the types of cells found in the secondary xylem (Table 4.1). The morphology of softwood cells is illustrated in Figure 4.1 and hardwood cells in Figure 4.2. For a definition of terms see Glossary on p. 74.

Tracheids

Axial tracheids are elongate cells found in both softwoods and hardwoods that can be up to 5mm long, or even longer in some species. In softwoods this cell type performs the conducting and mechanical functions. Thick-walled tracheids are responsible for maintaining mechanical rigidity, whereas the thin-walled tracheids have a water and nutrient conducting function in the living tree. The distribution of thick- and thin-walled tracheids in softwoods is not random: the thin-walled tracheids are laid down at the beginning of the season (early wood), whereas the thick-walled cells are laid

Table 4.1 Cell types in softwoods and hardwoods
(modified from Harada and Cote 1985)

Axial cells	Transverse cells
Softwoods	
Tracheids	ray tracheids
Axial parenchyma cells	ray parenchyma cells
Epithelial cells	ray epithelial cells
Hardwoods	
Vessels	
Tracheids	
Fibre tracheids	
Libriform fibre	
Axial parenchyma cells	ray parenchyma cells
Epithelial cells	ray epithelial cells

down later (late wood). The tangential diameter of tracheid cells in softwoods ranges between 20 and 70mm and they are closely packed together so that a transverse section through them resembles a honeycomb. The quality of a softwood depends upon the proportion of thick- to thin-walled tracheids. The higher the proportion of late wood, the stronger the wood. In softwoods, tracheid cells make up more than 90% of the total volume (Harada and Cote 1985).

Axial parenchyma
Axial soft tissue cells (known collectively as parenchyma) are the storage tissue of a living tree and are often seen as lines running more or less at right-angles to rays, or as a sheath surrounding hardwood vessels. In hardwoods, axial parenchyma is more abundantly developed and displays greater variation in arrangement and distribution. Axial parenchyma, which is independent of vessels (see below) is described as 'apotracheal' and can be further subdivided into 'diffuse', 'banded' and 'terminal'. A second arrangement of axial parenchyma in hardwoods is 'paratracheal', which is always associated with vessels, and can be divided further into 'aliform', 'confluent' and 'vasicentric' categories. In hardwoods, parenchyma cells are thin-walled, oblong or square in shape and have simple pits.

In softwoods, axial cells feature prominently in members of the Cupressaceae (juniper family) and Taxodiaceae (redwoods), but are absent or having a sparse distribution in members of the Taxaceae (yews) and Pinaceae (pines).

Epithelial cells
These cells are found in the axial and ray systems of both softwoods and hardwoods. They are usually thin-walled and are associated with the production and secretion of gums, resins, etc. Resin canals are a characteristic feature of many softwoods. These are not cells, but cavities in the wood, lined with an epithelium of a parenchyma cell. They run vertically in the stem and horizontally in the rays.

Vessels
These are found only in hardwoods and are primarily the specialised water conducting cells. They are the counterparts in hardwoods of the thin-walled, conducting tracheids of softwoods. Unlike tracheids, which are rounded and intact, vessel members are perforate and are composed of wide cylindrical cells. There are two types of perforation plate: simple and multiple and these are found at the junction between adjacent vessel members. Simple perforation plates are round and open, multiple perforation plates are scalariform (ladder-like), reticulate (network) or ephedroid (group of circular holes). The size and distribution of vessels are useful criteria for identifying hardwoods since three types of pore arrangement can be distinguished. Vessels are distributed singly, or in groups throughout the wood. As a general rule, those formed at the beginning of the growing season are wider and have thinner walls than those formed in late season. Most of the temperate hardwood species including beech, birch and poplar are described as diffuse porous, exhibiting little differences in the size and distribution of the vessels across the growth ring. In contrast, ring porous types such as ash, elm and oak produce large diameter vessels in early wood and small vessels in late wood of successive growth rings. Finally some wood species are described as semi-ring porous, possessing larger vessels in early wood but a more gradual decrease in size through to the late wood region of the annual growth ring.

The vessels of the heartwood do not conduct water, since these are often blocked by structures called tyloses. In heartwood of European oak, all the vessels are blocked with tyloses, rendering the line of demarcation between sapwood and heartwood distinct, even in archaeological samples. Tyloses are important because they will impede the absorption of conservation polymers such as polyethylene glycol (PEG) which, in hardwoods, travel mainly through the vessels. In softwoods, where tyloses do not occur naturally, the movement of conservation polymers is largely through the bordered pits in the tracheid walls.

Fibres
These cells are considered to be the mechanical tissue of hardwoods and consist of libriform fibres and fibre tracheids (Figs 4.3 and 4.4). Libriform fibres are narrow cells with finely tapering ends. Cells can be more than 1.5mm long with an overall diameter of between 20 and 40μm. Fibre tracheids are also elongate cells but are shorter than libriform fibres and have less pointed ends. The walls of fibre tracheids are not as thick and the cell lumen is therefore more conspicuous. The pit connections between fibre tracheids are described as reduced bordered with slit-like appendages and a central pit while those between libriform fibres are usually in the form of simple pits.

In hardwoods, the thickness of the fibre walls and their physico-chemical nature are considered the most

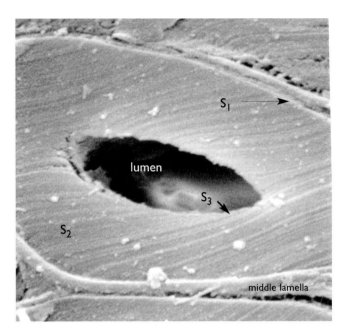

Figure 4.3 A well preserved wood fibre (oak) showing no signs of deterioration (SEM) (x3500)

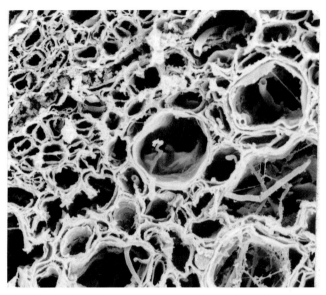

Figure 4.4 A sample of archaeological oak illustrating very decayed condition of cells in the outer surfaces (SEM) (x1500)

important factors in determining the strength, shrinkage and working properties of a ship's timber or wooden artefact.

Pits in softwoods and hardwoods

These serve as a communication between cells allowing the movement of liquids in and out of them. As might be expected, conducting cells have more pits than those concerned merely with the provision of mechanical rigidity. There are three principal types of pits found in softwoods and hardwoods namely simple pits, bordered pits and semi-bordered pits. Simple pits are small in diameter taking the form of straight-sided holes with a transverse membrane. These occur between parenchyma and parenchyma and also between fibre and fibre. In these cells the pit aperture at the luminal surface of the cell wall is slit-like, tapering to a full circle in the middle lamella.

Bordered pits are a regular feature of softwood tracheids. The entrance to the pit is domed and the internal chamber is characterised by a net-like membrane or 'margo' which supports a diaphragm or 'torus'. Differential pressure between adjacent tracheids causes the torus to move against the pit aperture, effectively preventing flow of liquid. As discussed below, these pits have a profound influence on the conservation of waterlogged archaeological timber. Bordered pits are also present in the cell walls of adjacent vessels in hardwoods, but their size, shape and arrangement is usually different to those observed in softwood tracheids. In hardwoods, the pit apertures may be oval and elongate and their arrangement can form distinct patterns in the cell wall. Patterns are described as 'scarliform', 'opposite' or 'alternate'. Unlike most softwoods, the bordered pit membranes in hardwoods

are impervious and composed of fine strands of cellulose.

Pit structures that are somewhat intermediate between simple and bordered pits are described as semi-bordered. These are characterised by the presence of a pit membrane but the torus is absent. Differences in size and shape of these pits are important anatomical features in the identification of softwoods. Finally, it must be pointed out that not all bordered pits have freely opened apertures and pit chambers. In some wood species, the pits are occluded by deposits or outgrowths and are described as 'vestured'. They create severe constriction in the pit canal and undoubtedly restrict the flow of liquids through the pit.

Wood cell wall ultrastructure and chemistry

Wood cell walls are structurally and chemically complex. The cell wall has been found to consist of several layers, which differ significantly in chemical composition. Most cell walls are composed of primary and secondary layers with a middle lamella, which forms a boundary between individual cells (Fig. 4.3). The thin primary wall develops first as cells undergo different-iation, while the thicker secondary wall layers are laid down inside the primary wall, usually after cell enlargement has ceased. A more detailed illustration (Fig. 4.5) shows that the secondary wall layer is made up of three layers; the S_1, S_2 and S_3. The transition between the middle lamella to primary cell wall is not clear, so the term compound middle lamella is used to describe both middle lamella and the adjacent primary wall layer.

The primary chemical components of these layers are cellulose, hemicellulose, and lignin that together account for 97–99% of the wood material (Fig. 4.5).

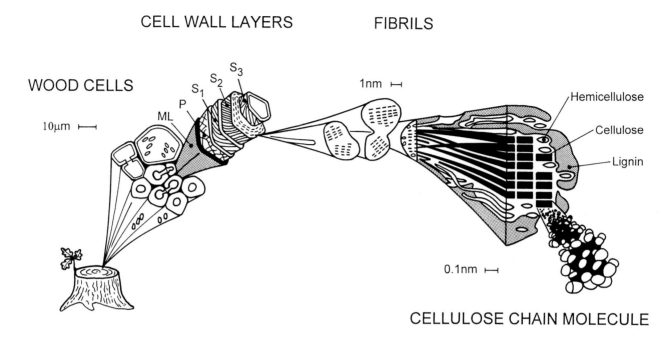

CELL WALL LAYERS FIBRILS

WOOD CELLS

10μm ⊢⊣

1nm ⊢⊣

Hemicellulose

Cellulose

Lignin

0.1nm ⊢⊣

CELLULOSE CHAIN MOLECULE

Figure 4.5 The structure of wood cell walls (modified after Hoffmann and Jones 1990)

Cellulose is present in greatest amounts, accounting for 40–55% of the total cell wall mass while hemicellulose content makes up approximately 25–40% and lignin about 18–33% of the total. In addition, the percentage chemical composition varies between hardwoods and softwoods.

Cellulose
Cellulose is the main structural polysaccharide of wood cells, making up approximately 40–50% weight of wood. Cellulose is made up of approximately 7000–12,000 glucose units joined together in a chain by the removal of one molecule of water between adjacent hydroxyl groups on adjacent monomers. Hydrogen bonding also leads to strong association with adjacent molecules, which form bundles known as fibrils. Glucose units are so regularly aligned that about 70% of the structure is crystalline, as demonstrated by x-ray diffraction studies. Cellulose fibril imparts great tensile strength and a low solubility in most solvents and is relatively resistant to hydrolysis.

Hemicellulose and pectins
The second major polysaccharide found in wood cells is hemicellulose, which accounts for 20–30% of the chemical mass. It is very soluble in aqueous alkali and is built up of branched chains of various simple sugars of approximately 100–200 sugar units per molecule. In softwoods the major component of hemicellulose is gluccomannan and it consists of unbranched chains containing mannose, glucose, galactose and an acetyl group linked to every third or fourth glucose and mannose units. The major hardwood hemicellulose is a glucouronoxylan which consists of xylose, 4-O-methylglucuronic acid and an acetyl group.

Pectins, a minor but important polysaccharide of wood cells, make up approximately 1% of the overall chemical mass. These are usually found in the middle lamella and are make up of galactouronic acid units often interspersed with the deoxy sugar rhamnose. Pectins are highly soluble in neutral water.

Lignin
These are amorphous cross-linked phenolic polymers that make up approximately 20–30% of the chemical mass cell wall component and have molecular weights ranging from thousands to hundreds of thousands. Lignins (Fig. 4.5) are produced from three cinnamyl alcohols. These structural units have propylphenyl carbon skeletons and differ from one another only by the number of methoxyl groups that are substituted on the benzene ring.

The types and relative amounts of cellulose, hemicellulose and lignin vary among wood cell types, between late and early wood and within individual cell walls. These differences affect the resistance of the various cells to degradation in the marine environment. All three polymers have distinct structural roles that are related to this architecture. Cellulose, which is predominantly crystalline in nature, provides the reinforcing framework of the cell walls. Hemicellulose and lignin function is to buttress the cellulose fibrils when wood is placed under stress.

Deterioration of archaeological wood

Examination of *Mary Rose* wood with polarised light showed that there was little residual birefringence of the surface layers. Birefringence increases with depth into the wood. This shows the marked decrease of the cellulosic components of the cell walls of waterlogged archaeological wood. Towards the inner regions of a timber or artefact, cellulose remained birefringent, indicating no microbial decay. In most cases, *Mary Rose* timbers have an outer layer of decayed cells, a transition zone containing decayed and undecayed wood cells and an inner sound core of well-preserved wood cells. This is typical of the wood recovered from the marine environment (Christensen 1970; de Jong 1977).

Similar observations were made with the scanning and transmission electron microscope. In the outer regions of wooden artefacts and ship's timbers, cell wall material was heavily degraded, especially the S_2 layers. Remants of microbial attack (bacterial and fungal) were observed, along with signs of chemical dissolution of cell wall material. A gradual improvement in condition of the wood is observed with increasing depth until an inner sound core of wood cells is reached. It was observed in hardwood species that fibre and ray cells were the most decayed wood cell types, while the vessels were the least degraded. In softwoods, tracheids and ray cells were the most decayed.

Exposed portions of the hull timbers and artefacts were, however, subject to a form of sand blasting by the abrasive action of the silt-laden currents of the Solent waters. This resulted in thinning and weakening of the outer surfaces.

In terms of the hull, the erosion of the uncovered superstructure caused port-side timbers to fall into an adjacent scour pit. Continued erosion finally led to the collapse of the ship's bow leaving only a few deck beams exposed to the sea water. A schematic summary of the sedimentary characteristics at the wreck site is illustrated in Figure 2.8, above.

Weakening of the *Mary Rose* timbers and wooden artefacts can also be attributed to the activities of biological organisms such as bacteria, soft rot fungi,

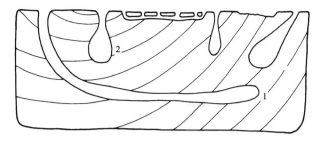

Figure 4.7 General morphology of the tunnels of 1) Limnoria sp. and 2) Teredo sp.

actinomycetes and wood-boring animals, as outlined in Chapter 2 (Figs 4.6, 4.7 and 2.13, above). Soon after being wrecked, the timbers of the *Mary Rose* absorbed sea water and were soon colonised by micro-organisms in probably the following sequence: bacteria, actinomycetes, soft rot fungi. The predominant bacterial types would have been rod- and oval-like in appearance and some of these organisms would have caused severe degradation to the outer surface of timbers during their early stages of exposure to sea water. Their long-term effect on both large and small wooden artefacts would have resulted in a pronounced increase in the permeability of the wood cell structure due to the degradation of the pit membranes. This phenomenon would have occurred within a few months of sinking.

Examination of the ship's timbers reveals ancient decay patterns of the wood cells that are suspected of being caused by marine bacteria (Fig. 4.8). The most common type of degradation is caused by erosion bacteria that can be distinguished by the appearance of lysis zones which are produced by the organisms themselves. Bacteria can be seen lying in the erosion trough, which conforms closely to the shape of the micro-organism. As we have described, this form of attack in *Mary Rose* timbers is very common and can occur in both aerobic and anaerobic conditions. Erosion troughs are probably the result of cell wall bound cellulases or extracellular activity attacking the cellulose component of the S_3 and S_2 layers of the wood cell wall. This results in partial or total conversion of these layers into an amorphous mass of residual cell wall and bacteria. The middle lamella is not degraded and is the best preserved cell wall layer.

Severe attack by erosion bacteria extends deeply into the ship's timber. A second type of bacterial attack found in the timbers of the *Mary Rose* is tunnelling, which takes place within the wood cell wall. A characteristic feature of this attack is the concentric wall like structures, probably composed of polysaccharides secreted by the tunnelling bacteria. A single bacterium can usually be seen in the front of each tunnel. Division of the bacteria leads to an increase in the number of these micro-organisms, some of which will initiate new tunnels in different directions. This results in a branched pattern of tunnels (Blanchette *et al.* 1990). The third type of bacterial attack of ships' timbers, called

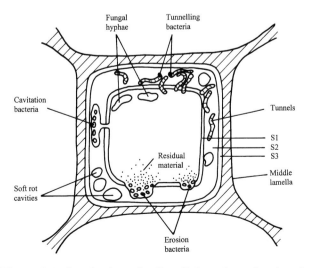

Figure 4.6 Attack of wood cell walls by soft rot fungi and bacteria (after Singh and Kim 1997)

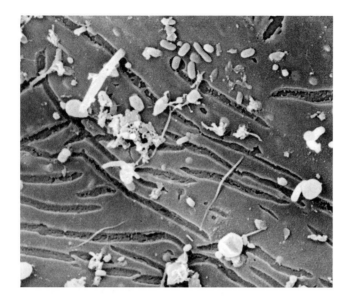

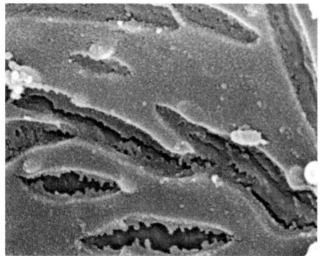

Figure 4.8 Examples of the effects of decay in the patterns of wood cells caused by marine bacteria (SEM) (x3500, x4000)

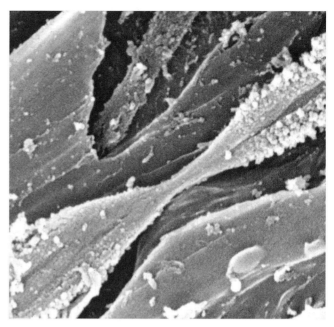

Figure 4.9 Longitudinal section of oak showing hyphae sitting within a soft rot cavity (SEM) (x3000)

cavitation, was not detected within timbers of the *Mary Rose.*

Finally, the difference in susceptibility of hardwood and softwood ship's timbers is worthy of comment. Identical decay patterns were produced in both hardwood and softwood types examined. However, softwoods, such as pine, would have been more resistant because they contained toxic substances which inhibit bacterial decay. However, once these toxins had leached out, softwood timbers were then rapidly colonised and degraded by bacteria. Bacteria, the initial colonisers, were then superseded by marine fungi in their role as the degraders of the wood cell wall layers (especially S_1 and S_2).

The first wood-rotting marine fungi to colonise exposed ships timbers are the soft rot fungi (Levy 1982). Marine soft-rot fungi grow in aerobic environments and require dissolved oxygen levels greater than 0.3 ml per litre. These fungi grow within the S_2 layer of the wood cell wall forming chains of distinct cavities with conical

ends. Cavities are usually formed along the length of the hyphae. In transverse sections, cavities within the S_2 layer appear as rounded holes. Enlargement of cavities through enzymatic activity eventually leads to the complete destruction of the S_2 layer. Cavity formation commences when hyphae growing in the cell lumen send a fine hyphal branch through the S_3 layer into the S_2 layer of the wood cell wall (Fig. 4.9). Once inside the S_2 layer the penetration hyphae branch to form T-branches with each branch growing parallel to the cellulose microfibrils and enzymatic breakdown of the S_2 ensues. The S_3 layer and middle lamella seem to unaffected by these fungi.

An additional type of attack by soft rot fungi was described by Corbett (1965). He demonstrated that some soft rot fungi can cause erosion of the wood cell wall. This form of attack has not been seen in *Mary Rose* timbers though soft rot attack by members of the Ascomycotina and Deuteromycotina has contributed significantly to the softening of outer surface layers (Jones *et al.* 1986; Mouzouras *et al.* 1990; Mouzouras 1990). As a result of bacterial and fungal decay, marine boring animals attacked the softened outer surface of exposed ship's timbers. As described in Chapter 2, at the wreck site, two main groups of marine borers were responsible for destroying large areas of exposed port-side timbers and exposed artefacts: the crustaceans and the molluscs.

The majority of wood-destroying crustaceans are members of the families Isopoda and Amphipoda. The adults have segmented bodies and legs and are able to crawl over timber surfaces allowing adults to move from one timber to another (Fig. 4.10). This contrasts with the wood boring molluscs which remain in their burrows for life (Fig. 4.11). The most commonly recorded wood

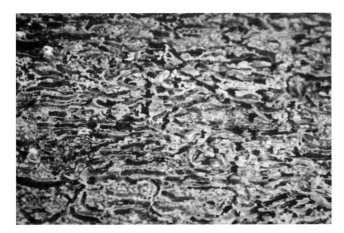

Figure 4.10 Damage to timber surface by Limnoria. *Note superficial tunnels formed beneath the surface*

Figure 4.11 Damage to exposed deck beam by the mollusc Teredo navalis

boring crustaceans at the underwater site are the genus *Limnoria* which are members of the Isopoda. Evidence of superficial attack by limnoriids of *Mary Rose* timbers and artefacts, soon after wrecking, is supported by the presence of a characteristic extensive network of galleries beneath the timber surfaces of recently excavated examples from Tudor sediments. Deck beams, carlings, planks, yew longbows and the so-called plotting board (see *AMR* Vol. 4, chapter 3) all show signs of attack by these crustaceans.

In the pine timbers of the Upper deck, the early wood appears to be attacked first leaving thin plates of late wood. Limnoridds are small animals, usually 2–4mm in length and greyish–white in colour. A large number of softwood and hardwood timbers and artefacts of the *Mary Rose* had been infested with these organisms resulting in long narrow tunnels 1–3mm in diameter with respiration holes present throughout the infested timber. The three species *L. lignorum. L. quadripunctata* and *L. Tripunctata* are common to the Solent waters and were isolated from exposed *Mary Rose* ship's timbers. These species are extremely aggressive degraders of wood and played a significant role in the destruction of the port-side timbers.

After a period of time, the hull and artefacts became covered by a hard layer of clay and crushed shells which sealed the ship and her contents for over 400 years.

Condition of archaeological wood

The condition of archaeological wood is not uniform and variations exist between the various wood species and conditions within a wreck site. Before a conservation method can be selected, the nature and extent of deterioration must be characterised. Changes to archaeological wood in terms of moisture content and cell wall chemistry have been used to determine the extent of deterioration by comparison with modern wood. Also, physical strength tests are often used to determine residual strength along with specific gravity

determinations. A useful scheme of classification for archaeological oak was developed by de Jong (1977; 1978) and used by Trust conservators. The scheme divides waterlogged wood into three distinct classes.

Class I: Wood containing over 400% water
Class II: Wood containing 185-400% water
Class III: Wood containing less than 185% water

Class I wood has lost almost all of its hard core. Class II has a relatively small hard-core present whilst Class III has a hard core present beneath a thin deteriorated surface layer.

Ship's timbers

A total of 134 ship's timbers were examined. Of these, 109 were oak, 12 elm, 9 poplar and 14 pine. The moisture content of every timber examined was determined and examples are listed in Table 4.2. These values are averages of three samples taken from each timber. Timbers were placed into one of de Jong's three categories (1977): 44% Class I, 50% Class II and 6% Class III (Fig. 4.3).

Additional data relating to moisture content was determined by taking 5mm cores from selected hull timbers. In each case the results represent a profile of the timber from surface to inner sound core, which is approximately 200–300mm below the outer surface. The direction of coring was through the tangential surface. All timbers examined were found to have moisture contents above 140% with values up to 760%. Moisture content values were found to be higher at the surface and decreased in value towards the centre of the timber. The majority of hull timbers have a hard, little degraded core below a thin, highly decayed outer surface.

Chemical analysis

Nuclear Magnetic Resonance Spectrometry (^{13}C cross polarisation magic angle spinning) and non-quaternary suppression spectrometry were employed by Trust

Table 4.2 Examination of a selection of hull timbers

Timber No.	Species	Moisture content (%)	Texture	Colour	Iron deposits
76/T52	oak	397	solid-spongy	dark brown	absent
77/T128	poplar	560	spongy	light brown	present
78/T180	elm	320	solid-spongy	brown	present
79/T332	elm	226	solid-spongy	brown	absent
80/T100	oak	329	solid-spongy	dark brown	absent
81/T227	pine	394	spongy	brown	absent
81T/350	oak	535	friable	dark brown	absent
81/T517	oak	262	solid	dark brown	present
81/T1137	oak	643	spongy	dark brown	absent
82/T44	oak	188	solid	dark brown	present
82/T400	oak	610	spongy	dark brown	spongy

conservators to determine chemical changes to *Mary Rose* wood (Pointing 1995). The NMR spectrometer used was a Bruker MSL 300 operating at the ^{13}C NMR frequency of 75MHz. The cross polarisation and decoupling r.f. field (B_{1H}) was 52KHz. The dephasing time used in NQS analysis was 50µs. The chemical shift was calibrated after each sample run using the reference adamantane sample (CH line at 38.56ppm and CH_2 line at 29.5ppm). From the spectra obtained, chemical changes to the wood structure and degradation products were identified for waterlogged archaeological oak (Class III heartwood, Class I heartwood and Class I sapwood) and pine (Class I sapwood). The spectra for the three oak samples show differences that can be related to the extent of degradation of the wood (Fig. 4.12). The spectra for Class III heartwood are similar to that obtained for recent oak supporting the 'slightly degraded' characterisation. There is a large loss of cellulose component in Class I heavily degraded oak heartwood and sapwood. The degradation product in the form of alkyl and cycloalkane carbon is seen in the 30ppm region of the spectrum for these samples. The remaining resonance in the cellulose region may be due to cellulose remnants or lignin/carbohydrate complexes as observed in recent softwoods. The absence of the 21ppm acetate methyl peak in these samples indicates hemicellulose degradation has occurred, but the lignin component (>110ppm) appears relatively unaffected in slightly and heavily degraded samples.

The spectra for archaeological pine are shown in Figure 4.13. Considerable difference was noted between this and published spectra for recent pine species (Leary *et al.* 1987), most notably a loss in the cellulose resonance lines. However, the cellulose region retains both crystalline and amorphous peaks indicating some intact cellulose remaining. The absence of a 21ppm acetate methyl peak indicates loss of hemicellulose. Lignins were relatively unaffected, but the spectra above 110ppm differed from that of oak, probably as a result of different lignin composition in softwoods (predominantly guaicyl units, as opposed to syringyl and

guaiacyl units in hardwoods; Hedges 1990). This study has highlighted the lack of structural coherence in Class I heartwood and sapwood for oak and pine timbers.

Physical properties

Wood cells weakened by cellulose and hemicellulose degradation are unable to resist drying stresses, and collapse (Stamm 1964) and surface cracking and splitting may occur as a result of drying gradients created as the surface of the timber dries but a wet core remains. Shrinkage data for four oak samples of varying degrees of degradation are given in Table 4.3.

In deteriorated *Mary Rose* archaeological wood there are two important changes that lead to excessive shrinkage and splitting no matter how much care is taken during drying (Noack 1965; Muhlethaler 1973). One of these is the loss of cell wall strength, making wood cells less resistant to drying stresses. The second change is that degradation of cellulose and hemicellulose is accompanied by a reduction of crystallinity. This not only leads to increased hygroscopicity, but also allows shrinkage parallel to the cellulose microfibril (Schniewind 1990). If the hull timbers were allowed to dry without conservation treatment, large changes in dimension would occur. Controlled air drying of the hull timbers without stabilisation would therefore be catastrophic.

The strength of wood samples taken from the *Mary Rose* was found to be greatly reduced (Table 4.4) in

Table 4.3 Shrinkage data for *Mary Rose* oak

Sample	Specific gravity (g/cm³)	Tangential shrinkage (%)	Radial shrinkage (%)	Longitudinal shrinkage
1	0.46	20	9	3
2	0.27	43	13	10
3	0.19	52	14	12
4	0.15	57	16	13
Recent wood	0.55–0.64	11	5	0.4

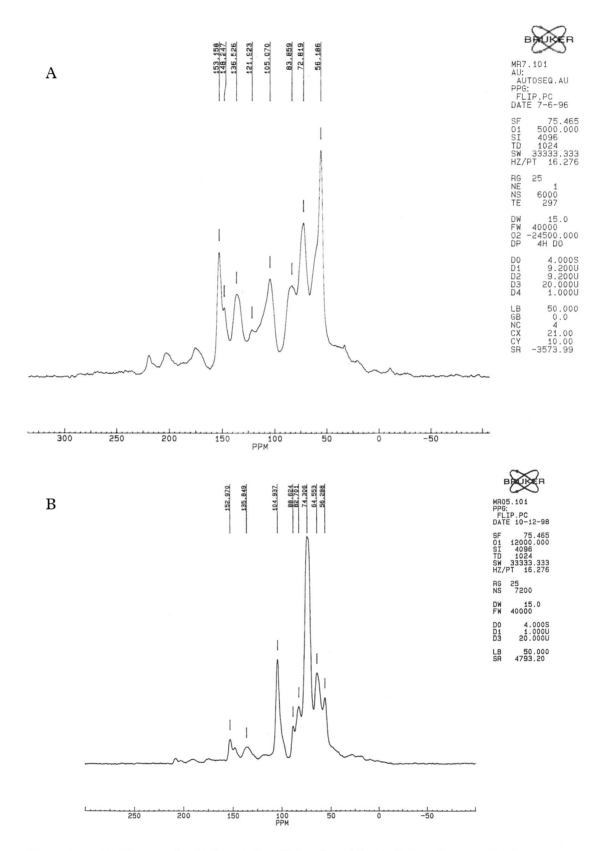

Figure 4.12 NMR spectra for A) degraded and B) undegraded oak. Peak assignments: 0–30ppm degradation products, 21ppm hemicellulose (acetate methyl), 56ppm lignin (methoxyl), 65–105ppm cellulose, 105–173ppm lignin (C_1–C_6), 173ppm hemicellulose (carboxyl of acetate)

comparison with modern material reflecting the degradation. Values compare favourably with published data on the strength properties of ancient wood (Schniewind 1990).

60

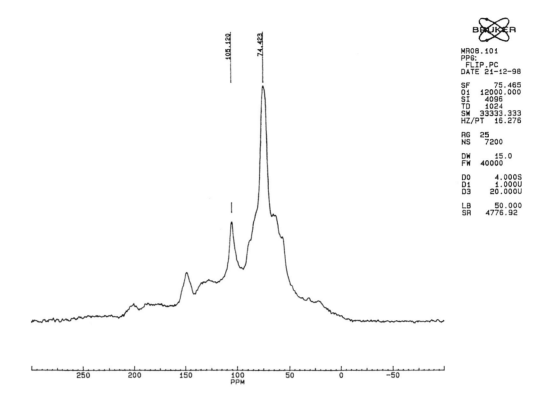

105.120
74.423

BRUKER

MR08.101
PPG:
  FLIP.PC
DATE 21-12-98

SF   75.465
O1   12000.000
SI   4096
TD   1024
SW   33333.333
HZ/PT   16.276

RG   25
NS   7200

DW   15.0
FW   40000

DO   4.000S
D1   1.000U
D3   20.000U

LB   50.000
SR 4776.92

250   200   150   100   50   0   -50
               PPM

Figure 4.13 NMR spectra for pine. See caption to Fig. 4.12 for peak assignments

Table 4.4 Physical properties of *Mary Rose* wood (N/mm²)

	Recent oak heart-wood	Recent oak sapwood	Recent pine sapwood	*Mary Rose* Class III oak	*Mary Rose* Class I pine
Compressive strength	21.75	24.94	23.00	17.43	1.15

The degradation of the *Mary Rose* hull and her wooden artefacts has been clearly identified by various analytical investigations. In order to retain the structural integrity of these waterlogged objects upon drying, active conservation techniques had to be employed to preserve this important assemblage for the enjoyment of future generations and a number of active conservation methods have been employed.

Conservation of Archaeological Wood

Grattan (1987) described conservation as an all-embracing subject, which is aimed at the safeguarding of material from nature's destructive influences. Conservation used in this specialised sense covers two important aspects: first, the arrest of ongoing decay and, secondly, the stabilisation of materials against further deterioration (Pearson 1987). Conservation of marine archaeological objects began during the middle of the last century, which coincided with a great surge in the

excavation of wetland and underwater historic sites. During this period, treatments tended to involve procedures founded upon the techniques of the scientific laboratories. Since then, conservation on a scientific basis has advanced enormously and, in Britain, the recovery of the *Mary Rose* hull and her artefacts led to a greater understanding of the techniques and processes required for the conservation of marine finds, including, wood, textiles, leather, ivory, stone, metals, glass and ceramics. There is, however, still a long way to go before conservators can confidently recommend a conservation treatment that can be guaranteed to effectively stabilise marine archaeological finds for the benefit of future generations (Pearson 1987).

The appearance of waterlogged archaeological wood can be highly deceptive, often disguising the fact that part or all of the object may now be a highly deteriorated matrix of lignin, carbohydrate debris and minerals which are held up by water. As a result of chemical changes that occur during exposure to the marine environment, wood is almost invariably weakened and fragile, unable to support its own weight, making it extremely susceptible to ambient conditions. Without considerable intervention, irreversible shrinkage will take place and destroy the object.

There are two chemical sources to the problems encountered with the treatment of ancient waterlogged wood. First, modification of chemical components of the object is the direct result of long exposure in the marine environment. Secondly, the object will have become contaminated by minerals from this complex environment. The first problem is considered irreversible, involving the loss of holocellulose by chemical (random polymer chain scissions) and biological processes. Conservation treatment of waterlogged wood will, therefore, try to control the various processes occurring as the object is transferred from the waterlogged to a dry and stable condition.

Conservation in the context of waterlogged wood must stabilise the size and shape of the object (Christensen 1970). Conservators at the Trust support the generally held opinion that the dimensions of a treated object should approach those of its waterlogged condition. In addition, the conservation treatment should be reversible and give long-term stability. All conservation methods used should adhere to the principle of minimum intervention, since the best treatment is that which interferes or modifies the wood to the least extent (Grattan 1987).

Definitions and aims

The types of chemical treatments that are involved in the conservation of waterlogged archaeological wood are (Barbour 1990):

* bulking treatments that enter the cell walls and reduce cell wall shrinkage,
* lumen filling treatments that fill the spaces within the wood with an inert chemical which provides structural support and prevents cellular collapse, and
* surface coating that covers the surface of a dry object.

Bulking treatments
Bulking treatment with chemicals used to enter the cell walls not only prevents cell wall shrinkage but also changes their mechanical properties (Barbour 1990). Only small molecules are able to penetrate the cell wall (Finney and Jones 1993). Low molecular weight bulking chemicals do not provide strength and will not prevent collapse of the cellular structure if little cellulose remains. These treatments will also act indirectly by reducing the vapour pressure of the water present in the micro-capillary system, and so retain water in these areas. This helps to keep the cells turgid, and so provides hydraulic support as the cell dries.

Bulking chemicals can be divided into non-reactive and reactive. Non-reactive chemicals enter the molecular structure of cell walls, replacing water, and help maintain cell size and shape. They react with cellulose by means of hydrogen bonding. Examples of non-reactive chemicals include polyethylene glycol (PEG) and sugars. In theory these chemicals can be removed from the wood matrix. All non-reactive treatments also reduce the stiffness of cell walls (Barbour 1990).

Reactive bulking chemicals form covalent bonding with the cell wall. Examples include alkylene oxides and low molecular weight thermosetting resins (Barbour 1990). Unlike non-reactive chemicals, treatment with these chemicals is non-reversible and they were not considered suitable for the treatment of Mary Rose wooden artefacts and timbers.

Lumen filling treatments (impregnation)
Large amounts of high molecular weight chemicals are introduced into the cell lumens and permanent voids to improve the mechanical properties of the object and prevent collapse. As a result, a treatment chemical must form a solid as water is removed.

Perhaps the greatest drawback to lumen filling treatments is that they can cause osmotic collapse if too great a concentration agent is employed across the wood cellular structure. Since the mass transfer of a chemical into the wood is proportional to this concentration gradient, the result is a very slow process. Determining a maximum sustainable concentration gradient, and the length of time taken for the object to equilibrate at each concentration step, is one of the major problems that conservators face when devising a lumen filling treatment procedure. Previously, this involved a certain amount of guesswork but, more recently, Trust conservators have experimented with nuclear magnetic resonance imaging equipment to help solve these interesting problems.

Examples of chemicals used include high molecular weight solvent-based polymers such as styrene, methyl methacrylate and butyl methacrylate. These are usually polymerised by heat or gamma irradiation. The problem is that they produce a composite artefact in which a larger part is the polymer. This often results in a considerable increase in object density. Objects treated in this way have to be carefully supported to prevent distortion occurring under their own weight.

Depending on the molecular weight and final concentration of the treatment solution, polyethylene glycol can also act as a lumen filling consolidant. High grade PEGs of about 1500–4000 molecular weight are often used to treat Class I archaeological wood. A major disadvantage with the use of high grade PEG is that the object tends to look waxy and wet, due to a reduction in intensity of internally reflected light from cells near the surface of the wood. Furthermore, unlike the solvent based polymers, PEG treated objects must be kept in controlled environments to prevent loss of PEG from surface cells.

Surface coatings
Small amounts of materials are applied to the surface of dried archaeological wood. Coatings are used to improve the surface quality and integrity of very fragile objects. Polyethylene glycol 6000 is frequently used to coat newly conserved Mary Rose artefacts. This grade of PEG also prevents the bleeding of low molecular PEGs (PEG200 and 400) from an object. The most common method of treatment is to apply a thin coat of molten PEG6000 to the surface of a dry object.

Drying

The removal of water without destroying the object is a significant conservation problem for conservators. There are three, physically distinct processes.

Air drying

This is the simplest drying technique, in which water undergoes a phase change to the vapour state, and is removed as such. This technique can result in unacceptable amounts of cell wall shrinkage and collapse. Some type of treatment is usually applied beforehand to prevent the dimensional response of an object to drying. Both bulking and lumen filling treatments were used by Trust conservators before controlled air drying. For slightly deteriorated objects (Class III), low grade PEG was used to prevent cell wall shrinkage and surface cracking. For the more deteriorated objects (Class I), a lumen filling treatment was used to reduce cellular collapse and improve strength properties. An object containing a highly deteriorated surface with a large undecayed core was usually treated with a combination of a bulking agent (PEG200 or 400) and a lumen filling consolidant (PEG4000).

Freeze drying

One way of preventing water from exerting surface tension forces is to freeze the object, and then remove the frozen water within the wood structure by sublimation (Fig. 4.14). This is the most commonly used drying technique used by Trust conservators to dry pre-treated waterlogged wood. However, this technique has the disadvantage of requiring the water within the object to undergo two-phase changes as shown in Figure 4.15. As water freezes it expands by approximately 9%, so a cryoprotectant such as PEG200 or 400 is required to protect the object during freezing. As small amounts of low grade chemicals (PEG) are required, the process of freeze drying is very much faster than the consolidation process required by controlled air drying.

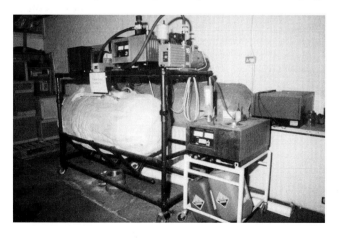

Figure 4.14 Small freeze dryer used to dry small PEG treated wooden artefacts

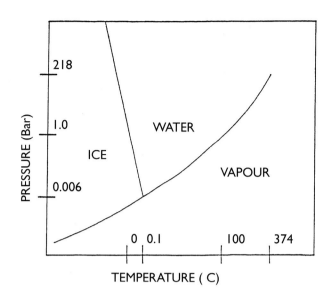

Figure 4.15 The phase diagram of water

Unfortunately the presence of PEG complicates the freezing process illustrated in Figure 4.15. Within a frozen PEG treated object, a complex mixture of phases can solidify during freezing. Of the various freeze drying procedures investigated by Trust conservators, pre-treatment with PEG400 worked well with slightly deteriorated objects. Very highly deteriorated artefacts responded best with a combination of PEG400 and high grade PEG4000. further information regarding freeze drying can be found in Pearson (1987).

Supercritical drying

In its simplest form, supercritical drying is an ideal technique to apply to deteriorated waterlogged wood. In principle the technique replaces water in the wood with carbon dioxide. The carbon dioxide is then converted into a supercritical fluid that can be removed by slow decompression (Kaye and Cole-Hamilton 1995), so avoiding all of the phase changes. Trust conservators employed this method to dry small wooden samples for studies involving scanning electron microscopy. During the early 1980s, commercially available supercritical drying equipment was considered too costly. Fragments of poplar arrows were tested in a small critical point drying chamber and the results were considered very promising. The first part of the procedure involved the replacement of water within the object with acetone. Acetone is then exchanged with liquid carbon dioxide and the temperature of the chamber increased to 40°C (37°C is the critical temperature needed to convert liquid carbon dioxide into gaseous carbon dioxide). Gaseous carbon dioxide is then vented off to the atmosphere. Some modification of the wood does occur during acetone exchange, as an amount of coloured material is leached out during this process. Kay and Cole-Hamilton (1995) found no evidence of holo-cellulose mobilisation.

Removal of mineral inclusions

The first step in the treatment of archaeological wood recovered from a wreck site is to remove or pacify contaminants that enter the object through long-term exposure to sea water and the burial sediments. Sea salts are passively absorbed into the object, but some ions, notably iron (III) are actively chelated (bound together) by cellulose and tannates, and high concentrations of iron corrosion products build up over time. As the wood becomes anoxic, the iron salts are converted into sulphides by the activity of microbes. A physical consequence of ion inclusions is that the wood microstructure becomes blocked making the object impermeable to future chemical treatment. Iron sulphide is unstable in the aerobic environment, and its oxidation can destroy the object (Fig. 4.16). As a consequence, the presence of high concentrations of iron salts (iron pyrites) in dry conserved archaeological wood results in structural damage and blooms of sulphate crystals develop on the object surface. In addition, the sulphuric acid produced inside timbers and wooden artefacts starts to hydrolyse the wood.

Iron compounds are removed from *Mary Rose* waterlogged wooden artefacts and ship's timbers while they are still waterlogged. Iron compounds commonly encountered are goethite (a–FeOOH), magnetite (Fe_3O_4), molysite ($FeCl_3$) and pyrrhotite (FeS).

In order to remove these compounds a chemical must be used that can dissolve the iron and not damage the chemical components of the wood (lignin and holocellulose). Conservators at the Trust consulted potential-pH diagrams for iron-water, iron-water-chlorides, and iron-water-sulphur, to determine pH conditions that will dissolve iron. A pH of below 5 is required. Disodium salt of ethylenediaminetetraacetic acid (EDTA; 5% in water) was used with limited effects. Wooden artefacts were usually soaked for periods of 24–36 hours; longer periods of immersion were often found to soften the outer wood surface. However, the use of EDTA did not remove iron pyrites. The standard treatment here is to soak the wooden object in dilute hydrochloric acid (0.1m). The problem with hydrochloric acid is that wood surface is severely softened. Its use by *Mary Rose* conservators was only contemplated for severely encrusted wood. Experiments involving low concentrations of PEG200 and 400 were also used to reduce the amount of iron. An important point about the removal of iron compounds from wood is that chances of successful removal are much higher if the wood is kept under slightly acidic anaerobic conditions (Grattan 1987).

Anions (negatively-charged ions) such as chlorides, should be removed before the object is dried. Failing to do so will leave the object vulnerable to slight changes in relative humidity encountered during display. Dried archaeological wood containing high levels of chlorides exhibit steeply increased hygroscopicity. By contrast, sea salt is readily removed by prolonged washing in fresh

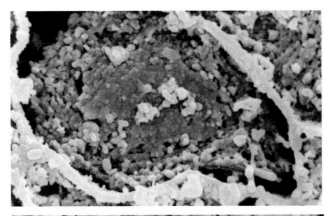
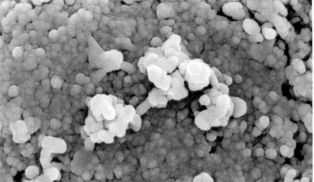

Figure 4.16 Mineral inclusion of wood cells with iron salts. Cells are completely blocked. Unless removed, these salts will act as a barrier to the penetration of treatment solutions such as PEG (SEM) (x2500, x3500)

water. *Mary Rose* objects were washed for periods of 8–12 weeks before commencing active conservation treatment. After this period of time, chloride concentrations were reduced to safe levels (20 ppm).

Removal of silts

For *Mary Rose* wooden objects, a typical washing procedure consisted of rinsing gently in tap water, followed by gently brushing with a fine bristle brush after which the object was soaked in regularly changed baths of tap water. This was found sufficient to remove most deposits which had adhered to the wood surface.

Cleaning of the *Mary Rose* hull involved both conservators and archaeologists. Silts trapped between the frames were removed carefully by hand and placed carefully into containers for further analysis. Hosing of areas inaccessible to the team was also undertaken with great success. Removal of all trapped silt took approximately three years to complete.

Active Conservation of *Mary Rose* Objects

Loss of structurally important cell wall material is one of the most problematic aspects of waterlogged wood conservation. It is very unusual for a wooden object to

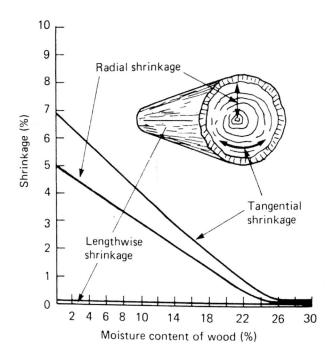

Figure 4.17 Wood shrinkage of fresh wood (after Grattan 1987)

survive drying even under controlled conditions without suffering from shrinkage, splitting, cracking and even collapse. The problem is that as water is removed from the object by evaporation, more water is drawn from the still saturated core into the dry layers by capillary action and as a result of surface hydration forces. This establishes a stress field within an object, with the surface cells placed under considerable tension whilst the core is compressed. These forces can cause severe distortion to an object and are greatly influenced by the anisotropic nature of wood (ie, its asymmetrical pore structure). With highly deteriorated waterlogged wood, tension forces in the outer surface results in extensive cracking and even structural collapse.

As waterlogged wood dries, the amount of shrinkage is greatest in the tangential direction, less in the radial direction, and very little along its length (Fig. 4.17). Traditional craftsmen understood this and, consequently, artefacts were usually sawn or split parallel to the axis of the grain. To prevent shrinkage and collapse, waterlogged archaeological wood must undergo active conservation which usually involves a bulking or strengthening agent. With the exception of the yew longbows, the majority of the *Mary Rose* objects required chemical intervention to retain excavated dimensions. In a comparative study of conservation methods, Trust scientists carried out a series of experiments involving solvent and water based polymers. Although several methods for treating waterlogged wood were found to be successful, Trust conservators concluded that most were unsuitable. Only treatments which were safe to use, reversible, inexpensive and left the objects in a stable condition under normal museum display and storage

environments (see Chapter 6) were considered. The conservation methods chosen included those which involved the replacement of water by a chemical which can be solidified at room temperatures such as PEG and sugar alcohols. Specific examples of the treatment of wooden objects are given in Table 4.5.

Polyethylene glycol (PEG) method

By far the most commonly used method for small (eg, sundials) and large (eg, gun carriages) objects is polyethylene glycol. Polyethylene glycols are polymers of ethylene oxide with the generalised formula shown below:

$$HOCH_2(CH_2OCH_2)nCH_2OH$$

All PEGs are designated with a number which represents their average molecular weight and range from 200 to 20,000. Polyethylene glycols with molecular weights ranging from 200 to 600 are clear viscous liquids at room temperatures and are readily miscible with water. Higher molecular weight PEGs (>1000) are white waxy solids at room temperatures, with decreasing solubility in water and organic solvents with increasing molecular weights. However, even PEG6000 is still soluble in water to concentrations of 50% by weight (Stamm 1956; Anon 1980).

Polyethylene glycols are considered inert and safe. They are used in a great variety of applications because of their chemical structure, low toxicity, solubility in water and their lubricating properties. In a data sheet produced by British Petroleum Chemicals Limited (Anon 1980) some 37 different applications are listed.

Since PEGS were found to be so versatile, Trust conservators recommended their use in the treatment of *Mary Rose* wooden objects. The advantages of using PEGs outweighed their disadvantages. It is well known that PEG methods require long treatment times and increasing hygroscopicity with decreasing molecular weight can be a problem when objects are stored under high relative humidity levels (>60%). This led to the use of high molecular weight PEGs (Gregson 1977). Polyethylene glycols with average molecular weights of approximately 1500 (Barkman 1975; Keene 1982) have been used to treat wet ancient wood. However, during the 1970s and 1980s, PEG4000 was considered to be the most effective consolidant in stabilising highly deteriorated waterlogged archaeological wooden objects (Christensen 1970; Barkman 1975; Gregson 1975; Titus 1982; Sawada 1985). Unfortunately, this high grade PEG requires long treatment times before optimum levels can be detected inside the wood structure.

Although there are variations of the PEG method between conservation laboratories, they all follow the same basic procedure. The wooden object is placed into a tank or container containing an aqueous solution of low concentration PEG at an elevated temperature of

Figure 4.18 Rigging block treated with PEG4000

Figure 4.19 PEG treated collection of wooden canisters belonging to the Mary Roses*'s Barber-surgeon*

60°C. The concentration is increased gradually by the evaporation of water or by the addition of more PEG, until 70–100% concentrations are reached for highly degraded wood or around 10–20% concen-trations for relatively sound wood (dried by vacuum freeze drying). Excess PEG is removed and the wood dried by controlled air drying by gradually decreasing the relative humidity (RH) within the drying area to that of a museum display condition (RH 55%). In some laboratories the process has been accelerated by dissolving PEG in solvents (Albright 1966) or methanol (Christensen 1970), again with some level of success for relatively small objects.

Before commencing active conservation, the condition of each object was determined by microscopic analysis. Since waterlogged wood is not uniform and variation exists between wood species, the PEG method adopted was based upon the nature and extent of deterioration, which was compared to sections of modern wood. As described above, moisture content was determined and the condition of an object classified according to de Jong (1977; 1978; de Jong *et al.* 1981). This scheme was specifically worked out for waterlogged wood treatments involving PEG4000. Wood belonging to Class I and II can be conserved well with PEG4000 but with objects of Class III conserving with PEG4000 is a problem. To treat Class III objects, de Jong (1978; de Jong *et al.* 1981) employed a treatment system that involved replacing the water in the wood with a tertiary butyl alcohol. This allowed PEG4000 to diffuse deeply into the sound inner core of objects (Figs 4.18, 4.19).

Although PEGs have been in use for the conservation of wood for a number of years, a standard treatment process has not yet been devised. To select a suitable treatment regime, Trust scientists carried out a number of laboratory based experiments on different wood species. This involved treating small wood samples with varying concentrations and grades of PEG3400 and 4000. For a discussion of the use of PEG in conserving the hull of the *Mary Rose*, see below.

Mannitol treatments

A number of wooden artefacts were treated with mannitol (sugar alcohol) and had varying degrees of success (Fig. 4.20). Trust conservators used mannitol as a pre-treatment to freeze drying (Table 4.6). However, short treatment times and the poor solubility of mannitol at ambient temperature resulted in the destruction of a number of wooden bowls and linstocks. Because of this, mannitol treatments were abandoned in favour of a two-step PEG treatment involving a low and high grade. However, other workers have had greater success with sucrose and sorbitol. Sorbitol is isomeric with mannitol, but much more soluble (because of the intra-molecular hydrogen bonding).

Figure 4.20 Linstock treated with mannitol. The object has split following freeze drying

Active Conservation of the *Mary Rose* Hull

New research on conserving timbers of the *Mary Rose* has built on the pioneering work on the use of polyethylene glycol for the stabilisation of large waterlogged timbers. To conserve the hull of the *Mary Rose* a two-step PEG treatment programme was developed by Trust conservators to stabilise the size and shape of all ship's timbers. This method of treatment was based upon several years of research involving samples and actual hull timbers. Funding for this important preservation activity comes from English

Table 4.5 Treatment of selected wooden items

Object	Comments	Treatment
Ram (ash) 80A0141	Stored initially in an aqueous solution of borax (5%)	Washed in fresh water to remove chloride ions. Immersed in a 5% PEG3400 solution for 4 months. Freeze dried for 1 month
Stave (oak) 80A0165	Stored initially in an aqueous solution of borax (5%)	Cleaned in a 5% solution of EDTA (di-sodium) treated with a 50% solution of PEG3400 for 6 months. Freeze dried for 1 month
Arrow (poplar) 80A0694	Stored initially in an aqueous solution of borax (5%)	Immersed in a 30% PEG4000 solution for 6 months. Freeze dried for 1 month. Surface cleaned to remove excess PEG
Pike handle (ash) 80A0840	Stored initially in an aqueous solution of borax (5%)	Cascade washed to remove chlorides. Soaked in a 5% solution of EDTA (di-sodium) to remove iron stain. Immersed in a 35% solution of PEG3400 for 12 months. Freeze dried for 3 weeks
Parrel ball (walnut) 80A0950	Stored initially in an aqueous solution of borax (5%)	Cascade washed followed by immersion in a 40% PEG4000 solution for 6 months
Rigging block (ash) 80A1079	Stored initially in an aqueous solution of borax (5%)	Cascade washed to remove chloride ions, immersed in a 25% solution of PEG4000 for 5 months. Freeze dried for 1 month and surface treated with PEG6000
Rigging block (ash) 80A1080	Stored initially in an aqueous solution of borax (5%)(2 months)	Cascade washed and immersed in a 50% solution of PEG4000 for 5 months. Freeze dried for 1 month. Surface treated with a 75% solution of PEG6000
Platter (beech) 80A1098	Stored initially in an aqueous solution of borax (5%)	Desalinated for 2 months, immersed in a 2% solution of EDTA (di-sodium) for 2 hours. Immersed in a 10% solution of PEG4000 for 3 months. Freeze dried for 2 weeks. Surface coated with PEG6000
Bowl (beech) 80A1156	Stored initially in an aqueous solution of borax (5%)	Desalinated and immersed in a 10% solution of PEG4000 for 6 months. Freeze dried for 1 month
Linstock (apple) 80A1193	Stored initially in an aqueous solution of borax (5%)	Desalinated by cascade wash, iron staining removed by immersion in a 5% solution of EDTA. Immersed in a 45% soluton of PEG4000 for 2 months. Freeze dried for 2 weeks
Tampion (poplar) 80A1286	Stored initially in an aqueous solution of borax (5%)	Cascade washed then immersed in a 40% solution of PEG4000 for 5 months. Freeze dried for 2 weeks and surface cleaned to remove excess PEG
Comb (boxwood) 80A1327	Stored initially in an aqueous solution of borax (5%)	Desalinated, immersed in a 5% solution of EDTA for 4 hours. Immersed in a 10% solution of PEG4000 for 3 months. Freeze dried for 2 weeks and surface cleaned
Comb (boxwood) 80A1396	Stored initially in an aqueous solution of borax (5%)	Desalinated, immersed in a 5% solution of EDTA for 4 hours. Immersed in a 10% solution of PEG4000 for 3 months. Freeze dried for 2 weeks and surface cleaned
Tigg (pine) 80A1477	Stored initially in an aqueous solution of borax (5%)	Desalinated and immersed in a 10% solution of PEG4000 for 3 months. Freeze dried for 2 weeks and surface cleaned
Longbow (yew) 80A1528	Stored initially in an aqueous solution of borax (5%)	Controlled air dried over 2 year period
Mallet (oak/ash) 80A1543	Stored initially in an aqueous solution of borax (5%)	Desalinated, immersed in a 5% solution of PEG4000 for 4 months. Freeze dried for 2 weeks
Feeding bottle (cherry or maple) 80A1555	Stored initially in an aqueous solution of borax (5%)	Immersed in methanol, then in a 20% solution of PEG4000/methanol for 3 months. Freeze dried for 2 weeks
Razor (yew) 80A1576	Stored initially in an aqueous solution of borax (5%)	Metal parts removed. Desalinated and then immersed in a 5% solution of EDTA for 3 hours. Immersed in 10% solution of PEG4000 for 4 months. Freeze dried for 2 weeks

Spatula (pine) 80A1587	Stored initially in an aqueous solution of borax (5%)	Immersed in a 10% solution of PEG4000 for 3 months. Freeze dried for 2 weeks
Sundial (boxwood) 80A1669	Stored initially in an aqueous solution of borax (5%)	Dehydrated in ethanol, then immersed in a 30% PEG4000/ methanol solution for 3 months. Freeze dried for 2 weeks
Log (oak) 80A1805	Sprayed with a 5% soluton of borax	Desalinated. Slowly air dried & surface coated with 50% PEG6000
Handle (chestnut) 81A0119	Stored initially in an aqueous solution of borax (5%)	Desalinated, immersed in a 5% solution of EDTA. Immersed in a 50% solution of PEG4000 for 1 month and freeze dried for 2 weeks
Tampion (poplar) 81A0184	Stored initially in an aqueous solution of borax (5%)	Desalinated. Stored overnight in a 5% solition of EDTA, intensively washed, then immersed in a 50% solution of PEG3400 for 2 months. Freeze dried for 2 weeks & surface coated with a 50% solution of PEG6000
Chest (pine) 81A2246	Stored initially in an aqueous solution of borax (5%)	Desalinated. Immersed in a 40% solution of PEG4000 for 3 months and freeze dried for 1 month. Surface treated with 50% solution of PEG6000
Kidney dagger handle (boxwood) 81A2197	Stored initially in an aqueous solution of borax (5%)	Washed in a 5% solution of EDTA, then treated with 35% soluton of PEG3400 for 2 months. Freeze dried for 2 weeks & surface coated with a 50% soluton of PEG6000
Shovel (beech) 81A2215	Stored initially in an aqueous solution of borax (5%)	Soaked in a 5% solution of EDTA for 24 hours. Washed & immersed in a 10% solution of PEG3400
Tigg (oak) 81A2307	Stored initially in an aqueous solution of borax (10%)	Washed with 5% EDTA for 4 hours. Desalinated and immersed in a 50% soluton of PEG3400 for 6 months. Freeze dried for 3 weeks

Heritage, the Heritage Lottery Fund and the *Mary Rose* Trust, the last of which is dependent upon public and corporate support. For example BP Chemicals supported the PEG requirements of the conservation department and this gift is a continuation of BP's long association with the Mary Rose Trust, which began in 1973. Such donations are welcomed or even actively sought, when the Trust can identify special needs. For example, the Trust had been using steel props to support the ship's deck beams. Conservators knew that steel would rust and give way, so a materials' properties search was undertaken and titanium alloy decided upon as the preferred material to support and maintain hull integrity. The Trust then enlisted the help of IMI Titanium Ltd, based in Whitton, Birmingham, to donate props and bolts to support and secure the hull timbers in perpetuity.

During the period of hull restoration, a research programme was set up to evaluate properties and behaviour of stabilising agents in relation to the properties of the hull timbers. The task, undertaken by Trust and university post-graduate students, was to carry out laboratory and pilot-scale trials to determine the preferred method to conserve the ship in the long-term.

Research by Trust scientists explored in great detail the morphological, physical and chemical properties of hull timbers and quickly noticed that the they were differentially decayed, as outlined above. The outer surface to a depth of 10mm was soft and heavily degraded, whilst the cells beneath this region were found be well preserved. According to research data, there can be as much as 20–50% shrinkage to the very decayed outer timber surfaces as waterlogged wood dries out. It was suggested that the badly damaged outer layer of the wood could be shaved off, leaving only the more sound inner layers which would not be so affected by exposure to air. This was considered unacceptable by Trust conservators and scientists because this would result in the loss of unique surface detail such as fabrication marks. Similarly, drying the hull timbers without stabilisation treatment would be an unsuitable treatment and the use of PEG for stabilising the hull as well as individual objects (as described above) was investigated.

The wide variety of properties of the PEG family, however, has complicated conservation efforts in the past. For example, low molecular weight glycols with relatively small molecules could move swiftly and efficiently into the wood cell walls, helping to stabilise them and prevent cell wall shrinkage. But they are hygroscopic and give a tacky feeling. Thus, up until recently, conservators would only use molecular weights greater than 1500; they might not have such a rapid uptake by the wood but they would not leave a tacky surface.

To overcome this problem, *Mary Rose* scientists began to experiment in 1984 with a wide range of

Table 4.6 Examples of mannitol treatments

Object	Comment	Treatment
Shovel (beech) 81A0196	Stored initially in an aqueous solution of borax (5%)	Desalinated, immersed in a 5% solution of EDTA for 5 hours. Immersed in a solution of mannitol (15%) for 4 days & freeze dried for 2 weeks. Surface coated with a 50% solution of PEG6000
Wedge (oak) 81A2004	Stored initially in an aqueous solution of borax (5%)	Immersed in a 5% solution of EDTA, desalinated & treated with 15% mannitol for 4 days. Freeze dried for 2 weeks
Stool (oak) 81A2029	Stored overnight in a 5% solution of EDTA	Desalinated and immersed in a 15% solution of mannitol for 10 days & freeze dried for 3 weeks. Surface cleaned & coated with a 50% solution of PEG6000
Beads (boxwood) 81A2295	Stored for 24 hours in a 5% solution of EDTA	Treated with 15% mannitol for 6 days. Freeze dried for 5 days
Handgun fragment (poplar) 81A2405	Stored initially in an aqueous solution of borax (5%)	Washed overnight in 5% EDTA. Treated with 15% mannitol for 5 days & freeze dried for 3 weeks
Ram head (ash/poplar) 81A2409	Stored initially in an aqueous solution of borax (5%)	Washed overnight in 5% EDTA & treated with 15% mannitol for 10 days. Freeze dried for 3 weeks & then surface coated with PEG6000

Figure 4.21 Pilot-scale spraying chambers containing hull timbers

molecular weights, comparing uptake rates and stabilising effects on small samples over three years. This laboratory based research programme indicated that a lower weight to start with, followed by a higher molecular weight was the best combination for stabilising waterlogged wood.

The conservation team then began scaled-up tests on original deck timbers (hatch-cover planks and half-beams). This programme of research was called the pilot-scale study and involved three treatment systems:

- PEG200 followed by PEG4000
- PEG600 followed by PEG4000
- PEG1500

The results achieved from the pilot-scale study (Fig. 4.21) supported the findings of Hoffmann (1985) that the hull timbers of the *Mary Rose* are best stabilised by a two-step PEG treatment system. The optimum suppression of shrinkage was recorded for PEG200 followed by PEG4000. This research lasted almost 10

years before Trust scientists and advisors adopted this method of treatment.

Active conservation commenced on 30 September 1994 with a two-step PEG treatment using PEG200 to stabilise wood cell walls followed by PEG2000 (spray) and PEG4000 (surface treatment) to consolidate the heavily degraded outer surface. Different mixtures of molecular weight PEGs were investigated and a comparative study involving small and large timber samples used.

Phases of hull active conservation programme

Phase One: Spraying the hull timbers with PEG200 (1994–2003)
This low grade PEG is used to bulk out the cell wall and prevent cell wall shrinkage. As described above, PEG is an example of a non-reactive bulking treatment in which the polymer enters the molecular structure of cell walls, replacing water and thus holding the cell wall in a swollen state (as in Fig. 4.3). The PEG is attracted to the cellulose component of the cell wall by hydrogen bonding only. This treatment also reduces the stiffness of the cell walls. At March 2003 the timbers are being sprayed with a 30%w/v PEG200 aqueous solution. Higher concentrations of PEG200 (40–50%) can result in internal cracking of the inner sound core.

Phase Two: spraying the hull timbers with PEG2000 and 4000 (2003–2010)
This treatment will help improve the mechanical properties of the outer surface layers by preventing cellular collapse. The permanent voids, which are very evident in the outer timber surface, will be filled with this grade of PEG. This helps improve the rigidity of the timber surface, preventing cellular collapse, and in some cases enhancing surface features. This high grade PEG will help seal in the low grade PEG. PEG2000 will also be sprayed onto the surface of every hull timber. Upon completion of treatment with PEG2000, the hull timbers will be surface treated with PEG4000.

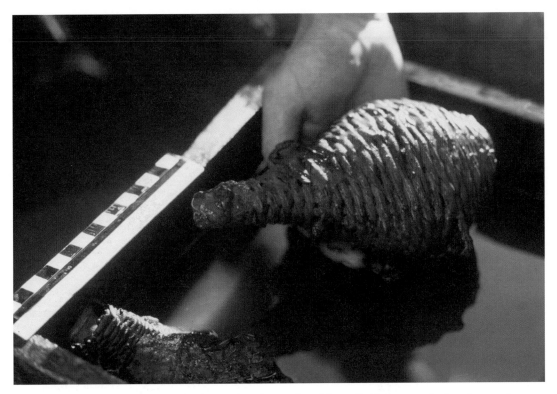

Plate 1 Wicker-covered ceramic bottles, as found, are placed into distilled water during the passive conservation stage

Plate 2 (left) A wooden chest full of longbows receives First Aid on board the Sliepner

Plate 3 (below) One of the great cooking cauldrons from the ship's galley, as recovered

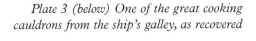

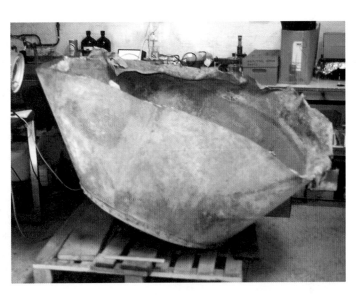

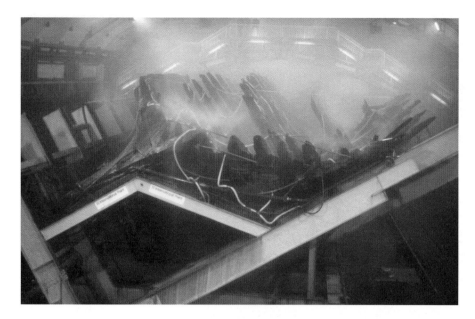

Plate 4 The hull, as recovered, lying on the cradle in the shiphall, being sprayed with chilled fresh water during the passive conservation stage

Plate 5 The hull during the passive conservation stage, in a non-spraying period. Notice the pipes and nozzles of the spray system festooning the hull

Plate 6 This low level view of the hull in the upright position gives an idea of the size and splendour of the great warship

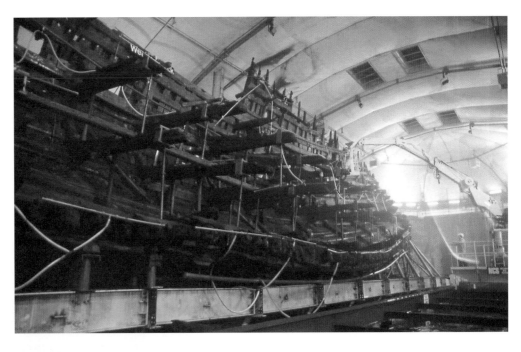

Plate 7 Replacing deck timbers previously removed during the excavation and stored in large hermetically sealed polythene bags

*Plate 8 (left) Example of shipworm (*Teredo sp.*) attack on archaeological ship's timber*

Plate 9 (right) Surface attack of a barrel stave by the white rot fungus Nia vibrissa

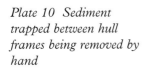

Plate 10 Sediment trapped between hull frames being removed by hand

Plate 11 Successfully conserved linstock – a long, decorated pole holding a fuse with which to light a gun at arm's length

Plate 12 Example of a well-preserved rigging block after treatment with PEG

Plate 14 (above) Reconstructing a leather bucket (photo: Tony Nutley)

Plate 13 (above) Surface cleaning a decorated wooden knife sheath. The 25 knife sheaths from the Mary Rose are virtually the only known Tudor examples ever recorded (Photo: Tony Nutley)

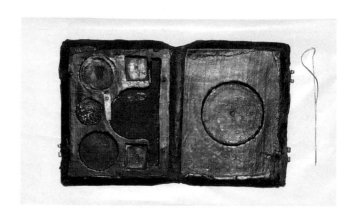

Plate 15 (right) A case carved to hold a delicate coin balance and weights. The wooden case is bound in decorated leather and closed by brass clasps. The central depression on the left bears the imprint of the silver coin weight it once held

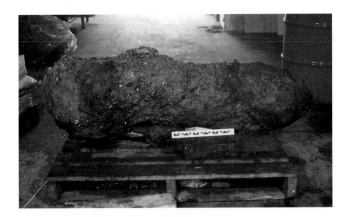

Plate 16 Three stages in the conservation of a wrought iron gun breech chamber; as found (top left) during mechanical removal of concretions (top right) and fully conserved (bottom)

Plate 17 A well-preserved pewter tankard during cleaning and fully conserved

Plate 18 The inside (wrist-side) of an archer's ivory wristguard with leather fastening straps (for the outside see Fig. 6.1)

Plate 19   Well over 300 individual shoes (including about 70 pairs) were recovered from the Mary Rose, in various conditions and states of repair

Plate 20   A selection of personal objects belonging to the crew of the Mary Rose made from a variety of woods and metals

Plate 21   Leather arrow spacer from a quiver and decorated leather wristguard

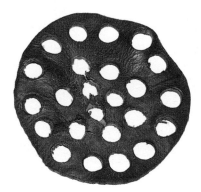

Plate 22 Fragment of woollen textile with gold braid

Plate 23 Fragment of woollen garment dyed with madder

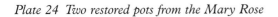

Plate 24 Two restored pots from the Mary Rose

Plate 25 A selection of clothing, including a replica jerkin, and other items that might have been used by a gunner on board the Mary Rose.

Plates 26–28 Three types of display in the Mary Rose Museum.

Plate 26 (left) Reconstruction of part of the Main deck of the Mary Rose, with Upper deck above

Plate 27 (bottom left) Glass-fronted, environmentally-controlled display case with reconstruction of the ship's galley, as found

Plate 28 (below) Bronze gun barrels on open display

Phase Three: controlled air drying of the PEG treated timbers (2010–2015)

Shrinkage related defects such as warping and checking, can be controlled by limiting the development of the very destructive moisture gradients that can exist in waterlogged archaeological wood. Polyethylene glycol helps limit these destructive forces, allowing archaeological wood to be dried without encountering serious problems. For the *Mary Rose* hull timbers, controlled air drying is therefore more successful when combined with a chemical treatment by decreasing the steepness of the moisture gradient and, in turn, reducing dimensional change. Drying of the hull timbers will take approximately three to five years and the drying regime will be based upon the finding of a three year controlled air drying research programme involving PEG treated timber samples. This work is nearing completion.

Controlled air drying research programme,
by G. McConnachie

As previously discussed, without appropriate treatment, waterlogged archaeological wooden objects can undergo dramatic dimensional change following exposure to air. Timbers from the hull of the *Mary Rose* are no exception and a number of studies have shown the extent to which they will shrink and collapse if dried without prior treatment (Dean *et al.* 1994; Jones and Rule 1991; Pournou 1999). Further analytical studies have revealed degradation of cell wall components (Squirrell and Clarke 1987; Jones and Rule 1991; Jones *et al.* 1986), leaving a weakened wood structure that cannot withstand the capillary tension forces, cell wall shrinkage and stresses that uncontrolled drying induces.

It is the aim of any conservation treatment to eliminate dimensional change during drying and leave the object in a stable and aesthetically acceptable condition. The crucial role of consolidating pre-treatments in achieving this is now widely understood. Polyethylene glycol is perhaps the most widely researched and versatile of consolidants and PEG impregnation in combination with vacuum freeze drying is undoubtedly the most commonly applied and successful technique for stabilising waterlogged archaeological wood. Like PEG impregnation, the freeze drying process itself has been thoroughly investigated and adapted to suit waterlogged wood conservation. In doing so, however, a number of limitations to the process have been highlighted, the most obvious of which is the size to which vacuum chambers can be constructed.

The sheer scale of the *Mary Rose* hull leaves only one feasible option for its eventual drying programme. Although controlled air drying is not a new technique, surprisingly little information is available on how post-PEG treatment air drying environments might be manipulated to further reduce dimensional change. The development and application of most conservation techniques has relied largely on an increased understanding of the nature of waterlogged archaeological wood and of its behaviour during the drying process. In developing a suitable post-treatment drying regime for the *Mary Rose*, full use will be made of this body of information, as well as findings from a focused in-house study, testing the drying behaviour of timbers from the hull.

Before examining the rationale behind this research programme, as well as some preliminary findings, it is worth looking in more detail at some of the reasoning behind the decision to air dry the hull. Presented below are brief accounts of the gross drying behaviour of waterlogged archaeological woods, more detailed reasons for ruling out freeze drying techniques for the drying programme and some mention of previous applications of controlled air drying.

The drying behaviour of waterlogged archaeological wood

The mechanisms and driving forces defining the drying behaviour of wood are numerous and complex. Key elements have been well researched, however, and we now have a good understanding of the underlying processes. It is known that water exits both archaeological (Barbour and Leney 1982) and fresh wood (Kollman and Cote 1968; Panshin and de Zeeuw 1980; Skaar 1988) in two stages, giving rise to two broad phases of dimensional change. 'Collapse' results from the removal of free water filling void spaces and cell lumina. 'Shrinkage' arises from the removal of chemically bound water occupying microcapillaries within the cell wall.

Collapse is attributable mainly to the development of capillary tension forces. As drying commences, receding columns of water are forced to pass through small openings in the cell wall. The high surface tension of water exerts enormous pressure as this happens and collapse occurs if capillary forces exceed the compressive strength of the cell wall material. Collapse is routinely encountered on drying archaeological wood, particularly in highly degraded outer layers (Fig. 4.4), where cell wall strength is greatly reduced.

Shrinkage begins after free water occupying voids and cell lumina has evaporated. Shrinkage associated with the cell wall results from the drawing together of cellulose fibrils and microfibrils, as chemically bound water leaves the microcapillaries between them. In archaeological wood, decrystallisation of cellulose within microfibrils leads to significant increases in longitudinal shrinkage values. Tangential and radial shrinkage values also significantly increase and, volumetrically, shrinkage can exceed 70% for highly degraded objects. Figure 4.22 shows the typical appearance of the three main structural wood types found within the hull of the *Mary Rose* after drying without prior treatment at 20°C and 55% RH.

In reality, the so called 'fibre saturation point', where collapse ceases and shrinkage begins in a drying timber, is highly theoretical. The drying front progresses from the outside of the object towards the core, so shrinkage may be evident in outer layers while the core is still fully

70

Figure 4.22 Typical appearance of timber samples in the waterlogged state (bottom) and after air drying at 55%RH/20°C (top). Woods are (left to right) oak, poplar and pine

saturated. Zonal degradation, structural anomalies and condensation inside cell lumina further complicate the drying pattern throughout an object. The result, is an uneven distribution of water, which leads to the development of drying stresses that in waterlogged archaeological wood can cause catastrophic failure.

Drying phase: the options
Freeze drying: By eliminating liquid water from the drying process, freeze drying prevents the capillary tension collapse that damages archaeological wood from the onset of drying. Consequently, the use of vacuum freeze drying in conjunction with PEG impregnation is perhaps the most popular and successful treatment for waterlogged archaeological wood. There are however a number of significant limitations to the technique which the conservator must consider:

1. It is limited by the scale of the material to be dried. The largest units used for archaeological conservation are around 20m³.
2. Highly degraded archaeological wood may require impregnation in high concentration solutions of PEG, which exceed their 'eutectic point' and will not freeze at the temperatures typically used in freeze drying.
3. The cost of vacuum freeze drying equipment can be prohibitive.

For most large composite structures such as ship hulls, vacuum freeze drying is clearly not a feasible option, although an alternative freeze drying technique does exist that is less restricted by scale. Ambrose (1975) describes the use of a simple laboratory scale freeze dryer that operates at atmospheric pressure and McCawley et al. (1982) built and tested their own unit. Other workers have freeze dried PEG treated timbers by

utilising natural environments exhibiting the low temperature and vapour pressure conditions required for freeze drying to occur (Grattan and McCawley 1978; Grattan et al. 1980).

Despite the long drying times reported for large objects, the technique has been applied on a large scale, notably to the 20 ton Roman wreck excavated in Marseille (Droucourt and Morel-Deledalle 1985; Amoignon and Larrat 1985). Although some surface cracking was reported, probably due to the absence of a pre-treatment, the process itself appears to have worked.

At around 280 tons, the hull of the *Mary Rose* is considerably larger than any of the timbers or structures dried in any previous atmospheric pressure freeze drying project. The practicalities of freezing such a volume of timber – and then maintaining an appropriate artificial drying environment – are enormous. The scale, probable drying time, access difficulties, plant installation and running costs are just some of the major factors that rule out this technique for drying the *Mary Rose*. Other conservation issues also exist, however. A small but significant number of highly degraded poplar timber elements exist within the hull. With moisture contents often in excess of 800%, these timbers require the excessive PEG bulking that may not respond well to freeze drying.

Controlled air drying: The development of shrinkage related stresses during drying may be alleviated if the rate of moisture removal is controlled, so as to reduce the moisture gradients that arise between inner and outer layers. This principle forms the basis for the seasoning of green timber, though application of the technique to waterlogged archaeological wood is more problematic. Archaeological wood is weaker than fresh wood, exhibits far higher shrinkage values and can undergo significant dimensional change as a result of even small moisture gradients. Since the process itself cannot prevent shrinkage or collapse, success of the technique is also largely dependent on pre-treatment with bulking and/or consolidating agents such as PEG. While no standard application of the technique has been suggested for archaeological wood, typically timbers are held in a high humidity environment, which is lowered incrementally. At each stage the timbers are allowed to reach equilibrium with the surrounding environment, until finally a humidity is reached at which the material will be stored or displayed.

Controlled air drying has been applied with varying degrees of success to a number of large archaeological structures and vessels. de Jong et al. (1981) describes the drying of a number of well preserved vessels excavated around Lake Yssel in Holland. Shrinkage values close to that of new wood are reported, though the lack of a pre-treatment resulted in damage to degraded outer layers. Seifert and Jagels (1985) incorporated a PEG540 blend surface application into their drying schedule for timbers from the bow section of the *Ronson*. Reasonable dimensional stability was reported but, again, more degraded surfaces showed extensive honeycombing and cracks. Even less desirable results were obtained using PEG surface application during the drying of timbers from the *Machault* (Jenssen and Murdock 1982).

Despite the interest these and other projects created, it is now recognised that achieving good dimensional stability through controlled air drying relies on thorough consolidating and/or bulking pre-treatments. Two-stage PEG treatments, as described above (Hoffmann 1985), are particularly suitable for use with air drying, since they address both shrinkage and collapse related dimensional change. High concentrations of PEG are often employed, particularly the high molecular weight second stage (Astrup 1994; Tran *et al.* 1997), since highly degraded cells must be completely filled if collapse is to be restrained. Instances where untreated material has yielded acceptable shrinkage values are generally the exception and results must be interpreted with care. Some archaeological softwoods for example, even when significantly degraded, can show surprisingly low shrinkage values (Schweizer *et al.* 1985). Only when very lightly degraded, on the other hand, will hardwoods exhibit shrinkage values similar to those of fresh wood. In practice, even very well preserved material usually has an outer decayed zone incapable of withstanding drying stresses without prior treatment. While de Jong *et al.* (1981) suggest that damage to the outer decayed zone may be acceptable in some cases, it can mean the loss of important archaeological information such as fabrication marks, as well as obvious structural and aesthetic considerations.

Undoubtedly the largest and best known of all air dried archaeological structures is the Swedish warship *Vasa*. Barkman (1975) carried out a number of preliminary investigations into the PEG treatment and controlled air drying of material from the wreck. He concluded that a high level of control would be necessary to successfully dry large finds of this kind after PEG impregnation. The actual approaches applied to the PEG treatment and drying phases (Barkman 1975; Hafors 1985; 1990) were revised a number of times during the process and it cannot be said that drying was truly controlled throughout. It is therefore not easy to assess the effectiveness of the drying process overall. The *Vasa* project has shown however, that conservation on this immense scale can be highly successful.

Controlled air drying is clearly the only feasible option for the eventual drying of the *Mary Rose*. Due to commence around 2009–2010, provision of a stable and controlled drying environment on this scale will require considerable forward planning. Detailed research is presently being carried out at the *Mary Rose* Trust, aimed at identifying the most appropriate drying regime for the PEG treated timbers of the hull. These data will provide a basis for the design specifications of the plant installations required to supply and maintain the correct drying conditions.

Controlled air drying of the Mary Rose *hull*
The problem: The enormous variability of archaeological wood can often make the choice of conservation treatment less than straightforward. Timbers from different archaeological sites will display unique patterns of degradation and may react very differently to any one treatment regime. Moreover, considerable variations in timber condition can be found throughout individual burial sites and within individual timbers.

The three main structural wood types found within the *Mary Rose*, oak, poplar and pine, all have very different physical properties, and this is reflected in their drying behaviour. Oak timbers, forming the bulk of the hull, and most pine timbers, typically have a soft, highly decayed outer layer surrounding a sound inner core. Each zone behaves very differently during drying, causing the development of considerable stresses. Lower density poplar timber elements are considerably more variable, some being highly degraded throughout and others retaining large proportions of a sound inner core. Timber variability has been addressed at the pre-treatment stage by adoption of the two-stage, high concentration PEG spraying regime which deals with sound core and degraded portions in turn. As stated, the exact design of this treatment programme was achieved by assessing the individual requirements of the material to be conserved and its reaction to a range of PEG treatments (Jones and Rule 1991). It is equally important that, before beginning to dry the hull, it is known how the timbers are expected to react and that the particular drying regime adopted will give the best dimensional stability achievable.

Research programme: A comprehensive programme of research is underway at the Mary Rose Trust, aimed at identifying optimum conditions for the stabilisation of the main structural wood types found within the hull. A series of controlled air drying experiments is being used to test a range of untreated and PEG treated timber samples through a series of different drying regimes. Rate and nature of water removal, shrinkage behaviour and the effect of PEG pre-treatment type are all being evaluated for each set of drying conditions used. Central to the study are two Weiss Technik climatic test chambers, purchased from a grant awarded by the Heritage Lottery Fund, capable of producing accurate and stable environmental conditions over prolonged periods. A smaller unit is the focus of initial studies, testing small untreated and PEG treated samples. Weight loss and dimensional change are being monitored throughout and data used to calculate drying rate, equilibrium moisture content and volumetric dimensional change of samples through each phase of each drying schedule.

A further set of experiments will make use of a large 'walk in' chamber (Fig. 4.23) to investigate moisture movement in larger samples and complete timbers. Progression of drying fronts will be monitored using

Figure 4.23 Walk-in climatic test chamber

Table 4.8 Volumetric dimensional change of samples dried at different temperatures and 55% RH

Temperature/RH%	Volumetric dimensional change (%) at 55% RH		
	Oak	Poplar	Pine
20°C/55%	27.00	83.36	9.55
40°C/55%	29.76	85.00	8.18
60°C/55%	33.26	83.40	10.67

resistivity probes inserted at different depths in each sample and shrinkage behaviour will again be monitored for a number of different drying regimes. A scaling up of sample size will provide valuable and realistic information on how complete timbers react to various drying conditions.

Preliminary results: A number of important studies are incomplete and it is not intended here to draw any conclusions about the drying behaviour of timbers from the *Mary Rose* or to indicate a potential drying regime for the hull. Nor is it intended to give a detailed account of experimental designs, methodologies or initial results. Preliminary studies have revealed a number of trends however, which although requiring further investigation, are worth mentioning here.

Drying behaviour of untreated samples: Fourteen drying schedules have been tested using multiple, small untreated samples, cut from representative oak, poplar and pine timbers. During all these initial tests, temperature has been held constant at 20°C and relative

humidity (RH) levels varied through each schedule, down to a final holding value of 55%. Schedules were designed to test sample behaviour over a wide range of humidity conditions, highlight any behavioural trends and identify those conditions giving most favourable results. By monitoring weight loss and dimensional change throughout each schedule it was possible to analyse the relationships between moisture content (moisture loss during drying) and dimensional change throughout the drying process. Detailed comparisons have been made of the moisture content/dimensional change relationships of samples for all schedules tested. Table 4.7 gives the final dimensional change values at 55% RH for a selection of schedules tested.

The effect of drying temperature on the behaviour of the same sample group has been evaluated in a separate series of tests. Initially the effect of temperature at 55% RH has been investigated and some final results are given in Table 4.8.

Overall, differences in final dimensional change values are very small for the different drying schedules tested. The small trends that are present, particularly for the oak samples, seem to suggest that schedules initiated at lower relative humidity levels and at lower temperatures yield slightly better results.

Drying behaviour of PEG treated samples: Further preliminary experiments have utilised samples treated

Table 4.7 Selected drying schedules of *Mary Rose* timber samples and resulting average volumetric dimensional change value at the final humidity level of 55% RH

Drying schedules at constant temperature of 20°C										Volumetric dimensional change (%) @ 55% RH – average of 2 drying schedules		
Relative humidity steps (%) used in schedule										Oak	Poplar	Pine
98	95	90	85	80	75	70	65	60	55	34.45	85.09	6.99
	95		85		75		65		55	29.90	84.73	9.48
	95								55	29.38	83.99	10.99
			85						55	28.94	79.40	9.17
					75				55	27.83	81.47	9.19
							65		55	24.80	80.36	7.42
									55	27.00	83.36	9.55

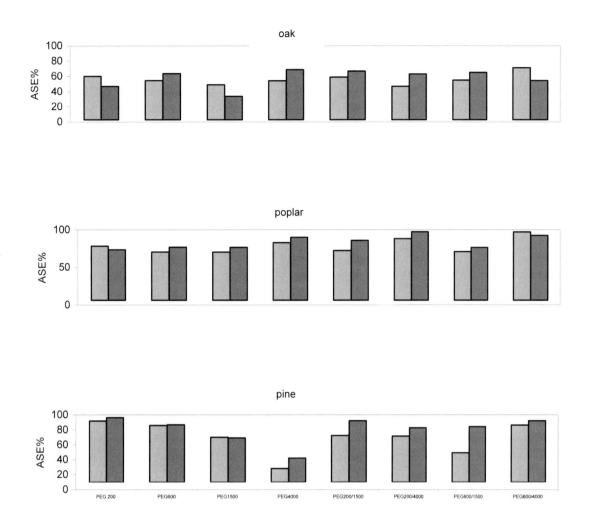

Figure 4.24 Anti-Shrink Efficiency Values for PEG treated Oak, Poplar and Pine timber samples dried under two contrasting drying schedules. Schedule 1: dried directly to 55% RH at 20°C; Schedule 2: 95%, 85%, 75%, 65%, 55% at 20°C

with different combinations of PEG200, 600, 1500 and 4000 in an accelerated treatment programme. Samples were impregnated with PEG for three months, with a maximum concentration of 50% w/v for both single and two stage treatments. Treated samples were then dried under a number of schedules, once again to assess differences in drying behaviour. Some results from these tests are presented in Figure 4.24.

Though actual shrinkage values are far lower for these treated samples, little variation in dimensional change is again seen between schedules. Figure 4.24 shows the anti-shrink efficiency (ASE%) values obtained from two contrasting drying regimes. Values for all three wood species are similar for both schedules.

These initial trials are beginning to underline the importance of adequate PEG treatment in the use of air drying and are suggesting that tight control of the drying environment at humidity levels above 55% may not prove crucial. A great deal more information needs to be gathered before any recommendations can be made, however. Further trials are underway, testing a wider range of PEG treatments and the behaviour of larger samples and complete timbers.

Future work
Much valuable information has already been gathered on the drying behaviour of untreated and PEG treated timber samples. Results have indicated which PEG grades, in what combination and concentration, are needed to best stabilise the different species encountered under specific drying conditions. Behavioural differences between species have been identified and some insight gained into how each timber type reacts to different drying conditions.

Ultimately, these results will be used to formulate a drying regime for the hull of the *Mary Rose*. Before this can happen however, more information is required. So far, tests have concentrated on the behaviour of small, 20x20x20mm, samples. While this has provided sufficient and comparative information on behaviour associated with collapse and shrinkage, the development of drying stresses may be limited in samples of this size. Initial studies using larger samples are already revealing increases in overall dimensional change in relation to size. This may be related to the development of stresses and it is essential that in considering a final drying regime, the behaviour of complete timber samples has been fully investigated.

Detailed accounts of methodologies and findings from these and other air drying trials will be published at appropriate stages throughout the research programme. It is hoped this information will be of use not just to the Mary Rose Trust but to the conservation community in general. Completion of this vital conservation programme will allow this majestic warship to voyage safely through the new millennium ahead.

Summary of hull treatment programme

Phase I (1994–2003): spraying of hull timbers with PEG2000.

Phase II (2004–2010): spraying of hull surface with PEG2000 followed by surface treatment of with PEG4000.

Phase III (2010–2015): controlled air-drying of hull.

Current problems with PEG treated timbers of the seventeenth century warship *Vasa* (Sangstrom *et al.* 2002)

Following treatment with PEG, the timbers of the *Vasa* are under threat by the internal formation of sulphuric acid. The cause of the problem is the presence of elemental sulphur and also sulphur compounds of intermediate oxidation states that exist within and on the surface of the PEG treated hull timbers. According to the *Vasa* scientists, the overall quantity of elemental sulphur could produce up to 5000kg of sulphuric acid when fully oxidised.

Sangstrom and his team of scientists suggest that the oxidation of the reduced sulphur is being catalysed by iron species released from the completely corroded ship fixings (iron bolts), as well as from those mild steel bolts inserted after recovery. Treatment to cure the *Vasa* by arresting acid wood hydrolysis is currently focusing on the removal of sulphur and iron compounds. Mary Rose Trust conservators are involved with *Vasa* scientists in helping to resolve this serious problem.

Initial analysis of *Mary Rose* timbers indicated much reduced levels of elemental sulphur. Furthermore, scientists at the Mary Rose Trust replaced original corroded iron fixings with titanium alloy bolts. In addition, PEG200 is washing out iron corrosion products from hull timbers. An additional safeguard undertaken by Trust scientists is to buffer the hull by raising the pH of the PEG200 spray solution to between 7 and 8.

Of the many thousands of wooden artefacts treated by Mary Rose conservators, only six objects are exhibiting signs of internal acid formation. The pH of these objects was found to be as low as 2.5. A 5% aqueous solution of sodium bicarbonate is being used to neutralise this effect, raising the pH to around 7.

Glossary terms: plant cell and associated structures

Apotracheal axial parenchyma
Banded: where parenchyma cells occur in lines or bands
Diffuse: where single strands or pairs of strands are distributed irregularly among the fibrous elements of the wood

Paratracheal axial parenchyma
Aliform: parenchyma surrounding or to one side of the vessel and with lateral extensions
Confluent: coalescing vasicentric or aliform parenchyma surrounding or to one side of two or more vessels, often forming irregular bands
Vasicentric: cells form a complete circular to oval sheath around a solitary vessel or multiple vessels.

Pits
Alternate: arranged in diagonal rows
Opposite: arranged in short to long horizontal rows
Scarliform: arranged in a ladder

lamella: a thin, plate-like layer: middle lamella, the layer between the walls of two adjacent plant cells.

lumen: the space enclosed by a tube structure or hollow organ

Tyloses: outgrowths from an adjacent ray or axial parenchyma cell through a pit in a vessel wall, partially or completely blocking the vessel lumen

Source: Wheeler *et al.* 1989

5. Conservation of Metals

by Des Barker

Almost 3000 metal artefacts were recovered from the *Mary Rose* and no attempt is going to be made in this chapter to discuss the conservation of each one. Moreover, all the possible methods of conservation of metals will not be discussed as this is beyond the scope of this book. Instead, typical examples of each metal class that are currently on display in the museum have been selected and the conservation procedures carried out will be examined in detail. Some of the traditional techniques of conservation were not considered because of the time required to conserve and fully stabilise the artefacts concerned. This was the case with, for instance, the large split-ring wrought iron guns where soaking in a suitable electrolyte would have taken five years to complete. A joint research project between Portsmouth Museum, the Mary Rose Trust and Portsmouth Polytechnic (now University) developed a large scale hydrogen reduction technique which reduced the conservation period down to one month.

The range of objects is remarkable and they come in all shapes and sizes. Objects include: guns, gun fittings and iron shot; hand weapons; all manner of containers and utensils concerned with feeding the crew, including the great cauldrons from the galley; the Barber-surgeon's medical equipment; the ship's bell; navigation tools; pitch pots; and a host of personal items such as buckles, jewellery, sewing equipment, coins and even a chamber pot. Many more metal objects and ships' fittings have not survived, though some are represented by parts made of other materials such as wood. Examples include the fine array of carpenters' tools from which virtually all the iron components have been lost.

It is first possible to divide the metals recovered into two distinct categories, Ferrous and Non-Ferrous. The former can be subdivided into i) wrought iron, ii) cast iron and iii) steels. The latter can be split down into i) copper and its alloys including brass and bronze, ii) tin and its alloys, iii) lead and its alloys, iv) silver and v) gold. The last mentioned should, in theory, not corrode in marine environments and hence will require only a minimal amount of conservation.

In this chapter, the conservation of each of these groups will be covered. In order to fully appreciate the reasons for carrying out the conservation method selected it is important to understand, in the first instance, how the metal or alloy was manufactured. From modern theories of corrosion of metals in marine environments (Tretheway and Chamberlain 1995), it is possible to predict the mode of corrosive attack that the artefact may have experienced while on or beneath the seabed. Any adverse effect on rate of corrosion on exposure to the atmosphere can possibly be predicted. From this knowledge, the most efficient methods of field treatments, storage conditions and conservation can be suggested.

In each of the sections below, the methods of obtaining the metal or alloy from its ores will be dealt with, followed by possible shaping processes to produce the finished object. The corrosion behaviour of the metal on the seabed will be covered and this will be related to conservation method selected.

General Principles of Extraction

Metals are rarely found in their native form, with gold being the main exception. They are present in the earth's crust as ores with the most important ones being metal oxides or sulphides. These ores are very stable and have existed for many thousands of years. It requires a great deal of energy to remove the oxygen or sulphur from the metal and the best way to achieve this is to heat the ore in the presence of a reducing agent. The reducing agent will then combine with the oxygen or sulphur part of the ore and free the metal. This can be represented by the following simple equation:

$$\text{ore} + \text{reducing agent} + \text{heat} = \text{metal} + \text{slag} \qquad (1)$$

Oxygen from the air must be prevented from mixing with the metal or else it will immediately react to produce fresh oxide. Additionally, the presence of oxygen may exhaust the reducing agent. This indicates that the design of the furnace required to heat the ore/reducing mixture must be such that there is a reasonably large region in which no oxygen is present. This is where the reaction in equation (1) takes place and the atmosphere is said to be *reducing*. The temperature at which the metal is produced varies from metal to metal and typical values for this are given in the relevant sections below. Moreover, the rates of the reaction will be faster if the reactants are in the liquid phase, ie, the metal and slag are molten. This will depend on the melting point of the metal. One of the main limitations of the early metallurgists was that they could not generate particularly high temperatures in their furnaces. Thus the low melting point metals, such as tin, lead and copper, were produced in large quantities much earlier than the higher melting point ones such as iron. In reality, the production of wrought iron was carried out virtually by solid-state reduction with the end products being 'blooms' (Tylecote 1962). These were solid mixtures of iron and slag from which the slag was removed by hammering. It was not until the beginning of the fourteenth century that furnace designs allowed the temperature to reach the melting point of cast irons, and even later before steels, with an even higher melting point, could be manufactured on a large scale.

Once the metal had been extracted from the ore, the method of shaping depended on several factors. If the metal or alloy could be kept molten then it would have been possible to pour it into specially shaped moulds (similar to pouring jelly into a mould). The moulds were made from clay or sand and were destroyed after use. This process is referred to as 'casting' and the bronze cannons from the *Mary Rose* are good examples of objects manufactured in this manner.

Pure metals are fairly soft and ductile and hammering or beating at room temperature can achieve the desired shape. This is called 'cold working', with copper and/or lead objects being good examples where this was regularly carried out. Some metals, such as wrought iron, are not so easy to shape at room temperature and have to be continually softened by heating to approximately 2/3rds of their melting point. This is called 'annealing'. If the shaping is carried out hot, above the annealing temperature, it is called 'hot working'.

General Principles of Metallurgy

As stated above, pure metals are very ductile. The reason for this is that the crystal shapes that the metals adopt are very simple – such as simple cubes. Ceramics and glasses have extremely complicated crystal shapes and, as a result, are very hard and brittle at room temperature. If a polished piece of metal is placed in a suitable chemical (etchant), grains will be visible under an optical microscope. The size of these will vary from a few microns up to 3–4mm in diameter. If an alloying element is added to the parent metal and can fit into the original crystal structure, the two metals are said to be soluble in one another (similar to milk in tea). Under the microscope, the grains will appear the same as the pure metal. Although the resultant alloy is slightly harder and less ductile than the unalloyed one, it is still possible to manufacture the alloy by hot or cold work. These alloys are often referred to as 'single-phase' alloys.

If the two metals that form the alloy are insoluble in one another, they will exist as two separate phases often in alternate layers, as is observed in tin-lead alloys or cast irons, for example, where the carbon is often found as minute tadpole-like shapes (flakes) adjacent to the

pure iron. These types of 'two-phase' alloys are extremely difficult, if not impossible, to shape by hot or cold working. Fortunately, these alloys have a melting point well below that of the pure parent metals and are very suitable for shaping by casting into moulds. Casting, compared to attempting to manufacture the same item by mechanical shaping, can fairly easily produce complicated shapes. This is the reason why the large wrought iron split ring guns were superseded by cast iron ones soon after the *Mary Rose* sank in the Solent. These types of alloys have two important limitations in that, first, they are very brittle when subjected to impact loads and, secondly, their corrosion resistance is inferior to pure metals or single-phase alloys (Higgins 1993).

General Principles of Corrosion

The aqueous corrosion of metals is due to an electrochemical cell being formed between two different metals in electrical contact or two separate metallic phases present on a metal surface. Consider a strip of copper (copper electrode) joined to a strip of iron (iron electrode) by a copper insulated wire and immersed in sea water. The iron will start to dissolve (corrode) and release electrons according to equation (2):

$$Fe = Fe^{++} + 2e \qquad (2)$$

In corrosion science, the iron electrode is referred to as the *anode* and this is always the place where corrosion takes place. The electrons travel through the wire to the copper electrode surface where they react with dissolved oxygen in the water to form an alkali, hydroxyl ions, according to equation (3):

$$O_2 + 4e + 2H_2O = 4OH^- \qquad (3)$$

The copper electrode is called the *cathode* and never corrodes. Cathodes are always protected.

The electrical circuit is completed by the sea water electrolyte, which carries a charge by movement of ions through the solution via the movement of chloride and sodium ions in the sea water.

Single metals and alloys, such as wrought iron, bronze and lead will corrode even though they are not joined to a different metal or alloy. In reality, anodes and cathodes are set up on the surface of the metal. This will be due to the different phases present in the alloy, eg, iron will be the anode and graphite the cathode in a cast iron and/or impurities present in the metal. Pure metals are not really 100% one metal, even today, and certainly not in Tudor times. A corrosion cell will be formed between the impurity and the parent metal. The reactions taking place on the anode and cathode will be the same as above (2) except the anode may be a different metal if the object is not iron. With a copper artefact, for example, the anode reaction will be:

$$Cu = Cu^{++} + 2e \qquad (4)$$

where Cu^{++} denotes that copper is now present in the solution. The cathode reaction will be the same as equation (3) for all metals and alloys in natural environments such as sea water. Cathodes and anodes will also form on metal surfaces if moisture films condense on them on a damp day, or if the humidity (inside a museum for instance) is very high.

From the above, the following five factors are required for corrosion to occur:

Anode: where corrosion will take place.
Cathode: where the electrons are consumed. The cathode is protected.
Electrolyte: sea water, which carries the charge and completes the electrical circuit.
Electrical contact between anode and cathode: carries the electrons from anode to cathode.
Cathode reactant: dissolved oxygen, which mops up the electrons at the cathode.

Wherever one observes corrosion, the above five factors must be present. Removal of any one of these will prevent corrosion. For example, sachets of silica gel are put into packaging of cameras, radios, etc, to prevent corrosion by stopping an electrolyte from condensing on the metal surfaces. In museums, a considerable number of objects are put on display in humidity-controlled cabinets where moisture will not condense on metal surfaces. If two dissimilar metals are joined together and immersed in sea water, the use of insulators between the two will stop the flow of electrons and hence stop corrosion (Tretheway and Chamberlain 1995).

It is amazing to think that wrought iron guns, bronze cannons, pewter plates, etc, can survive for over 500 years below the surface of the sea. The reason for this is that one of the five factors mentioned above has not been present. A considerable number of objects were recovered from the *Mary Rose* with a calcium carbonate scale formed over the entire surface. This is called a concretion and has excluded oxygen from getting to the metal surface – no cathode reactant, therefore, no corrosion. Even the very large wrought guns became engulfed in sediment. No air (oxygen) could penetrate, hence no cathode reactant, so corrosion ceased.

This highlights the importance of carrying out conservation very quickly once the metal object has been brought to the surface as oxygen can now once more reach the cathode sites and corrosion immediately recommences – in the case of the *Mary Rose* after a gap of over 400 years. This is particularly important when chloride ions are present in the surface layers adjacent to the metal surface. As sea water contains 3% weight sodium chloride, all metal artefacts recovered from this environment will have chlorides associated with their corrosion products. These ions were considered to be very deleterious for objects recovered from the *Mary*

Figure 5.1 Copper alloy cauldron before conservation

Rose as they would rapidly corrode most of the metals, with the exception of the gold coins.

There are several reason for this excessive rate of corrosion. The first is that chlorides will readily dissolve into any moisture films that condense on the artefact during display or in storage and increase the conductivity of the water. This means that the charge can pass more easily through the electrolyte and results in a higher flow of current in the corrosion cell. The second reason is that chloride-containing compounds in the corrosion products tend to be more soluble than oxides or hydroxides, which are the predominant compounds formed in the absence of chlorides. Liquid corrosion products will not hinder the arrival of oxygen to the metal surface and the cathode reaction is less impeded. The chloride-containing compounds are also quite deliquescent and this means that they readily attract water. To maintain completely dry surfaces on the metal artefact, it is necessary to keep the humidity as low as 16% RH. This is difficult to achieve in most circumstances in museums or storage rooms. Finally, corrosion reactions involving chlorides can produce acids such as hydrochloric acid. These reactions may take place in crevices or pits on the metal surface and the pH can drop from 8.1 (sea water) down to 2.5 at the base of a pit. Metals will invariably corrode faster in acids than in neutral electrolytes and hence corrosion will be accelerated at the base of these pits. From the above it is apparent that, if the artefact is to survive long after it has been excavated, the removal of the deleterious chloride is essential. This is one of the main tasks in the conservation of metals as once these have been removed, the metal is said to be stabilised.

Conservation

The main aims of conservation of metals are as follows:

1. Arrest the corrosion process.
2. Remove the chlorides from the corrosion products.
3. Leave the shape of the artefact unaltered.
4. Maintain the metallurgical structure of the artefact.

Before removal of the chlorides from objects recovered from the *Mary Rose*, concretions were very carefully removed by mechanical means using chisels, dentist drills or shot blasting with a very mild abrasive such as magnesium carbonate. If the extent of corrosion of the artefact while buried was uncertain, a radiograph could be taken to ascertain the amount of metal left uncorroded. This was often helpful in deciding the most suitable method for subsequent conservation.

The removal of the chloride ions is the essential requirement – but the conservator must consider the other three aims when deciding what method to use. For example, there are several proprietary solutions on the market, or ones that can be made up in a laboratory, which will dissolve all the corrosion products and leave the metal intact. This method is not suitable, however, if the artefact has thick layers of corrosion products on the surface as the shape will be lost. Even worse, if the artefact was composed of solid corrosion products only, there would be nothing left after immersion in these solutions! This method is only really suitable if there are only very thin layers of corrosion products left on the surface after recovery.

A relatively simple method is to dissolve out the chloride ions by immersion in a suitable solvent. Water has been used, with the water being changed every month until no further chlorides are detected. This can take up to five years for marine artefacts with high levels of chloride buried within deep rust layers. Moreover, the metal will continue to corrode while the artefact is immersed in the water for this length of time. By altering the pH of the solution, it may be possible to dissolve out the chlorides without corroding the metal. This is achieved by the formation of a thin passive film, approximately 10nm ($\sim 10^{-9}$m) thick on the exposed metal. For example, wrought iron will form a passive film in a solution above pH 9. Hence sodium hydroxide, sodium carbonate or ammonium hydroxide would be suitable for this class of artefact. The disadvantage of these solutions is that they still take a long time to remove all the chlorides and one is not absolutely certain that all the chlorides have been removed after a period of five years (Arrhenius *et al.* 1973).

A quicker process is to use electrolysis, whereby the artefact is made the cathode in an electrolytic cell with a stainless steel or lead sheet becoming the anode. A current is passed between the two electrodes when they are immersed in a suitable electrolyte, such as sodium carbonate. The chloride ions dissolve in the electrolyte and are attracted to the anode. This can reduce the conservation time down to two years but electrical connections have to be made to the artefact. In addition, one must also ensure that there is no vigorous gas evolution on the cathode surface that may lead to the spalling of the rust layers and, hence, destruction of the shape.

Thermal methods are much quicker but will alter the metallurgical structure of the artefact (Archer and Barker 1987). A large-scale method was developed in Portsmouth for the conservation of the numerous wrought iron guns recovered from the *Mary Rose*. This involved slowly heating the artefacts in an atmosphere of hydrogen to 850°C. At this temperature, the chlorides are removed from the corrosion products in the form of gaseous hydrochloric acid, which is blown out of the retort. Chemical reactions are significantly faster in the gaseous phase and by doing this, the time for complete removal of the chlorides could be as short as seven days. At the time, these wrought iron guns were the largest artefacts to be conserved by this technique. As there were a large number of similar artefacts, it was not imperative that the metallurgical structure remained unaltered, as one example was conserved by the washing method so that any examination in future may be carried out on it (O'Shea *et al.* 1982).

After conservation by any of the methods outlined above, the corrosion products, which are now free from chlorides, are very friable and have to be consolidated by impregnation with a suitable resin. Low viscosity polyesters and epoxies were extensively used on *Mary Rose* metal objects as these can flow into the porous corrosion products and set hard, thus making the artefact much more stable and easier to handle (Barker 1985).

Treatment of Ferrous Artefacts

Metallurgy

Ferrous materials can be divided into three types:

a) Wrought iron.
b) Cast iron.
c) Steel.

Wrought iron is essentially pure iron but with particles of slag from the refining method still included in the structure. Wrought iron melts at 1535°C and is relatively soft and ductile and, therefore, is able to be shaped by techniques such as forging and hammering. As the result of these shaping processes, the slag orientates itself in the direction of working (streaks of slag) and the end result is a fibrous structure (Tylecote 1962).

Cast iron is an alloy of iron and carbon, with the latter ranging from 3% to 4.5%. The melting point of this alloy is 1150–1200°C, which is considerably lower than wrought iron. Carbon is found in the cast iron as graphite (termed grey cast iron) or, in some instances, as iron carbide (Fe_3C) or cementite, in which case, the alloy is called white cast iron. Both forms of carbon make the cast iron a very brittle material and thus impossible to shape it by forging or hammering. Fortunately, due to the lower melting point of cast iron, it is possible to melt it and cast it into the required shape.

Steels are alloys of iron and up to 1.7% carbon, although they are not usually found with more than

1.2% carbon. The melting point of steels is only a few degrees lower than that of pure iron so it was impossible to produce temperatures in furnaces used in the sixteenth century that were anywhere near that required to melt steel, ie, ~ 1600°C. The mechanical properties of steels are greatly influenced by carbon content. As the carbon increases in the steel, the ductility decreases while the hardness and tensile strength go up. A further important consideration is that hardness of steels can be dramatically increased to even higher levels by a process of heating to above ~ 800°C and quenching in water, or some other fluid such as urine, and then tempering at 200–300°C. This produces the ideal mechanical properties for cutting instruments such as knives, blades scissors, razors, etc, which require sharp cutting edges and do not blunt easily.

Extraction

There are four main economic ores from which iron can be extracted, namely haematite (Fe_2O_3), limonite ($Fe_2O_3.3H_2O$), magnetite (Fe_3O_4) and siderite ($FeCO_3$). The iron content of these ores can range from 50% down to 20%. The extraction of the pure metal from these ores is far more difficult than it is for producing pure copper or pure tin. The reason for this is that the oxygen is more strongly bonded to the oxides of iron and requires more stringent reducing conditions within the furnace to achieve separation. The minimum temperature at which the oxide is removed is 800°C, which is well below the melting point of iron. Another consideration is that the ore is mixed with a large amount of unwanted material, called gangue, and this has to be separated from the metal by a process of slagging. The unwanted material is melted by combining with silica (sand) and is drained away from the iron. The melting point of this slag is approximately 1200°C.

Shaft furnaces were employed to reduce the iron ores to the metal. The ore was mixed with charcoal (reaction 5) and the temperature raised to c. 1000°C by means of manually operated bellows. This temperature is below the melting point of iron so reduction occurred within the solid phase according to the following reactions:

$$2C + O_2 = 2CO \tag{5}$$

$$Fe_2O_3 + CO = 2FeO + CO_2 \tag{6}$$

$$FeO + CO = Fe + CO_2 \tag{7}$$

Reaction 6 took place higher up the shaft while reaction 7 occurred near the hearth. The end result was a mixture of iron and slag which was hammered while hot to produce a bloom of wrought iron. This was called the bloomery process for the production of wrought iron. The wastage of iron was very high, with over 70% of available iron lost in the slag.

The introduction of mechanically operated bellows and taller shaft furnaces allowed higher temperatures to be achieved. These were called charcoal blast furnaces but they did require the use of an excessive amount of fuel to achieve temperatures up to 1200°C. The walls of the furnace were well lagged to keep the temperatures up while the extra height allowed the iron ore to be in contact with the carbon monoxide gas for a longer period of time. At this higher temperature, the solid iron slowly dissolved the charcoal and thus lowered the melting point of the iron. When the carbon content became around 4.5%, the metal became liquid at the maximum furnace temperature and formed a layer beneath the now molten slag. This molten metal had the composition of cast iron. The slag was able to be separated from the cast iron by draining the top liquid layer of slag away.

The slag produced by this blast furnace had a much lower iron content so, this was a much more efficient method for producing ferrous material. The molten cast iron was run off from the furnace into blocks called pigs or into the desired shaped clay moulds. The first blast furnace built of this type in England was at Sussex in 1496 and the earliest artefact of cast iron has been dated to 1509. The main use of cast iron was for ordnance purposes but no large guns made from this material were recovered from the *Mary Rose*. All the large ferrous guns were manufactured from wrought iron staves and bands put together by welding (referred to here as 'split-ring guns'). The guns produced from cast iron were easier to produce and were more pressure tight than the split-ring guns. In addition, they were far cheaper than the bronze ones found on the ship.

Wrought iron could be produced from cast iron by blowing air over the surface of molten cast iron. This caused the carbon to oxidise to carbon dioxide and hence this was continued until all of the carbon had been removed.

The temperatures of the furnaces at this time were still not high enough to produce steel. This could only be made in the blacksmith's forge. During the annealing of wrought iron at temperatures between 800°C and 900°C, the charcoal (carbon) will very slowly diffuse into the pure iron. This is precursor to the modern method of solid case hardening of steel. Times of up to 20 hours would have been required to produce 0.8% carbon to a depth of 2mm. Because of this, only the surface layers of a cutting material would have been converted to steel or else tiny strips of wrought iron would have been converted to steel and these strips subsequently twisted and beaten into the required shape.

Corrosion

Very pure iron has superior corrosion resistance to cast irons or steels as only one phase is present at room temperature, namely pure ferrite. Examples of artefacts that have exhibited this effect include the Delhi pillar in India (Shrew *et al.* 1994). Wrought iron contains small amounts of slag that appear as fibrous inclusions in the ferrite structure. Preferential corrosion occurs along these inclusions leaving the object with a ridged appearance. The cathode sites are probably the areas of slag while the adjacent ferrite phase is the anode and corrodes. The ridges or layers of corrosion often indicate to a conservator that the artefact has been manufactured from wrought iron. If the artefact has been exposed to elements for a long time, these layers may break away and leave only a thin layer of rust by the time the object is excavated.

The structure of grey cast iron consists of flakes of graphite surrounded by grains of ferrite. The graphite flakes act as the cathode sites and are protected while the ferrite grains are the anodes and corrode. The graphite flakes prevent the corrosion products (red rust) from diffusing into the sea water and the rust is trapped between the graphite flakes. The shape of the artefact is maintained but the corroded layer is very soft and has virtually no mechanical strength. This type of corrosion is called graphitisation of cast iron and has to be treated with care in the conservation process because of its fragile nature.

Steels will also corrode in sea water because a corrosion cell is set up between the ferrite and the cementite (Fe_3C), which is the form that carbon takes in this alloy. The rust layers are not held in place as the cementite has an extremely fine structure compared to the course flakes of graphite found in cast iron.

The electrochemical reactions taking place at the anode and cathode sites in sea water are as given in equations (2) and (3) on p. 76. The products from these two reactions, ferrous and hydroxyl ions, then diffuse away from their respective sites and combine to form ferrous hydroxide ($Fe(OH)_2$). If there is any oxygen gas dissolved in the water, this will oxidise the ferrous compound to an insoluble ferric one, namely $FeO.OH$, which is familiar to us all as red rust. In reality, there are over 35 possible compounds that can be found in rust on ferrous metals but it is beyond the scope of this present discussion to describe them all (Turgoose 1982). If there was an absence of chloride ions in the electrolyte, the rate of corrosion of the ferrous artefact will be of the order of $30\mu m$ a year. This is obviously not the case in sea water as it contains approximately 3% salt. The presence of chloride ions in the electrolyte, or contained within the rust layers, will accelerate this rate of corrosion. The general rate of corrosion may now be up to $125\mu m$ a year with the possibility of pitting attack at certain sites giving rates of 2–3mm per year.

The reason for this accelerated attack is that chlorides may cause soluble corrosion products to form that are less protective than the insoluble ones formed in the absence of chlorides. The presence of chlorides will increase the conductivity of the electrolyte between the anode and cathode sites allowing much higher currents to flow through the electrolyte between these two sites. A higher current flow means that more electrons will be produced at the anode sites and thus be consumed at a faster rate at the cathode site. The net effect of this is that there is a large increase in the rate of corrosion. Another contributory factor is that chloride corrosion products may break down to generate hydrochloric acid. This lowers the pH from 8.1–8.3 in sea water down to approximately 2.5 inside pits, crevices, etc. Corrosion is obviously enhanced in acidic conditions. Finally, when an artefact is excavated and exposed to air, the presence of chloride-containing compounds will cause water to condense out at very low humidities. These compounds are said to be very deliquescent and moisture will condense out even on very dry days or when an artefact is exposed to an allegedly dry atmosphere within a museum.

Concretions

In a similar manner to other groups of metals and alloys recovered from the *Mary Rose*, ferrous artefacts were covered in layers of concretion or calcium carbonate. As the corrosion rate of these groups of metals is higher than for the copper-based ones, for example, the thickness of the concretions is far greater than on the non-ferrous metals. Concretions ranging between 5mm and 150mm thick have been observed on the wrought iron guns recovered from the Solent.

The mechanism for the formation of the concretions is exactly the same as it is for brass objects (see below). Concretions can arise from two sources. The first is due to the corrosion reactions taking place on the surface of the metal. In sea water, the cathodic reaction in aerobic conditions is the reduction of dissolved oxygen to hydroxyl ions as given by equation (8)

$$O_2 + 2H_2O + 4e = 4OH^- \qquad (8)$$

The increase in pH (more alkaline conditions) at these local cathodes causes the soluble calcium bicarbonate, which is a constituent of sea water, to be converted to the insoluble carbonate which forms a scale (inorganic calcite) over the metal surface as shown in equation (9). This will slow down or arrest the corrosion process altogether.

$$Ca(HCO_3)_2 + 2OH^- \longrightarrow CaCO_3 + H_2O \qquad 9)$$
$$\text{(calcite)}$$

Once this inorganic carbonate film has formed, it may be possible for the marine organisms to colonise the artefact and an organic carbonate film may form over the initial inorganic layer.

When this layer covers almost the entire surface of the artefact, oxygen is excluded from getting to the cathode sites and corrosion is arrested. Another reason why the ferrous metals survived for over 450 years under the sea is that the guns became enveloped in the silts of the Solent seabed. This is an anaerobic environment (no oxygen) and hence corrosion will be stopped because, once more, there is no cathode reactant and hence the anode reaction will no longer be able to take place.

The major problem with these ferrous artefacts is that, once they are brought to the surface, air (the source of oxygen) can reach the metal surface and corrosion will recommence; hence the need for urgent conservation treatment. In addition, the deleterious chloride ions will concentrate on the metal surface if the artefact starts to dry out and this will further exacerbate the corrosion process. For those artefacts that are completely mineralised, such as grey cast, where the shape is only maintained by the graphitised structure, dehydration of the corrosion products will involve a volume change. This will set up mechanical stresses within the corrosion products that may cause them to spall and the shape of the artefact to be lost.

Ideally, the artefacts should be immersed in an electrolyte as soon as they are brought to the surface. This was very impractical for the large guns recovered from the *Mary Rose* so they were immediately packed in wet sawdust or cloths to stop them from drying out. Some of the smaller objects were also placed into sealed plastic bags in an attempt to exclude oxygen from the surface.

Conservation

The aim of conservation is to stabilise the rust layers and prevent any corrosion while the artefact is on display or kept in store. For artefacts recovered from the *Mary Rose*, it is essential to remove all traces of chlorides from the corrosion products and to consolidate these once the chloride has been removed. The well established method of conservation for ferrous metals is aqueous washing in suitable electrolytes. The electrolyte selected must not corrode the metal but, at the same time, it must dissolve the chloride ions from the layers of rust. Provided the electrolyte has a pH greater than 9.5, any exposed iron will be covered with a very thin protective film. This is called a passive film and is only about 10nm (10^{-9}m) thick. Typical electrolytes employed by conservators include 0.5M sodium hydroxide, 0.2M sodium carbonate and 0.2M sodium sesquicarbonate. The chlorides slowly dissolve in these solutions and they are replaced every month until no chlorides are detected in them by conventional analytical techniques. The problem with aqueous washing is that it can take up to five years to remove all the chloride ions and, even after this period of time, it is not certain that all the chlorides have been removed from deep crevices or pits at the metal/rust interface.

A faster conservation method is electrolytic reduction. In this, the artefact is made the cathode in an electrolytic cell with a mild steel or stainless steel anode. This has a two-fold action, the first being the reduction of the corrosion products (red rust) to magnetite according to equation (10):

$$3FeO.OH + e = Fe_3O_4 + OH^- + H_2O \qquad (10)$$

This involves a 30% reduction in volume of corrosion products and thus allows the electrolyte to penetrate into the rust layers.

Chloride removal is the second action of electrolysis. Under the influence of the applied electric field, the negatively charged chloride ions migrate away from the cathode (rust layers on the artefact) into the electrolyte and towards the anode. There the chloride ions may react to form chlorine gas, if the cell potential is high enough. The treatment time is reduced to a maximum of two years depending upon the amount of chloride in the rust. 0.5M sodium carbonate and 0.2M sodium sesquicarbonate have been used as electrolytes with a cell voltage of 2.5–4.0V. The small amount of hydrogen gas that is produced at the surface of the cathode (artefact) also helps to break up the layers of concretion into powdery deposits, which can be subsequently lightly brushed away from the surface.

Figure 5.2 A hydrogen reduction furnace

Table 5.1 Treatment of selected iron objects

Object	Comment	Treatment
Wrought Iron objects		
Split ring gun 70A0001	Concreted	Pre-cleaned by electrolysis. Hydrogen reduction furnace for 100 hrs at 850°C. Further cleaning & impregnated with low viscosity epoxide varnish & given final wax coat
Breech gun 81A2650	Heavily concreted, radiograph taken	Pre-washed in ammonia solution. Mechanically cleaned. Hydrogen reduction furnace for 100 hours at 850°C. Further cleaning & impregnated with epoxide varnish & given final wax coat
Split ring gun 71A0169	Concretion all over surface	Pre-heated in hydrogen furnace at 400°C to assist in removal of concretion, which then mechanically removed. Hydrogen reduction furnace for 100 hrs at 850°C. Further cleaning & impregnated with epoxide varnish & given final wax coat
Breech gun 81A2604		Mechanically cleaned. Pre-washed in ammonia solution. Hydrogen reduction furnace for 100 hrs at 850°C. Further cleaning & impregnated with epoxide varnish & given final wax coat
Swivel gun 79A0543		Soaked in 2% NaOH. Mechanical removal of concretion. Hydrogen reduction furnace for 100 hrs at 850°C. Further cleaning & impregnated with epoxide varnish
Swivel gun 82A4076		Pre-washed in ammonia solution. Mechanically cleaned. Hydrogen reduction furnace for 100 hrs at 850°C. Further cleaning & impregnated with epoxide varnish
Swivel gun 82A4077		Pre-washed in ammonia solution. Mechanically cleaned. Hydrogen reduction furnace for 100 hrs at 850°C. Further cleaning & impregnated with epoxide varnish
Cast iron objects		
Hail shot gun 79A1088	Covered in concretion – c. 60% of original metal content lost	Mechanical removal of concretion. Soaked in 5% NaOH for 3 weeks. Hydrogen reduction furnace for 50 hrs at 850°C. Vacuum impregnation of polyester resin & baked at 210°C for 2 hrs
Hail shot gun 80A0544	Gun in 2 parts. After conservation repaired with araldite	Soaked in 2% NaOH. Mechanical removal of concretion. Hydrogen reduction furnace for 100 hrs at 850°C. Further cleaning & impregnated with epoxide varnish & given final wax coat
Shot 80A0358		Soaked in 2% NaOH. Mechanical removal of concretion. Hydrogen reduction furnace for 100 hrs at 850°C. Further cleaning & impregnated with epoxide varnish & given final wax coat
Shot 80A1346		Soaked in 2% NaOH. Mechanical removal of concretion. Hydrogen reduction furnace for 100 hrs at 850°C. Further cleaning & impregnated with epoxide varnish & given final wax coat
Derived steel objects		
Handle 81A1984	Only wooden parts remained but prob. derived steel by intended use	As for wood
Axe 81A3830	as above	As for wood
Auger 81A3066	as above	As for wood
Razor 80A1525	As above	As for wood

As there was a large number of artefacts recovered from the *Mary Rose* and these included the large wrought iron guns, this would have meant having an excessive number of soaking tanks in order to carry out conservation in an effective manner. Moreover, the time scale for conservation, 2–5 years, meant that the immediate impact of these finds for publicity or other purposes, would be seriously delayed. The hydrogen reduction process became operational in 1975 (Fig. 5.2). The basic principle of this technique is to heat the artefacts in a furnace under an atmosphere of hydrogen (Barkman 1977). First this causes the volatile chlorides to sublime off from the rust and, secondly, the oxides of iron are reduced eventually to metal. This is accompanied by a volume change of the surface layers thus allowing the deeply buried, trapped chlorides to escape into the furnace atmosphere. The time taken to conserve artefacts was approximately 14 days (Kendall 1982).

The ferrous artefacts were stored in an alkaline solution with the pH above 9.5 to prevent any further corrosion prior to treatment in the hydrogen furnace. At first, 2% sodium hydroxide was used as the electrolyte (eg, swivel gun 79A0543) but subsequent problems arose during hydrogen reduction. The sodium hydroxide converted some of the chlorides in the rust layers to sodium chloride. It was virtually impossible to reduce this by hydrogen reduction and this meant that it was very difficult to ensure the complete removal of all the chlorides from the corrosion products, which is one of the main aims of conservation. A switch was then made to ammonia-based electrolytes for pre-storage prior to the artefact undergoing conservation. The chlorides are now converted to ammonium chloride that is reduced in the hydrogen furnace. An example of this was swivel gun 82A4076 in Table 5.1.

The large guns were separated into the different materials which included the wooden gun carriage and metallic sections such as the gun barrel and chamber. The wood would be conserved by a totally different method of freeze-drying as discussed in Chapter 4. The metal parts would first have the concretion removed. This was mostly carried out by mechanical means using chisels or scalpels (Fig. 5.3) or, in selected instances, by electrolysis as with the split-ring gun 70A0001. Light concretions were removed during the treatment in the hydrogen furnace and could easily be brushed off at the end of conservation. The final pre-treatment was to make quite sure that the barrel of the gun was clean so that the atmosphere within the furnace could freely reach all parts.

The length of the gun barrels recovered from the *Mary Rose* dictated the size of the furnace employed for the conservation. The maximum length recovered is nearly 3m with the chamber sections being 1m long. Subsequent to building this furnace, chambers 1.5m long were excavated which meant that the barrels would be approaching 4.5m. Fortunately for the conservators, no barrels of this dimension have been recovered!

Once cleaned, the artefact (eg, gun barrel) was secured onto a stainless steel base and a Nimonic alloy retort clamped down over it so as to ensure an air tight seal. The effective working area of the retort was 2.5m high by 0.7m in diameter. The retort was wheeled into an electrically-heated furnace, 4m by 2.2m in diameter. The retort was purged with nitrogen until the last traces of oxygen had been removed. Anhydrous liquid ammonia was heated to 850°C and passed over a nickel catalyst, whereby the ammonia was completely dissociated into hydrogen and nitrogen and this mixture was fed into the retort. The furnace was switched on and the temperature allowed to slowly rise to 850°C over a period of approximately 24 hours. This ensured that the artefact was not subjected to any significant thermal shock. The temperature remained at this value until the chlorides in the exhaust gases coming out of the furnace were undetectable by analytical methods used at that time (Draeger tubes). This could be anything from 100–200 hours depending upon the original levels of chloride within the rust layers. At this point, the cracked ammonia was replaced by nitrogen in the furnace and cooling down to room temperature was carefully controlled once more to minimise thermal stresses. This normally took 48 hours. The artefacts were removed from the retort and given a brush to remove any powdery deposits (Barker *et al.* 1982).

Figure 5.3 Conserving an iron gun: (top and middle) conservation staff removed concretion from the surface with hammers and chisels; (bottom) the exposed remains of the wrought iron gun

At the end of this process the original rust layers had been converted mostly to a mixture of magnetite and metallic iron. This is very friable and has to be consolidated with an organic resin. Initially, the barrels, etc, were soaked in a tank or brushed with a polyester resin but this was soon switched to an epoxide one. The final part of the conservation programme was to give a top coat of wax, although this was optional (Fig. 5.4) (Archer 1991).

Figure 5.4 Wrought iron gun barrel after conservation

Treatment of Copper and its Alloys (Excluding Bronze and Brass)

Metallurgy

Copper based ores are found in Scotland and Ireland and on the west coast of England and Wales. The main ores are malachite ($CuCO_3.Cu(OH)_2$, chalcocite (Cu_2S) and chalcopyrite ($CuFeS_2$). The oxide-based ores are usually found on top of the deposit while the sulphides are found underneath. The production of copper from its ores is far easier from the oxide than the sulphide bearing ores. The basic mechanism for the production of the metal from the ore is best represented by equation (11):

$$Ore + reducing\ agent + heat = metal + slag + gas \quad (11)$$

The reducing agent has a greater affinity for oxygen than the metal. In the period around AD 1500 charcoal was used so that the active reducing agent would either be carbon itself or, more likely in the presence of just sufficient air, carbon monoxide, CO (reaction 12).

$$2C + O_2 = 2CO \quad (12)$$

In this process the slag is the unwanted material, which may be in the form of some silicate or oxides of other metals found associated with the metal being extracted. For the production of copper, the malachite is mixed with charcoal and placed in a furnace with some type of bellows arrangement to increase the temperature in the furnace to 700–800°C. The ore is reduced to metal according to equation (13):

$$CO + CuCO_3 = 2CO_2 + Cu \quad (13)$$

In the furnaces employed at the time that the *Mary Rose* sank, the copper usually remained in the furnace as a solid ingot, as the temperatures could not easily reach the melting point of pure copper (1083°C). If there was an excess of air in the furnace, the carbon monoxide would be oxidised to carbon dioxide (equation (14)) and there would be insufficient carbon monoxide present to reduce the ore to copper. Hence the copper

artefacts often contained quantities of unreduced Cu_2O in their structure.

$$2CO + O_2 = 2CO_2 \quad (14)$$

The sulphide ores had first to be roasted to form oxides as the sulphides are too difficult to reduce to the metal. The chalcocite or mixed copper/iron sulphide ore was placed over burning wood in shallow cavities for up to 30 days to convert the sulphides to oxides of copper according to equation (15).

$$Cu_2S + O_2 = 2CuO + SO_2 \quad (15)$$

The oxide so produced was then treated as for the oxide bearing ores. There is very little iron found in copper obtained from chalcopyrite as the iron is more difficult to reduce than copper and ends up in the unwanted slag. The main impurities that are found in the copper produced by this method are arsenic and antimony as these metals are reduced under similar conditions to the copper together with any silver or gold that may have been associated with the copper deposits.

Pure metals, such as copper, are easy to shape by hammering, beating or bending because they are very soft and ductile. This can be carried out hot (above the annealing temperature), in which case the mechanical properties are not significantly altered, or by shaping at ambient temperatures. The latter is again called cold working. The hardness is increased but this process decreases the ductility. There is a limit to the amount of change of dimensions that the metal can withstand by cold working as eventually it will become so hard that it will crack if any further deformation is carried out. Cold working was thus a very simple way to harden a pure metal but the increase would not be sufficient to manufacture a sharp knife, for example.

The addition of alloying elements will increase the hardness without sacrificing too much loss in ductility provided the alloying additions are able to dissolve in the crystal structure of the parent metal. Arsenic found in copper alloys (often referred to as arsenical copper alloys) was such an alloy that was produced from ores containing this metal. The hardness of 4% arsenic/copper alloys was approximately double that obtained from pure copper.

Cold worked copper or its alloys could have their ductility restored by annealing them at temperatures above 200°C. The time taken to anneal copper depends on the degree of cold work and the annealing temperature. Nowadays, temperatures in excess of 550°C are used, but temperatures as low as 300°C would have produced a significant alteration in the ductility of severely cold worked materials. Temperatures of 300°C are relatively easy to maintain with wood fires.

A fragment of a cauldron recovered from the *Mary Rose* was examined using a metallurgical microscope. The structure showed large equiaxed grains with large inclusions of copper oxide (Cu_2O) distributed throughout the structure. This illustrated that not all of the copper ore had been reduced during the metal winning stage and the large grains indicated that the copper had been annealed. This is not surprising as the cauldron was used for melting tar, the temperature of which would be well into the annealing range for copper or its alloys (Barker *et al.* 1992).

Spark emission analysis of the tiny fragment indicated the presence of antimony and lead in the copper. These were probably associated with the ore used to produce the copper in the first place and were not deliberate alloy additions.

Corrosion

The corrosion of copper and its alloys is very similar to those discussed for brass and bronze (below) with bronze disease and pitting corrosion being the most important aspects to eliminate if conservation is to be effectively carried out.

Conservation

Most of the artefacts listed in Table 5.2 were first mechanically treated by a scalpel and a small glass fibre brush to remove loose corrosion products (Fig. 5.5). To remove the chloride ions from the remaining solid corrosion products, a washing technique was employed in either distilled or de-ionised water. The water was changed daily and the rate of chloride removal followed by chemical analysis. In order to reduce the risk of corrosion of the artefact during this washing period, the temperature of the water was maintained at 50 or 80°C. This higher temperature reduced the amount of dissolved oxygen in the water and hence the rate of corrosion of the underlying metal as the rate of corrosion in neutral water is directly proportional to the amount of dissolved oxygen. A further advantage of using higher temperatures is that the rates of diffusion of the chlorides from the corrosion products into the water will be increased thus speeding up the conservation

Figure 5.5 The Barber-surgeon's shaving bowl cleaned of corrosion products

Table 5.2 Treatment of selected copper/copper alloy objects

Object	Comments	Treatment
Sheave 77A0009	Yellow appearance. Thick layers of green & green-black corrosion products.	Washed for 27 days in de-ionised water. Chloride levels dropped from 106 ppm to 10 ppm. Dried and soaked in 1%BTA for 1 day. finished off with 3 coats of Incralac
Thimble ring 81A6784	Some holes where the dimples were situated on the object	Mechanically cleaned and hot washed in distilled water at 80°C for 1 month. Chloride levels reduced below 10 ppm. Soaked in 3% BTA for 1 day & given 1 coat Incralac
Chain 81A4999	Bronze coloured. Light covering of black corrosion products	Mechanically cleaned. Soaked in 3% BTA for 1 day and coated with Incralac
Buckle 81A4186	Various coloured corrosion products. Metal underneath appeared yellow	Mechanically cleaned with a scalpel followed by soft glass fibre brush. Hot distilled water wash at 80°C for 1 month until chloride levels below 1 ppm. Dried in IMS for 8 hrs, stabilised in 3% BTA for 24 hours & given 1 coat of Incralac
Powder scoop 81A0241	Several holes and tears. Signs of active corrosion spots	Mechanically cleaned. Hot washed in distilled water at 50°C for 1 month. Dried and stabilised in 1% BTA for 8 hrs & given 1 coat of Incralac
Dividers 81A0084	A new bronze rivet added after damage on display	Immersed in modistic gel for 4 hrs in ultrasonic bath. Water washed for 5 days, solvent dried and surface coated with Incralac

BTA = Benzotriazole (Oddy 1972; 1974); IMS = Industrial Methylated Spirit; Incralac = Solution of acrylic resin disolved in toluene

Note: Without chemical analysis it is difficult, if not impossible, to identify if an artefact is made from copper or one of its alloys. The items listed here are, at present, classified as copper based until chemical analysis has been undertaken

process. Chemically, when the copper or its alloys is immersed into water, the chloride containing compounds within the corrosion layers are hydrolysed to hydroxide with the release of the chloride into the water according to equation (16):

$$CuCl_2 + 2H_2O = Cu(OH)_2 + 2HCl \qquad (16)$$

The formation of hydrochloric acid emphasises the need to change the water frequently to prevent the pH of the water becoming too low. A chloride level below 10 ppm was deemed to be satisfactory in preventing the onset of bronze disease provided the humidity of the surrounding air was maintained below 40% RH while the artefact was on display or in store. After soaking in water, the artefacts were treated in a similar manner to that discussed for brass and bronze.

Treatment of Bronze Artefacts

Metallurgy

Archaeological bronze is an alloy of copper and tin. The composition of these alloys typically ranges from 3% to 14% tin together with trace impurities such as lead and iron depending on the chemical content of the original ores. The alloys were made by mixing tin ore (cassiterite, SnO_2) with pure copper, covering the mixture with a layer of charcoal and heating to approximately 800°C. Liquid alloy was tapped from the furnace.

Alloys with a tin content up to 6% were capable of being cast and subsequently hammered into their final shape. This is because the tin is soluble in the copper crystal structure which allows the alloy to be deformed at room temperature. The composition of tin is not uniform across the whole object as the diffusion rate of tin through copper is slow. This is called coring and can be eliminated by annealing the object at 600°C. Above 7%, a brittle intermetallic phase (δ - $Cu_{31}Sn_8$) is formed which hardens the alloy considerably but makes it unsuitable for producing wrought products. The higher

Figure 5.6 The ship's bell

levels of tin lower the melting point of the alloy and increase the fluidity, thus making these alloys ideal for shaping by casting. This is the method used for producing the range of bronze cannons recovered from the *Mary Rose*. Adding zinc improved the fluidity of the alloy and allowed less tin to be used. This was particularly important if there was a shortage of tin or it became too expensive. These ternary alloys were the precursor to modern Admiralty Gun Metal, which is a 88/10/2 alloy of copper/tin/zinc. High levels of phosphorus (>0.1%) in a straight copper/tin alloy increased the tensile strength of the bronze and this is now called a phosphor bronze. This addition was useful in that it helped to deoxidise the melt thus preventing the formation of tin oxide in the alloy.

Chemical analysis of a gun (79A1232) gave 89.7% Cu, 6.8%Sn, 1.1%Pb and 1.9%Fe. This compares quite well with other cannons recovered from different sites dating from the same period (Pearson 1987) where the tin content ranged from 7.6–13.9% and the lead from 1.3–1.6%. A small fragment of metal from the ship's bell (83A2297) (Fig. 5.6) showed there to be 15% tin and 1.68% lead, with the remainder being copper. Bronzes for the manufacture of bells are often in the range 15–25% tin, which agrees with these findings.

Corrosion

Bronzes have a superior corrosion resistance to brasses because tin forms a protective layer of SnO_2 over the surface of the alloy, when exposed to well aerated sea water, which virtually stifles further attack. If the sea water is not well aerated then this protective layer will not form over the entire surface and corrosion of the copper rich area in the micro-structure will take place. This results in the presence of corrosion products normally associated with the corrosion of pure copper.

Selective removal of tin – called destannification – is not so prevalent as is the removal of zinc in brasses. Very few examples have been reported and those that have been observed are from sites where the artefacts have been excavated from anaerobic sites (Pearson 1987). It is thought that arsenic and antimony will inhibit this form of de-alloying and, as these are common impurities found in bronze artefacts, this is the reason for this form of corrosion not being commonly observed.

The most important corrosion phenomenon associated with bronze artefacts is bronze disease. On artefacts recovered from land-based sites, this manifests itself by the break out of mounds of green rust on the alloy surface. On artefacts recovered from marine sites, this effect can occur over the entire surface. On removal of bronze objects from marine sites, the corrosion products may be considered to consist of layers of different compounds. Adjacent to the metal surface is a layer of nantokite (CuCl) followed by a layer of cuprite (Cu_2O) then a layer of malachite ($Cu_2(OH)_2CO_3$). In the absence of oxygen, as is the case on the *Mary Rose*

Table 5.3 Treatment of selected bronze objects

Object	Comments	Treatment
Gun (Demi-culverin) 79A1232	Good evidence of bronze disease. Heavily corroded	Concretion removed by chisels, vibro-tools & brushes. Chemically cleaned with Sepiolite. Soaked in 3% BTA in IMS. Surface waxed with Waxoyl. Mechanical cleaning of bore. Iron shot removed. Electrolysis of bore in 5% NaOH at 10A. Removal of corrosion products in 5% EDTA. Bore washed with de-ionised water for 7 weeks. Washed in 3% BTA in IMS. Dried with acetone
Gun (Demi-cannon) 81A3002		Electrolysed in 3% Na_2CO_3 for 32 days at $0.5A\ ft^{-2}$. Washed in distilled water at 30°C for 5 days. Steam cleaned using distilled water. Waxed with Carnauba
Gun (Cannon Royal) 81A3003	Concreted. Extensive bronze disease	Concretion reomoved mechanically. Electrolysis in 5% NaOH at 2–3 V for 441 hrs. Cleaned with glass fibre brush, rotary soft brush & vibro-tools. Soaked in 3% BTA in IMS. Coated with 20% Incralac in acetone. Coated with micro-crystalline wax
Bell 82A2297	Complete & in fair condition	Cleaned, soaked in BTA and coated with Incralac. Coating stripped, object cleaned & recoated
Sheave 82A0009	Good condition, encrusted areas	Electrolysed in 0.5% Na_2CO_3. Washed in water. Light mechanical clean. Coated with Incralac
Pitch pot 82A4455	Corrosion over most of metal sur-face, dark blue in places	Electrolysed in 5% Na_2CO_3 for 3 days. Soaked in oxalic acid for 4 hrs. Washed in tap water for 5 days. Oven dried. Immersed in 3% BTA for 24 hrs. Coated with Incralac
Pot 82A0982	Clay in bottom of pot. Con-cretion on top half	Mechanically cleaned. Electrolysed in 5% NaOH for 7 days. Washed in tap water for 7 days. Soaked in 3% BTA in IMS for 12 hours. Coated with Incralac

site, or water, the corrosion reactions are stifled. On exposure to air and damp conditions, the cuprite layer may crack and allow moisture to the underlying nantokite layer. This results in the dissolution of the outer surface of the chloride layer into the water while, at the same time, more copper is converted into CuCl at the metal interface. Electrode reactions then take place above and below the cuprite layer with the reduction of oxygen above being the main cathode reaction together with the oxidation of cuprous to cupric ions. The net effect is that basic copper (II) chlorides such as paratacamite and atacamite form large green mounds

on the surface layers. The reaction is self perpetuating as long as water and oxygen are present. For this reason, the humidity of the air in contact with bronze artefacts should be kept below 35% RH to prevent the formation of water films on the surface. If this is difficult, then complete removal of all of the corrosion products is the only means of eliminating this form of corrosive attack on bronze objects.

Conservation

All of the bronze objects listed in Table 5.3 exhibited extensive bronze disease. This necessitated the removal of chloride ions from the corrosion products or removing all of them completely to ensure that the artefacts were stable and that break out of corrosion would not occur while on display or in store. The concretions were removed mechanically using brushes, vibro-tools or, in the worst cases, chisels. The bronze objects were then made the cathode in an electrolytic cell with a stainless steel anode. The electrolyte was either 5% NaOH or 0.5–5% Na_2CO_3 if there was no zinc or lead in the object being electrolysed.

Treatment of Brass Artefacts

Metallurgy

Brass is an alloy of copper and zinc in which the zinc is completely soluble in the copper lattice. The Ardennes region (now part of Belgium) was the major site for the production of brass at the beginning of the sixteenth century with Isleworth just commencing its brass production. The manufacture of this alloy was achieved by taking pieces of copper and mixing them with Calamine ($ZnCO_3$), a zinc ore and charcoal and placing in a crucible. The crucible was heated to 950–1000°C to reduce the Calamine to zinc vapour which dissolved in the pure solid copper. The temperature of the crucible was raised to melt the alloy, the temperature being dependent on the amount of zinc dissolved in it. A 20% zinc alloy had a melting point of 1000°C while a 30% alloy had a slightly lower one at 904°C. A gunsight from the *Mary Rose* (80A0965) was found to have 15.3% zinc, 2.52% lead, 1.87% tin and 77.8% copper. The major impurities were iron, antimony and arsenic.

The advantage of adding zinc to copper was that the tensile strength and hardness of the resultant alloy was superior to that of pure copper. Depending upon the impurities present in the alloy, the ductility was also improved. This last mechanical property allowed the brass to be shaped by hammering or beating at room temperature and the term 'wrought brass' was often applied to this type of alloy. Bronzes of this period were not so ductile and hence tended to be cast into shape as they were brittle and would crack if repeatedly hammered.

Table 5.4 Corrosion products of brass

Corrosion product	Chemical name	Formula
Oxides		
Cuprite	Copper (I) oxide, cuprous oxide	Cu_2O
Tenorite	Copper (II) oxide, cupric oxide	CuO
Cabonates		
Malachite	Basic copper carbonate	$Cu_2(OH)_2CO_3$
Azurite	Basic copper carbonate	$Cu_3(OH)_2(CO_3)_2$
Chlorides		
Nantokite	Cuprous chloride	$CuCl$
Paratacamite	γBasic copper (II) chloride	$Cu_2(OH)_3Cl$
Atacamite	δBasic copper (II) chloride	$Cu_2(OH)_3Cl$
Sulphides		
Chalcocite	Cuprous sulphide	Cu_2S
Covellite	Cupric sulphide	CuS

Corrosion

Copper ions in solution can exist in two different oxidation states: cuprous (I) and cupric (II). This results in the possible formation of a wide range of corrosion products that can be found on the surface of copper alloy artefacts. A list of the more common ones are given in Table 5.4 . No analysis has been carried to date on the corrosion products from brass artefacts recovered from the *Mary Rose*. It is unlikely that many zinc-containing compounds would be observed as most zinc salts would be quite soluble in sea water. There is a possibility that traces of zinc carbonate may be identified.

A common observation on brass artefacts recovered from high chloride containing environments such as sea water is the selective removal of zinc from the surface layers. The outer layer, where there is no zinc, is copper coloured while the inner, uncorroded area has the typical yellow brass colour. Porous copper layers up to 12mm deep have been observed on brass artefacts recovered from marine sites. This is called dezincification and, although the shape of the artefact is not altered very much, the porous copper layer is considerably softer and is easily damaged if not handled with great care during conservation. There is still some doubt about the mechanism of dezincification. Some scientists believe that the zinc diffuses out of the alloy into the sea water leaving behind a porous copper layer, while others suggest that the copper and zinc dissolve and the copper subsequently replates out onto the artefact. On some brass artefacts from the *Mary Rose* there was little evidence of dezincification. This is rather surprising but the answer is probably due to the presence of certain impurities in the brass that inhibit this form of corrosion. Typical impurities include arsenic, antimony and phosphorus. This is overcome in modern brasses by the addition of tin. Inspection of the analysis data for the gunsight given above indicates the presence of several of these elements and accounts for the lack of dezincification observed in the brasses recovered from the *Mary Rose*.

Where brass is joined to wood, there is a distinct possibility that a differential aeration cell will be established between the area of the brass exposed to the sea water and the part embedded in the wood. The former will be in contact with high oxygen concentrations while the latter will be in contact with an electrolyte with low oxygen concentrations. This sets up a potential difference on the surface of the brass which causes the low oxygen region to become the anode and to corrode. A thinning of embedded brass artefacts is a common observation. Another reason for the increased corrosion of the embedded part of brass into wood is that the wood may release organic acids, ammonia and amines into the electrolyte held within the wood. These compounds are known to corrode copper containing alloys. There were several artefacts made from a combination of wood and brass including a sundial (81A2026), a knife and sheath (81A0793) and a gunshield (82A0992)

Because copper and its alloys form corrosion products that are toxic to marine organisms, brasses are often only covered in thin layers of concretion. The mechanism for the formation of these concretions is the same as for other metal artefacts, as described above.

Conservation

As most of the brass artefacts were only covered in a thin layer of concretion, simple mechanical methods of removal were used. This included air blasting or very careful treatment with wire wool. For those artefacts with a thicker layer of concretion, a softening process was carried out by immersing the brass in a Modalene.

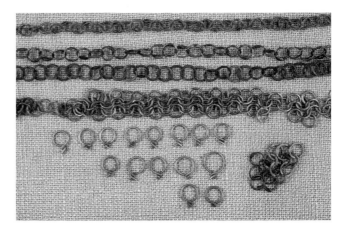

Figure 5.7 Brass chain

Table 5.5 Treatment of selected brass objects

Object	Comments	Treatment
Reamer 79A1011		Mechanically cleaned. Soaked in 1% BTA for 2 weeks. Stored with silica gel. 2 coats Incralac with Gasil 23C matting agent
Thimble 81A0807	Complete object	Soaked in Modalene to soften concretion. Water washed, dried. Soaked in BTA for 24 hrs. Coated with Incralac
Chain 81A1210	Complete object	Soaked in Modalene to remove concretion. Rinsed & dried. Coated with Incralac
Compass 81A0071	Made from brass, glass and wood (poplar)	Brass cleaned by ultrasonics/mechanical cleaning. Soaked for 3 days in 5% BTA. Air dried. Coated with Incralac

After this, the carbonate scale was easily removed by one of the above techniques (Fig. 5.7).

The next step was to remove the chlorides in the corrosion products and incorporate a corrosion inhibitor into these in order to prevent the onset of bronze disease which can occur on any copper-based alloy which has chloride incorporated in its corrosion products. From Table 5.5, it can be seen that this was achieved by soaking in a solution of benzotriazole (BTA). Either a 1% solution of BTA in water or 3%.

BTA in an organic solvent such as industrial alcohol was employed while for more severely corroded objects, a 5% solution was used. The BTA functions by slowing down the anodic and cathodic reactions in the corrosion cell formed on the surface of the brass. It is also thought to form a very thin film of polymer over the artefact which retards the diffusion of water and oxygen to metal surface. These are two of the important factors in the corrosion cell as outlined in the introduction to this chapter.

After the BTA soaking, the artefacts were dried and coated with silicone oil or a clear acrylic lacquer containing BTA (Incralac). One or two coats of the latter were applied depending on the condition of the artefact. The BTA treatment is no guarantee that bronze disease will not appear while the artefacts are in store or on display. It is essential, therefore, that the treated articles are kept at humidities below 40% RH to slow the onset of this type of corrosion.

Treatment of Lead Artefacts

Metallurgy

Lead was one of the first metals to be smelted and used by man. The main ore is galena (PbS) and is the mineral most often used in the production of the metal. The low melting point (327°C), softness, malleability and ductility indicated the ease with which it could be cast and formed. This is reflected in its use for lead weights (density 11.35g/cm^3), net sinkers, sounding weights, sheeting, piping and window frames. The main ores in England are to be found in the Mendips, Derbyshire, Co. Durham and Northumberland. Over half the silver extracted annually came from these ores as this metal is one of the major impurities found in them. The Romans established lead production sites in these areas and there was no alteration in the manufacturing techniques until after the *Mary Rose* was lost.

Galena could be readily smelted in a charcoal or dry wood furnace. This fuel would have easily generated the conditions for the winning of lead from the ore as the lead melts at 327°C and is reduced by carbon just below 800°C. At the top of the furnace, where there was an abundant supply of oxygen, the sulphide was roasted to the oxide according to equation (17):

$$2PbS + 3O_2 = 2PbO + 2SO_2 \qquad (17)$$

Once the ore was roasted, the conditions within the furnace changed from oxidising to reducing as the ore moved down the furnace. The remaining unreacted lead sulphide mixed with the oxide acted as a strong reducing agent and converted the oxide to metallic lead as shown in equation (18):

$$2PbO + PbS = 3Pb + SO_2 \qquad (18)$$

The molten lead was run off at the bottom of the furnace into clay moulds.

If silver content of the metal was high (0.04–0.4%), it was recovered from the metal (see below). During this recovery, the lead would have been oxidised to PbO and the only way to convert this back to pure metal would have been by the reduction of the oxide by carbon monoxide. Although this was more difficult than the reduction of the sulphide/oxide mixture, it was still relatively easy compared to other metals because of the low temperature required for reaction to take place:

$$PbO + CO = Pb + CO_2 \qquad (19)$$

Figure 5.8 Lead sounding weight

Table 5.6 Treatment of selected lead objects

Object	Comments	Treatment
Weight 77A0125	Complete	Washed in EDTA, cleaned, air dried & coated with micro-crystalline wax. Excess wax removed with hot air dryer
Shot 72A0081	Complete	Washed in EDTA, cleaned, air dried & coated with micro-crystalline wax. Excess wax removed with hot air dryer
Shot 81A6827	No significant corrosion. Surrounded with straw when excavated	Washed in 1–2% HCl for 24 hrs. Washed in cold followed by hot water to remove last traces of acid
Lead from window 82A5161	Covering of concretion over glass & lead	Cleaned in 10% EDTA for 3 hrs. Washed in water & dried in IMS for 1 hr. Concretion removed mechanically. Lacquered with 1 coat 5% Paraloid B72 in xylene

If an artefact had been cast, the microstructure of the lead would be dendritic with any impurities situated in the arms of the dendrites. If the lead had been shaped by beating or hammering, the microstructure would be equiaxed grains as the annealing temperature for lead is room temperature. This is why it is impossible to harden pure lead by cold work. Alloying is the only way to increase the hardness of lead.

A micro-section of a small fragment from a lead collar attached to a bronze cauldron recovered from the *Mary Rose* could be seen to consist of a dendritic structure indicating that the artefact was cast. This was the most usual method for fabricating lead sheet at this time. The analysis of the metal showed only trace amounts of silver which suggests that the silver had been recovered prior to manufacture of the cauldron. The major impurities were copper 0.46%, zinc 0.25% and tin 0.42%. This is consistent with other results taken from items recovered from similarly dated sites (Barker *et al.* 1992).

Corrosion

In natural environments, lead forms a series of relatively insoluble compounds such as $PbSO_4$, $PbCl_2$ and $PbCO_3$ and PbS, depending upon the nature of the environment. These form adherent films on the metal surface which insulate the metal from the electrolyte and prevent further attack. This results in lead artefacts being recovered in very good condition even after several hundreds of years buried in marine environments. Examination of Table 5.6 shows this to be the case for those recovered from the *Mary Rose* where the majority of items were complete with only thin layers of corrosion products 1–3mm thick.

Analysis of the concretion from the lead cauldron collar showed it to be a mixture of $PbCO_3$ (Cerussite) and $CaCO_3$ (Calcite). This it at variance with results from lead samples recovered off the coast of Australia where $PbSO_4$ (Anglesite) was found mixed with the Calcite rather than the lead carbonate (Pearson 1987). Analysis of the compounds adjacent to the metal surface indicated traces of $PbCl_2$ and tin compounds although it was difficult to be specific about the nature of the tin compound due to the very small amount of tin (0.42%) in the original metal (Barker *et al.* 1992).

Conservation

The lead artefacts were first immersed in an electrolyte to remove the concretion enveloping the metal. Those with very thin layers on them, such as the shot (eg., 81A6827), were immersed in a very dilute solution of hydrochloric acid for 24 hours. The acid dissolved the calcium carbonate part of the concretion and made the lead carbonate fall away from the surface. Once bare metal was exposed, no further attack could take place as the acid reacts with the lead to form insoluble lead chloride ($PbCl_2$) in a thin tenacious film over the metal. The artefact was then thoroughly washed in cold followed by hot water to ensure that no trace of acid was left on the surface or in any pits or crevices on the metal surface (Fig. 5.8).

With thicker layers of concretion, such as in the case of weight 77A0125 and the shot 72A0081, the artefacts were immersed in a 10% solution of EDTA. This electrolyte dissolved away the concretion and corrosion products without attacking the underlying metal. The time this took varied from 3–24 hours depending upon the extent of corrosion and the thickness of the concretion. Any loosely adhering particles were removed mechanically. To prevent attack of the cleaned artefacts in storage or on display, they were coated with a micro-crystalline wax with the excess wax being removed by means of a hot air dryer.

One of the major problems with lead objects is that they are corroded by organic acids such as citric, tartaric, acetic, etc. Prime sources of these acids are wood, cardboard, glues and decaying organic matter such as marine growths. With the exception of the last, these are the major construction materials used for display cabinets and storage systems. This is why the lead is coated with the micro-crystalline wax to retard this type of attack. Nevertheless, it is important to ensure that the relative humidity is maintained at around 40% to prevent moisture films from forming on the metal surface and to pay particular attention to the materials used in the construction of the storage and display cabinets which will house these objects.

Treatment of Pewter Artefacts

Metallurgy

The main tin-bearing ores are found in Devon and Cornwall with the chief ore being Cassiterite or Tinstone (SnO_2). As the ore is already in the oxide form, roasting does not need to be carried out and the cassiterite is directly reduced by the carbon in the fuel (charcoal or dry wood) to produce tin. The temperature required for this reaction is approximately 600°C and the molten tin (melting point 232°C) runs out of the bottom of the furnace into clay or stone moulds. It is important that the ore and the fuel are well mixed as they are loaded into the top of the furnace in order to ensure that the reaction takes place.

The main problem with pure tin is that it transforms from one crystal form to another at 13°C as shown in equation (20):

$$
\begin{array}{c}
13°C \\
\text{White tin (ß)} \Leftrightarrow \text{Grey tin (α)} \qquad (20) \\
\text{Density 7.3g cm}^{-3} \qquad \text{Density 5.75g cm}^{-3}
\end{array}
$$

Prolonged exposure of tin to temperatures below the transition temperature will result in the white tin transforming to powdery grey tin, with the result that the artefact will crumble into a powder mass. Fortunately, this reaction is very slow at temperatures just below 13°C and is not usually a problem if the tin is exposed for relatively short periods of time. Once the process, which is first observed at grain boundaries, has started, the reaction is catalysed and the rate of the transformation increases until all of the tin artefact is completely converted to the grey form of the metal. Storage above 13°C is recommended for these artefacts. This transformation is inhibited by the addition of lead to the tin.

One of the major uses of tin was in the production of pewter ware. The composition of these metals can be subdivided into lead-free alloys and those containing lead. English pewter at the time of the *Mary Rose* was said to contain 20% lead while the French limited the lead content to 18% maximum because, above this level, the lead rich phases in the alloy would dissolve into the wine! In reality, the lead content varied enormously, and some alloys were similar to modern day plumbers' solder of 33% tin and 67% lead. Others had only low levels of lead with copper present. The copper made the pewter harder and it is used extensively as an alloying addition in modern pewter. The production of plates and most of the high lead-containing alloys was by casting, as the presence of two separate phases in the microstructure sharply reduced the ductility of the alloy and made cold working very difficult, if not impossible. The low lead solders would be able to undergo some cold work as the majority of the microstructure would

Table 5.7 Metal content (by %) of pewter objects listed in Table 5.8

Object	Tin	Lead	Copper	Antimony	Bismuth
Pear flask 80A1406	95.2	0.39	3.80	0.03	0.28
Plate 80A0919	93.5	3.62	2.47	0.06	0.18
Canister lid 81A5981	91.8	6.11	1.83	0.07	0.15
Flagon 72A0031	90.6	0.70	2.27	0.01	0.06
Plate 82A1906	93.6	0.47	5.50	0.05	0.10

be a single phase of relative pure metal with only a small amount of the brittle eutectic structure.

Analysis of some of the pewter from the *Mary Rose* is shown in Table 5.7, from which it can be seen that the artefacts listed belonged to the low lead group. The presence of copper in all the alloys is the reason for them being fairly hard and stiff.

Corrosion

In aerobic conditions tin corrodes to form a grey film of SnO_2 over the metal surface. This film is not very protective and corrosion can continue underneath this layer, particularly adjacent to inter-metallic particles within the microstructure. This results in mounds or pustules forming on the artefacts and is very commonly observed on items made from this metal. In most cases, there is very little, if any, metal left although the SnO_2 will preserve the shape of the artefact. This makes the artefact very fragile. It must be handled with care and removal of the oxide is best avoided. Sometimes the

Figure 5.9 Poorly preserved pewter objects after conservation

Figure 5.10 Well preserved pewter objects after conservation

Table 5.8 Treatment of selected pewter objects

Object	Comments	Treatment
Pear flask 80A1406	Most of surface pitted with several holes. Black surface with no metal evident	Washed in distilled water, electrolysed in NaOH at low current density. Washed in dilute sulphuric acid to remove alkali, dried, immersed in acetone & coated with silicone wax
Plate 80A0919	Fair condition. Initials stamped on rim. Scratchmarks on bowl through use	Electrolysis in 0.5% EDTA. Washed in distilled water. cleaned with metal polish. Degreased in tricholoethane & coated with wax
Canister lid 81A5981	Good condition	Electrolysis in sodium sesquicarbonate followed by water wash. Mechanically cleaned with 5% oxalic acid followed by another wash. Air dried and polished
Flagon 72A0031	Covered in corrosion products, colour varying white to grey to brown. Pustule growths in many areas	General clean as excessive mechanical cleaning may have broken object as not much of original metal may have been left
Plate 82A1906	In good condition with a green tinge to corrosion products	Electrolysis in 0.5% EDTA. Washed in cascade of distilled water for 2 months. Cleaned with metal polish. Degreased in trichloro ethane & coated with wax

corrosion products may be coloured brown or black. This is due to alloying additions/impurities in the tin dissolving into the SnO_2. Copper is one of the main elements to cause this alteration in colour. In anaerobic conditions a sulphide film may form over the surface which is far more protective than the oxide. Artefacts recovered from sites where the oxygen levels are very low are usually in very good condition with only superficial corrosion, even after several hundred years of burial.

The corrosion of pewter will depend on the lead content of the alloy. Those artefacts that are lead free will corrode in a similar manner to pure tin. Hence, those found in aerobic sites will be covered in grey, black or brown corrosion products with pustules all over the surface. There will often be very little of the original metal left intact. Those buried in anaerobic silts, for example, will have only a superficial film on the surface and will be in excellent condition. The corrosion behaviour of lead containing pewters will be very similar to that observed for pure lead with a protective film of lead sulphate forming in oxygenated sea water and lead sulphide in oxygen starved conditions. In both cases, the pewter should have most of the metal left and require minimum conservation.

Examination of Table 5.7 indicates that those artefacts that had not been deeply buried would have suffered the most corrosion as there was insufficient lead present to form a protective layer of lead sulphate over the surface. The pear flask (80A1406) had numerous pustules over its surface and there was evidence that complete mineralisation had taken place in some parts of the flask. Other artefacts in the table had green, brown or black corrosion products; consistent with the copper content in the original alloys (1.83–5.5%).

Plates that had been buried deep under the Solent silt and had experienced anaerobic conditions were found in good condition due to the protective nature of the sulphide films formed in the absence of oxygen. This is consistent with the theory outlined above.

Conservation

The flagon (72A0031; Fig. 5.9) was very severely corroded and any extensive mechanical cleaning would have damaged the artefact. As there was not much remaining metal, it would have been difficult to make electrical contact with the flagon and this ruled out the use of any electrolysis. Furthermore, any hydrogen gas liberated on the cathode surface of the remaining metal could have spalled off the corrosion products and the shape of the object would have been destroyed.

The other objects listed in Table 5.8 had sufficient surviving metal to make electrical connections and were, therefore, electrolysed to remove chlorides from the corrosion layers and convert any lead compounds back to the metal (Fig. 5.10). It is very difficult to convert tin compounds back to metal but the hydrogen gas produced during electrolysis will assist in the physical dislodging of light corrosion compounds from the surface of the artefact. Alkaline media were selected in most instances, such as sodium hydroxide or sodium sesquicarbonate, although EDTA was chosen in one instance (plate 80A0919) to assist in the dissolution of the corrosion layers. After electrolysis the artefacts were thoroughly washed to remove the last traces of the electrolysing electrolyte, loose debris removed and, if there were large areas of metal exposed, the object was polished. After drying in an organic medium, a micro-crystalline wax coating was applied to the conserved artefact.

Treatment of Silver Artefacts

Metallurgy

Silver is extracted from sulphide-bearing ores of lead and copper. To be viable, the silver content should be in the order of 0.033%. When it is realised that, in Tudor times, the relative price of silver/copper/lead was in the ratio 1000:10:1, it is easy to see why it was economic to recover silver from ores with this quantity of metal present in them. In England most of the silver came from lead-bearing ores but there was a reasonable proportion recovered from copper ores. In the latter, the silver-bearing copper matte was placed in a hearth and lead loaded on top. The temperature was raised and the silver in the copper matte dissolved in the lead and formed an immisicible layer which was separated from the copper. Thus all the silver was dissolved in the lead. This was then treated in the cupellation process, as was the lead recovered from lead ores. The lead silver alloy was heated in hearths with bone ash to a temperature of 1000°C (melting point of silver = 960°C) and air blown over the surface. The lead, together with any other base metal, was oxidised while the silver remained unaffected. The oxidised lead (PbO – litharge) was

Table 5.9 Treatment of selected silver objects

Object	Comments	Treatment
Coin 80A1712	Poor condition	Stabilised in hydrogen reduction furnace
Coin 80A1766	Severely corroded	Stabilised in hydrogen reduction furnace
Ring 81A0366	Severely corroded	Water washed & scrubbed twice. Agitated in silver dip. Air abrasion to bring out detail on ring head
Ring 81A1347	Completely mineralised	Extended agitation in silver dip. Cleaned by air abrasion. Arc of cross repaired using Araldite
Coins 80A1440	Completely mineralised but shape maintained	Washed in 1% BTA & stabilised in hydrogen reduction furnace

skimmed off and a small button of metallic silver was left in the hearth.

The silver recovered in this way was too soft to be used for coinage and copper was added to increase the hardness and wear resistance. A typical analysis of coinage silver, which did not vary for many centuries, was 6.19% copper, 0.8% lead and 0.3% gold together with other trace impurities such as arsenic and antimony. The coins were probably forged from cast sheets of the metal or by blanking or punching, a process which had just been introduced at the time that the *Mary Rose* capsized. As copper is almost insoluble in silver at room temperature (0.1%), the copper forms inter-metallic precipitates which often form along the grain boundaries. These precipitates account for the increase in hardness of the alloy and are a form of precipitation hardening as employed in the modern day development of aluminium alloys for the construction of aeroplanes. The precipitates do have, however, a significant influence on the subsequent corrosion behaviour of the alloys.

Corrosion

In aerated sea water environments silver is easily corroded to form silver chloride (AgCl – cerargyrite) while under de-aerated conditions, silver sulphide (Ag_2S – argenite) is the main corrosion product. Unfortunately, neither of these two compounds forms a protective film over the metal surface and corrosion continues underneath either the chloride or sulphide layers. This is rather surprising as silver chloride is a very insoluble compound with a solubility product of 1.56×10^{-10}. This requires only an activity of approximately 10^{-10} of silver ions to precipitate out the chloride. The reaction does not take place on the anode surface but slightly away from it thus not blocking the corrosion process.

A similar situation exists for the sulphide formation. To make matters worse, as far as corrosion is concerned, a corrosion cell is set up within the alloy between the copper rich phase which is the anode and the silver rich phase which is the cathode. As the copper rich phase in early times was mostly situated at the grain boundaries, the first stage in the corrosion of the artefact would be inter-granular corrosion which caused the artefact to start to disintegrate. A further problem is that, unlike copper, silver is not toxic to marine growths. There is often quite a build up of concretions on top of the layers of corrosion products. This layer will be a mixture of calcium carbonate, copper and silver corrosion products.

Overall, the majority of silver finds from the *Mary Rose* have been virtually all mineralised due to the unprotective nature of the corrosion products. The redeeming factor is that the boundary between the concretion and corrosion product layers is very weak and it is possible to separate the two by very careful mechanical means. Secondly, the silver chloride/

94

Figure 5.11 A silver bosun's call

sulphide does maintain the shape of the original object and inscriptions, engravings, etc, are retained even if all the metal has corroded.

Conservation

As most of the silver artefacts had very little, if any, metal left uncorroded, the main aim of conservation was to stabilise the objects and then consolidate if necessary. Simple washing and immersion in a silver dip was one method employed (Table 5.9). The slight amount of reduction of silver compounds to silver metal tends to reinforce the mineralised layers and makes handling slightly easier although the objects are still exceptionally brittle even after this treatment (Fig. 5.11).

An alternative reduction technique employed on silver artefacts was the hydrogen reduction method which was developed for the conservation of ferrous based objects. The corroded objects were placed in the hydrogen furnace and the silver corrosion products were partially reduced to silver under an atmosphere of hydrogen at elevated temperatures. Once more, the partial reduction to metal consolidated the object and it

Figure 5.12 A gold coin, perfectly preserved after more than 450 years

was not deemed necessary for any further consolidation to be carried out.

Treatment of Gold Artefacts

Pure gold does not corrode in sea water or marine sediments. Consequently, the gold artefacts (coins) recovered from the wreck did not require any stabilisation treatment. In general terms, surface silts were removed by washing in warm soapy water (Fig. 5.12).

6. Conservation of Ivory, Horn Leather and Bone

Ivory, horn, leather and bone finds can be divided into two groups and include both artefact and non-artefact types. Over 1000 items recovered from the wreck of the *Mary Rose* are made from these materials (and a few from other skin products), including archery equipment (leather arrow spacers and archers' wristguards, ivory wristguard and horn nock), items associated with weaponry (scabbards and sheaths), personal items (book covers, leather drinking flasks, purses and pouches), clothing (leather jerkins and mittens) and footwear (shoes and thigh-length boots). Beyond their visual impact, these artefacts inform us of the use of these organic materials during the reign of Henry VIII. Non-artefact material recovered from the wreck site includes the skeletal remains of the men who bravely served aboard the *Mary Rose,* and cooked and uncooked remains of provisions which include the skeletal remains of cattle, sheep, pig and deer.

Ivory, horn, leather and bone all share a common origin as parts or by-products of living organisms. Thus, such structures are made up of complex polymers, which are formed by the bonding of very small units called monomers. These polymers join together in a chain which align with others to form micro-fibrils which, in turn, combine to form fibrils. Thus is formed a basic structural unit which is tough and solid.

Freshly excavated ivory, horn, leather and bone from the wreck of the Mary Rose appeared to be markedly well preserved. However, closer examination suggested that these materials actually came into the conservation laboratory in various states of deterioration. In general terms, the more deteriorated they were, the more rehydrated they had become. Accordingly these objects were considered to be a high conservation priority because their hygroscopic and anisotropic nature meant that moisture changes could impose stress leading to surface cracking, shrinkage and distortion similar to the problems encountered with *Mary Rose* timber. If conservation had not been employed these objects would have deteriorated very quickly and it was necessary for *Mary Rose* conservators to undertake considerable research in order to determine a suitable treatment. The success of the treatments employed may be amply judged by the range and quality of organic items on view in the museum.

The conservation treatments discussed in this chapter were carried out almost 20 years ago, and some of these methods may now be considered to be obsolete. It is therefore important that conservation treatments described in this chapter should only be undertaken with due regard to current practices.

Treatment of ivory

The upper incisors of elephants are composed of 1:3 collagen:hydroxyapatite (90%) and water (10%) and are commonly known as true ivory. It is tougher and is considered more resistant than enamel with hardness values of 2.25–2.75 Moh's. Throughout history, ivory has been used for both utilitarian purposes and works of art. Elephant tusks from Indian and African elephants have been commonly used for knife handles and ornaments for many centuries. A single ivory object, namely an archer's wristguard or bracer, was recovered from the wreck of the *Mary Rose.*

Unlike bone, ivory has a laminated structure and a refractive pattern described by Boyd (1968) as a checkerboard or engine-turning appearance. The colour of ivory varies according to its origin: African ivory is transparent, Indian is yellowish white or opaque.

Conservation

The two components that make up ivory are preserved at opposing pH. It was not surprising to find the ivory bracer in a good state of preservation. This is due to the

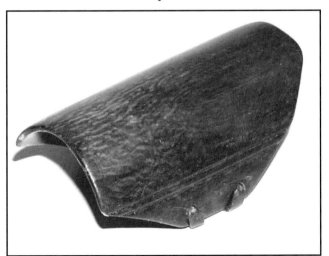

Figure 6.1 Ivory wristguard or bracer

preservative nature of the wreck sediments, which had a pH of 7.5–8.0. Chemical analysis of the bracer suggested slight bacterial attack of surface organic collagen with minor loss of inorganic hydroxyapatite. SEM/EDS examination of a surface sample was undertaken in order to identify the presence of soluble sea salts. Results indicated a high concentration within the outer surface layers. Fortunately the ivory bracer (Fig. 6.1) was not contaminated with iron salts.

To conserve the ivory bracer, it was essential to remove any soluble salts from the object before it was dried. These salts are very hygroscopic and can also cause physical damage if allowed to crystallise from solution. Removal of soluble salts from the bracer was achieved using a water cascade, as described in Chapter 8 (Fig. 8.2) in which the object was washed in progressively dilute salt solutions, eventually finishing in clean water. As the water passes down through successive levels of the cascade system it progressively accumulates an increasing level of salt, which reaches a maximum at the bottom tank. To prevent osmotic shock to the ivory bracer (and other artefcts treated in this way), it was first placed in the bottom tank and, when sufficient salts had been removed, it was transferred into the tank at the next highest level. There it encountered a wash water system with a lower concentration of dissolved salts. When it had come to equilibrium at that concentration it was lifted to the next highest level, and so on. When it was removed from the top tank the salts had been removed. SEM/EDS was used to make sure that the surface was free of salt.

Although ivory is both hygroscopic and anisotropic in nature and prone to cracking and splitting during drying, the well-preserved nature of the ivory bracer enabled *Mary Rose* conservators to air dry this unique object without prior consolidation.

Treatment of Horn

Only a few horn or possibly horn objects (including a 'nock' from a longbow and an ink pot) were recovered from the wreck of the *Mary Rose* and all were of cattle origin. These objects are made up of non-living

Figure 6.2 Horn nock from a longbow (top) original and (bottom) modern replica

keratinised cells which are formed from epidermal tissue that surrounds the basal bony core (Florian 1987). Keratin is a sulphur-containing protein composed of amino acids, bonded together to form a chain. Further strength is provided by the presence of inorganic calcium salts.

Horn objects are strong and resistant to abrasion. Keratin is highly reactive and under certain marine burial environments can often be found in a highly deteriorated state. A marine burial environment, which is alkaline in nature and contains high levels of metal ions, can lead to the total loss of horn artefacts. Under burial conditions keratin firstly undergoes hydrolysis and then becomes chemically altered by any one of the following reactions: oxidation, reduction, methylation, esterification or alkylation. In general, horn artefacts recovered from the *Mary Rose* were found to be severely deteriorated, extremely fragile and highly hydrated.

Conservation

Simple mechanical devices such as fine brushes were used to clean horn objects. Soluble salts were then removed by washing in water in the simple cascade system described above (and see Figure 8.2, below).

Little work had been previously carried out on the active stabilisation of horn subjected to long-term marine burial. As there were so few surviving horn objects, they were considered to be of great historic importance. *Mary Rose* conservators decided, after careful consideration of data available, to control air dry these objects without stabilisation. Surprisingly both objects were successfully dried without any signs of delamination (Fig. 6.2). After drying, horn objects were coated with almond oil to restore the optical properties of the remaining keratin.

Treatment of Leather

A considerable number of leather artefacts were recovered from the *Mary Rose*. These artefacts are the skins of various vertebrate animals that had been made into functional items such as shoes, book covers, ship scuppers, flasks, purses, scabbards, and clothing (Fig. 6.4). Leather finds recovered originate from the skins of cattle, calf, sheep, goat, deer and pig.

These skins (Fig. 6.3) are made up of innumerable fibrils of protein (collagen) held in bundles which interweave in a three dimensional manner through the skin. The fibre bundles differ in size depending on the level within the skin. The largest bundles are found in the central corium, but these subdivide to become very fine as they approach the skin surface. The outer surface of all mammalian skin is covered by hair, which is found in a layer that extends from the outer surface to the base of the hair follicles. This layer is commonly referred to as the grain layer and contains not only the hairs but also

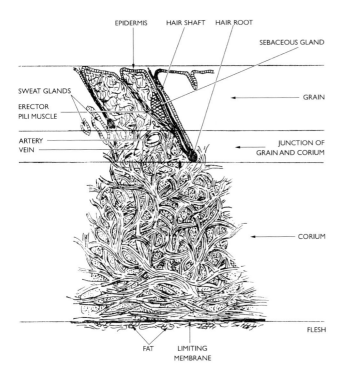

Figure 6.3 General structure of hide (ox) (after Robertson 1957)

the sebaceous and sweat glands and the epidermis. In the early stages of leather processing, the epidermis and the hairs are removed chemically and this results in the exposure of the very fine fibrils at the surface. Towards the flesh surface, the fibre bundles become finer and lie in a horizontal manner to form the flesh layer separating the skin from the underlying muscles.

There are distinct differences in skin structure between cattle, sheep, deer, pig and goat: the skins differ in thickness, in the size of the corium bundles, in the proportion of the total thickness occupied by the grain layer and in the compactness and pattern of the fibre weave.

Cattle

The skins of mature cattle are usually 4–6mm in thickness, the corium fibre bundles are relatively large at about 0.1mm in diameter and the grain layer occupies one sixth of the total thickness.

Calfskin

A calfskin is a miniature of the adult skin, 1–1.5mm in thickness; the proportion of the grain layer to the total thickness remains at one sixth, but the overall thickness and size of corium bundle fibres both increase with age.

Goatskin

Goatskins range from 1–2mm in thickness. The corium fibres are very fine and compactly interwoven. The grain layer occupies one third of the total thickness of the skin and the corium fibres interweave well into the grain layer.

Sheepskin

The skins are 2–3mm in thickness with a grain layer that occupies one half of the total thickness of the skin. The corium fibres are fine and less compactly interwoven. Natural fat deposits are stored in a layer of fat at the junction of the corium and grain.

Deerskin

These skins range from 2–3mm in thickness. The grain layer occupies one sixth of the total thickness. The corium fibre bundles are somewhat coarser than those of a young calf or goatskin and the weave is more loosely interwoven.

Conservation

Leather artefacts recovered from marine burial sediments come in different states of deterioration. Water-soluble vegetable tannins, oils and fats have a tendency to leach out leaving the collagen fibres very susceptible to hydrolysis. If waterlogged leather is allowed to air dry without treatment the deteriorated collagen fibres move together resulting in severe dimensional change (shrinkage). Shrunken leather is very brittle, weak and is susceptible to further damage by bio-deteriogens and environmental agents such as light, air pollutants and changes in relative humidity. High soluble salt content, which makes the leather artefact hygroscopic, can also cause internal abrasion. Several variables, such as the burial environment, the genus, the hide's original manufacture and the individual history of each artefact, add to the tendency of these objects to deteriorate and to their subsequent drying behaviour. Of the various skins identified, cattle skin artefacts were found to be slightly decayed. Pig, goat and deer were moderately deteriorated, whilst sheep and calfskin artefacts were found to be very fragile.

While awaiting conservation treatment the leather artefacts were kept in polythene bags, which were subsequently stored at 5°C. A domestic type refrigerator was found to be most suitable for this task. The deep-freezing of waterlogged leather is unsuitable as freezing without a cryo-protectant has been found to have a dimensional effect on the cellular structure of skin. Occasionally, leather artefacts were treated with a 1% aqueous solution of panicide (dichlorophen), which prevented the growth of fungi. Thorough cleaning of the leather artefact is essential as a first step in treatment, as examination and conservation cannot proceed until burial sediments and soluble salts have been completely removed. Leather artefacts were washed by hand in a gentle stream of water. Small brushes and sponges were used where appropriate. Ultrasonic equipment in a water bath containing Lissapol N was used to assist with the removal of stubborn soil deposits. Soluble salts were then removed by a water wash system over a 4 week

Table 6.1 Treatment of selected leather objects

Object	Condition	Treatment
Wrist guard 81A1158	Good	Washed with 5% oxalic acid for 1 hr. Cascade washed in water for 3 days. Immersed in 10% Bavon 520S for 2 weeks. Freeze dried for 4 weeks then coated with dilute Pliantine Special G (1:1) in Genklene
Pouch 81A1991	Good	Cascade washed. Immersed in 10% Bavon 520S for 2 weeks then freeze dried
Shoe 81A1471	Good	Immersed in EDTA (di-sodium) for 4 hrs. Washed in water for 4 weeks. Immersed in 10% Bavon 520S for 2 weeks then freeze dried. Excess Bavon removed with solvent
Flask 81A1214	Good	Washed in water. Immersed in 10% Bavon 520S and 10% Fat Liquor for 2 weeks. Freeze dried. Excess lubricants removed with Genklene
Mitten 81A3292	Fragile	Concretion removed, soluble salts removed by cascade wash for 4 weeks. Immersed in 10% Bavon for 2 weeks. Freeze dried. Surface cleaned with Genklene
Jerkin 81A3055	Fragile	Water washed. Immersed in 10% Bavon 520S for 2 weeks. Freeze dried & given 1 coat of Pliantine Special G
Leather jerkin flap 81A2918	Poor	Water washed. Immersed in 10% Bavon 520S. Freeze dried & given 2 coats of 25% Pliantine Special G
Book cover 81A4123	Poor	Water washed. Immersed in 10% Bavon 520S for 2 weeks. Freeze dried & coated with Pliantine Special G
Shoe 81A0053	Fair	Iron stains removed with 5% oxalic acid. Cascade washed. Immersed in PEG400 for 4 weeks. Freeze dried
Scabbard 81A1709	Poor	Washed initially with 5% EDTA for 2 hrs. Water washed for 3 days. Immersed in PEG1540 for 2 months then freeze dried
Wrist guard A0901	Good	Soaked in 5% EDTA overnight. Water washed for 1 day. Impregnated with 10% PEG400, then freeze dried. Surface coated with Pliantex
Shoe 81A0048	Fair	Washed in 5% oxalic acid. Cascade washed for 1 day. Immersed in 10% PEG400 for 1 month. Freeze dried
Clothing 81A0600	Fair	Pre-treated with 5% oxalic acid for 1 hr. Cascade washed. Impregnated with 10% PEG400. Freeze dried
Clothing frag 80A1505	Fair	Desalinated in EDTA (tetra-sodium). Cascade washed. Immersed in 10% PEG400. Freeze dried
Clothing frag 81A0419	Fair	Iron stains removed with 5% solution of oxalic acid. Treated with 10% PEG400 for 1 month then freeze dried

period. Iron corrosion products often encountered on the leather artefacts were treated with a 2% solution of oxalic acid followed by thorough washing in deionised water (Table 6.1).

Leather artefacts can only be considered stable when the collagen is able to bind with another material such as a tanning agent. When such bonding takes place, the reactive sites on the collagen fibre are prevented from reacting with each other or with an aggressive agent such as water. To maintain flexibility, this type of bonding must be recreated. Therefore, a successful active conservation treatment must be able to introduce stability and flexibility to the artefact, retain the shape and form and not alter the chemical and physical nature of the leather.

Before commencing active conservation, a series of experiments were carried out by *Mary Rose* conservators to determine a suitable stabilisation treatment. This work was led by Ian Panter who studied the suitability of several chemicals for the stabilisation of waterlogged archaeological leather. Conservation treatments investigated are described below.

Treatment 1. Syntans

These are man-made tanning agents, which are based on phenols, formaldehydes and acrylic resins. The syntan used during this study was Tannesco HN (Ciba-Geigy) which is a phenol sulphonic acid/formaldehyde compound containing chrome oxide. A 5% aqueous solution was used, and ten samples were treated for two weeks followed by vacuum freeze-drying at -25°C and a pressure of 5m Torr.

Mixed results were obtained; treated samples resembled cardboard. There was also a tendency for syntan to recrystallise on the surface of the leather. Shrinkage values obtained ranged from 6–14%.

Treatment 2. Aluminium salts

Aluminium salts such as Mystolene ALT (Basic Aluminium Chloride containing 20% AL_2O_3) are a form of mineral tannage, which form weak bonds with the collagen fibres. Leather samples were immersed in a 5% solution for a period of one week and then freeze dried. Similar results to those obtained for syntan were recorded. Leather samples were also found to be very brittle. Shrinkage values obtained ranged from 6–15%.

Figure 6.4 Fragments of a leather jerkin

Treatment 3. Chrome salts

This is another example of a mineral tanning agent, and has been in use since the late nineteenth century. The tanning process is complete when the skin or hides contain about 3% of its weight. This makes the treated process both cost effective and quick. Leather samples were immersed in a chrome-tanning agent called Chromeduol SP3. Concentration of the stabilising solution was approximately 5% by weight and the period of immersion lasted just one week. Leather samples were then freeze dried. Overall the results obtained were promising. Shrinkage values ranged from 5%–12%. However, recrystallised salts were present on the leather surface and flexibility of the leather samples was considered poor.

Treatment 4. Fat liquor

These are emulsions of soaps and oils, used in the tanning industry to impart softness and pliability to the finished skins or hides by coating the collagen fibres. A synthetic anionic compound named Invasol SF was tested. Ten leather samples were immersed in a 10% aqueous solution for two weeks and then freeze dried. Good results obtained with shrinkage values ranging from 7–11% but long-term stability problems may lead to undesirable long-term effects.

Treatment 5. Glycerol

Glycerol has been widely used in the treatment of waterlogged archaeological leather. It has been used in the leather industry in conjunction with chrome salt. A standard 5% solution was used with an immersion period of two weeks. Shrinkage values obtained ranged from 6–17%. Customary objections to its use are high hygroscopicity leading the excessive uptake of water, greasy feel and its inability to consolidate decayed leather artefacts.

Treatment 6. Polyethylene glycol 400

Leather samples were placed into a 10% solution of PEG400 for two weeks followed by freeze drying. This method was considered successful for the treatment of wet archaeological leather samples. The flexibility of the tested samples was good and the shrinkage values ranged from 5–12%. *Mary Rose* conservators employed this treatment for better preserved leather artefacts.

Treatment 7. Bavon

Bavon is the trade name for a leather-lubricating compound. There are two related proprietary compounds which were used to determine their stabilisation properties. Bavon ASAK ABP is an alkylated succinic acid derivitive soluble in white spirit and Genklene (1.1.1 trichloroethane). This compound bonds to the polar region of the collagen fibres causing the hydrophobic portions of the fibres to repel water and allow mechanical slippage. A water-soluble compound named Bavon 520S, which is an emulsified version of Bavon ASAK ABP was also tested. A 10% solution of Bavon 520S was used and the immersion period was two weeks. For the solvent grade (Bavon ASAK ABP), the samples were placed into a 15% solution in Genklene for 36 hours prior to air drying. Samples treated with Bavon 520S were then freeze dried.

Both grades of Bavon produced good results with shrinkage values ranging from 6–10% for Bavon 520S and values of 6–12% for Bavon ASAK ABP. While Bavon ASAK ABP produced excellent results, safety hazards associated with the use of Genklene prohibited its use at the *Mary Rose* conservation laboratory. On the other hand, Bavon 520S was considered the more favourable brand and a large number of leather artefacts were treated with this lubricating compound.

As a result of these experiments, two leather treatments were regularly employed by conservators at the *Mary Rose* conservation laboratory:

Lubrication with Bavon 520S followed by vacuum freeze drying (Table 6.1):
- Immersion in 10% Bavon 520S for two weeks
- Freeze drying at -25°C and a pressure of 5mTorr for four weeks
- Removal of excess Bavon 520S by Genklene
- One coat of Pliantine (traditional leather dressing)
- Display environment: 18–20°C, 55% RH.

Freeze drying with Polyethylene Glycol Pre-treatment
- Immersion in 10% PEG 400 for two weeks
- Freeze drying at –25°C and a pressure of 5mTorr for four weeks
- Removal of excess PEG

Figure 6.5 Pig bones

- One coat of Pliantine
- Display environment: 18–20°C, 55% RH.

Treatment of Bone

Bone is a hard connective tissue, which is heavily impregnated with salts of calcium to produce a rigid material. The bone matrix contains two components: an inorganic lattice base amounting to about 65% of the weight of dry bone and an organic base of connective tissue amounting to about 35%.

The inorganic component of bone consists of submicroscopic crystals of hydroxyapatite $[Ca_3(PO_4)_2]_3.Ca(OH)_2$. In addition to calcium and phosphorus, bone also contains magnesium, sodium, carbonate and citrate. The organic component is called bone collagen or ossein. The bone collagen fibres, which exist in bundles are cemented together by osteomucoid.

Deterioration of bone in the marine environment can occur by bacterial attack of the organic component (protein) and acid attack of the inorganic base. The porosity of the bone also allows the inward passage of both marine microbes and sea salts and the substitution of inorganic material by inorganic salts from the sea. In some severe cases iron corrosion products that percolate near by may replace the hydroxyapatite component.

Recovered human and animal bone was found to be in a remarkably good condition upon excavation. This was due to anoxic non-acidic conditions that existed in the sediments of the wreck site.

Conservation

All bones were desalinated in a water cascade system to remove soluble sea salts, which are hygroscopic and liable to acid formation. Such salts can also cause physical damage upon recrytallisation from solution.

Bone, like other organic material, is prone to cracking and splitting. Fortunately, dimensional stabilisation of well preserved bone is readily achieved (Fig. 6.5). The well preserved, little deteriorated bone (both human and animal) recovered from the wreck did not require active intervention with either PEG or PVAC: conservation simply involved slow air drying. After drying, all bones were stored at 18–20°C and at a relative humidity of 50%. These values are rigorously controlled within purpose-built storage areas.

7. Conservation of Textiles

The term 'textile' in this chapter is used to mean any item made from plant or animal fibres as defined below (as opposed to skin, horn or skeletal products – see Chapter 6). There are two main categories of textiles from the *Mary Rose*: those representing the remains of personal belongings, in particular clothing and clothing accessories on the one hand, and those representing the remains of ship's equipment, such as sailcloth, straps, sacking and ropes on the other.

More than 260 textile fragments in the first category were recovered from the wreck. The largest piece measures 1620 mm in width but 70% have a maximum surviving dimension of under 100mm. A few pieces retain their (presumably) original colour. Wool and silk are the principal materials representing fragments of, for instance, hats, jerkins, breeches, socks, ribbons, braids, decorative borders and shoe linings (see *AMR* vol. 4, chapter 2).

Many fragments of sailcloth and rope were recovered, the former generally in a very fragmentary state. Specific areas of the Orlop deck seem to have functioned as rigging stores and included at least one sail. Fragments of sacking were also recorded, mainly in the Hold. Rope survived in a much better condition generally, partly no doubt because much of it had been impregnated with tar to help preserve it during use and several large coils of heavy rope were recovered as well as many shorter lengths of varying dimension and, presumably, function. One of the coils is on display in the Museum and, to this day, smells of tar. Various fragments of flat woven straps or strops were also found; these would have been used for a variety of purposes on board, including for strapping down objects when the ship was at sea.

Table 7.1. Chemical composition of cotton fibre
(after Siu 1951)

Constituent	% dry weight
Cellulose	94.0
Protein	1.3
Pectin	0.9
Ash	1.2
Wax	0.6
Molate, citrate & other organic acids	0.8
Total sugars	0.3
Pigment	trace
Other	0.9

All textile fragments were unstained, unconcreted and relatively easy to clean. Textiles are made up of fibres and the identification of the fibre and the extent of deterioration is a prerequisite to formulating and undertaking appropriate conservation treatments.

Collier (1970) divided natural fibres into three groups according to their origin: plant fibres, animal fibres and mineral fibres. The plant fibres are based on cellulose and include cotton, jute, hemp and linen. Animal fibres are proteinaceous in nature and include wool from animal hairs, and silk from the cocoon of the silk worm (*Bombyx mori*). Mineral fibres, such as asbestos, are of no concern here. All fibres have moisture in their structure; plant fibres tending to have a lower moisture content than animal fibres.

Plant Fibres

The simplest form of plant fibre comes from the tips of cotton seeds and consists of a flattened, twisted tube of which the primary and secondary walls and the lumen are the main structural components. Table 7.1 shows the typical composition of the cotton fibre, and indicates that the majority of the fibre is composed of cellulose.

Other fibres of plant origin include, jute, flax and hemp, and are all known as stem fibres since they comprise bundles in the fibrous region beneath the bark of dicotyledonous plants, which serve to maintain the plant's structural integrity. The fibres are bound in a non-cellulosic matrix and are separated from this by a natural fermentation process known as retting. Table 7.2 lists the chemical composition of hemp, the most frequently recovered textile fibre for ships' equipment that survived marine burial at the *Mary Rose* wreck site. Although comparatively short, hemp fibres are extremely strong and can be woven into rough cloth to a variety of shapes and sizes. A small, rudimentary loom of a type known as a fiddle loom was recovered from the ship (see *AMR* vol. 4, chapter 8) indicating that some of the strapping, at least, was probably made on board.

Table 7.2 Physical and chemical composition of hemp (after Esau 1953)

Hemp (*Cannabis sativa*)		
	Cellulose	56.0–64.0
	Hemicellulose	15.0–17.0
	Pectin	1.8–3.8
	Lignin	2.0–2.5

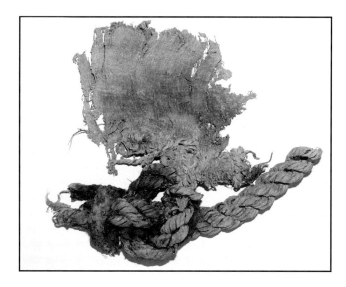

Figure 7.1 Fragment of sailcloth and rope

Deterioration

The plant textile fibres consist mainly of cellulose microfibrils which are embedded in a matrix of hemicellulose, pectin and small amounts of lignin and are vulnerable to both bacterial and chemical deterioration. Generally speaking, it is the most readily water-soluble or biodegradable cell wall components such as cellulose and hemicelluloses that will deteriorate first. It is usually the lignin component that remains intact.

Cellulose is the most abundant single polymer in plant textile fibres. It is a linear polymer of D-anhydroglucopyranose units linked by ß 1-O-4 glycosidic bonds, the number of glucose units per cellulose molecule averaging 8000–10,000. A highly ordered arrangement of molecules is evident from X-ray diffraction and polarising microscopy. Cellulose is highly polar because of its many hydroxyl groups, which have a high affinity for water. Absorption of water by cellulose results in swelling and consequently in changes in overall dimension that can be dangerous for the textile artefact. When swelling is severe, the micellar structure (Florian 1987) is destroyed and the cellulose is no longer crystalline.

The deterioration of cellulose in the marine environment is both chemical and microbiological. Non-biological depolymerisation will only occur under extreme conditions rarely found in sea water and marine sediments. It may occur very slowly by oxidation or hydrolytic processes.

Biodeterioration of plant fibre textiles within the marine environment is a far greater problem. The obvious reason is that the cellulolytic bacteria are extremely active within both sea water and marine sediments. These organisms are capable of producing cellulases. Degradation of *Mary Rose* cellulosic textiles occurred initially in sea water by aerobic bacteria (*Cytophaga* sp., *Cellulomonas* sp. and *Vibrio* sp.).

Table 7.3 Treatment of selected hemp objects

Object	Origin	Condition	Treatment
Sail cloth 81A4354	Hemp	Poor	Water washed. Dehydrated in acetone. Immersed in an acetone solution of TEOS, air dried
Rope 81A4718	Hemp	Fair	Water washed. Dehydrated in acetone. Immersed in acetone solution of TEOS for 4 days. Lacquered with 1 coat Bedacryl (1% in toluene)
Rope 81A2921	Hemp	Good	Water washed then air dried. Single coat of lacquer (Bedacryl 1:1 in xylene) brushed on to surface
Rope (no number)	Hemp	Poor	Water washed. Soaked in acetone for 24 hrs. Immersed in acetone solution of TEOS for 4 days then air dried. Lacquered with 2% Bedacryl in xylene
Rope Handle (no number)	Hemp	Poor	Washed in water cascade. Dehydrated in acetone. Immersed in acetone solution of TEOS then air dried. Lacquered with 2% Bedacryl in xylene

Following burial, anaerobic bacteria became the main degraders of plant fibre textiles.

The combined effect of non-biological and microbiological deterioration results in losses of tensile strength, fibre toughness, flexing endurance and abrasion resistance. Hemp (Fig. 7.1) contains non-cellulose substances such as hemicelluloses, pectin and lignin. The presence of these components slows down the rate of decay. Hemicelluloses are relatively short, branched homo- and heteropolymers, made up of glucose and other hexose and pentose sugars and their uronic acid derivatives. Hemicellulose has a degree of polymerisation that seldom exceeds 200. These polymers are soluble in alkaline conditions and a proportion of the polymer can dissolve away in sea water. Enzymatic degradation by microbial activity will occur in the marine environment. Details of the marine organisms responsible for hemicellulose degradation are given by, for instance, Holt (1971).

Pectin substances, which are located within the middle lamella and primary wall are hydrophilic and act as a molecular colloid in cell walls. They are linear polymers composed of units of polygalacturonic acids and are usually called polyuronoids. Pectin is made up of two chemically different components, namely pectic acid which is insoluble in acid, and pectic acid that is soluble at low pH. The pectin substance are readily

Figure 7.2 A knitted 'scogger': a woollen tube which served as a detached sleeve or, possibly, a leg covering

hydrolysed by both acids and enzymes produced by bacteria and fungi (Florian 1987). Loss in pectin may result in the loss of fibre integrity and brittleness.

The fourth component of stem-based textile fibres is lignin, a complex three-dimensional polymer of phenyl-propane units that is completely amorphous and serves as an encrusting material surrounding microfibrils. Because of its strong negative charge and acidic nature, lignin absorbs cations ($Fe^{2+,3+}$, Mg^+, Na^+ and Ca^+) that exist in sea water. A high concentration of cations can influence conservation treatments. Lignin is insoluble in seawater but is sensitive to alkaline degradation. This is the most resistant component found in plant fibre textiles.

Animal Fibres

Animal fibres are basically proteinaceous in nature and form the main constituents of animal wool, hair fibres and silk. Wool is generally fine and short, whilst hair is thicker and longer. Wool and hair fibres are based on the protein keratin. It is somewhat harder than collagen and

Figure 7.3 The Barber-surgeon's hat. This red velvet and braid cap or coif was found inside the chest containing the Barber-surgeon's equipment within his cabin on the Main deck of the ship

is very insoluble as a result of high degree of di-sulphide bonds cross-linking between chains. It is composed of amino-acid units, bonded together in a chain.

A wool fibre is composed of three main regions: the cuticle and scale cells, the cortex, and the medulla. The outer region contains irregular, overlapping scales, which fit closely together. The strength and elasticity of the fibre is due to the basic arrangement of the cortical material. The keratin making up the woollen protein contains a relatively high concentration of cysteine, a sulphur-containing amino acid. Individual molecules are thus held together by di-sulphide linkages and also by salt linkages, resulting from the association of free carboxyl and amino groups.

Silk is non-cellular and is produced as a continuous filament of the protein fibroin mixed with a simiar protein called sericin. The sericin is evenly distributed along the thread length and there are no sulphur-containing amino acids present in fibroin, and hence no di-sulphide bridges as in wool. Silk molecules are fully extended and are closely packed into crystalline regions joined by amorphous regions. Hence, silk fibre is very strong but has little elasticity since the molecules are unable to unfold.

Some of the woollen clothing fragments from the *Mary Rose* were found associated with human remains – presumably the clothing being worn at the time of the sinking – while others were stored inside personal chests. Knitted caps, jerkins, breeches, shoulder capes or 'tippets', hose (stockings); socks and a 'scogger' (see Fig. 7.2) are all represented. Other fragments may represent blankets and wraps.

Among the silk artefacts are the fine velvet cap belonging to the Barber-surgeon with its braid fastenings (Fig. 7.3); ribbons, including several attached to bosun's calls that were presumably being worn when the ship sank; decorative braids, borders and fastenings; and lengths of thread and yarn.

Deterioration of wool and silk artefacts

Following exposure in the marine burial environment, keratin absorbs excessive amounts of specific metal ions. Under certain conditions, keratin undergoes hydrolysis,

104

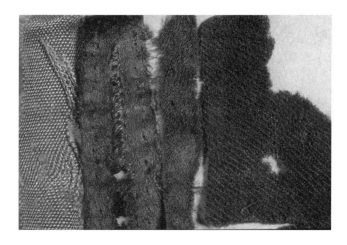

Figure 7.4 A selection of textile fragments

oxidation, reduction, methylation, esterification and aklyation reactions (Florian 1987). Woollen artefacts have undergone deterioration by one or other of these reactions. Enzymatic degradation by bacteria is also evident on wool fibres examined under the scanning electron microscope. These organisms secrete proteolytic enzymes, which break down the protein so that the amino acids can be utilised as a source of nutrients. Pseudomonas and *Bacillus* species are considered the primary degraders of woollen artefacts in the marine environment. Burgess (1934) discovered that bacterial attack and protein degradation was enhanced if the woollen fibres were maintained in a slightly alkaline pH. He concluded that under these conditions, protein hydrolysis occurs leading to the formation of soluble nitrogenous compounds. No data are available on the deterioration of *Mary Rose* silk artefacts. This is currently under investigation by Trust scientists.

Conservation treatment of hemp and wool

Fibre identification is a prerequisite for the formulation of a conservation treatment. Plant and animal fibres behave differently with respect to stabilisation chemicals and to moisture in terms of twist, direction, shrinkage, tensile strength and moisture regain (Florian 1987).

Cleaning
Waterlogged textiles recovered from the *Mary Rose* (Figs 7.2–7.4) were found to be physically weak and required careful handling by conservators at all times. Prior to cleaning, dye analysis was carried out on certain textile artefacts. The dyes madder (red), weld (yellow) and kermes (red) were identified. Since chemical treatment can remove these, all textiles were washed in water containing no chemical agents (such as calgon (sodium hexametaphosphate), sodium pyrophosphate, EDTA or acids).

Before commencing the cleaning process, animal and plant fibre textiles were carefully unfolded underwater in

Table 7.4 Treatment of selected woollen items (all sheep wool)

Object	Condition	Treatment
Clothing frag 81A2911	Good	Washed in deionised water. Cleaned with soft brush while wet. Air dried between cotton towels and blotting paper
Braid 81A1168	Good	Water washed to remove soluble salt. Cleaned in ultrasonic bath. Air dried between cotton towels
Knitted stocking 81A1936	Good	Washed in water with synperonic detergent. Rinsed in water. Air dried between cotton towels
Sacking 81A1219	Good	Water washed. Air dried between cotton towels
Clothing frag 81A1725	Poor	Water washed. Air dried. Surface treated with CMC

a shallow container; a method which did not stress the textile artefact. During the cleaning process, the textile was supported on a synthetic net frame. Conservators used soft brushes and sponges to remove the burial sediments from the surfaces. On occasions, ultrasonic cleaning was attempted on a number of well-preserved artefacts. The method was considered extremely efficient and useful. Removal of soluble salt was achieved by a water cascade system (see Chapter 8). Final soaking and rinses were carried out in deionised water (Tables 7.3, 7.4).

Drying
All *Mary Rose* textile artefacts were dried successfully by slow air drying. Conservators placed the textile artefact between dry paper towelling, weighted between glass plates. There was little evidence of fibre collapse.

Post-drying consolidation
A number of textile artefacts required post-drying interventions with a suitable consolidant. These textiles exhibited shedding and brittleness following drying and required consolidation. Treatment by re-immersion is usually inappropriate at this stage, therefore solutions were added by brush or spraying. Aqueous solutions of carboxymethyl cellulose (CMC) were used for consolidation. The long-term stability of this cellulosic compound is unknown beyond the fact that it is prone to oxidation.

Pre-treatment with tetraethoxy silane (TEOS method)
By this method, the textile is fully dehydrated by acetone and then placed in an acetone solution of tetraethoxy silane (TEOS) $(C_2H_4O)_4Si$. After impregnation, the

Figure 7.5 Silk yarn

solvent is allowed to evaporate; hydrolysis of the tetraethoxy silane to deposit silicon dioxide occurs.

Preventing further deterioration

Storing textiles under ideal environmental conditions prevents further decay. Low light levels are maintained within museum display cases or totally excluded within storage rooms (see Chapter 9) and dirt and dust prevented from gaining access to fibres. Maintaining a relative humidity within a range of 50–55% controls further microbial activity and prevents dimensional change to the textile fibres.

Conservation of silk

All silk artefacts were cleaned within an ultrasonic bath containing a 1% non-ionic detergent to remove adhering silts and soluble salts. Great care was taken with the pH of the washing water to prevent further deterioration; pH solutions of above 10 may damage proteins. Final soaking and rinses were carried out in deionised water. Following cleaning, the silk artefacts were dried carefully between blotting paper weighted between glass. Further cleaning of the surface involved careful vacuuming (Fig. 7.5).

8: Conservation of Ceramic, Glass and Stone

by Keith Watson

The conservation work discussed in this chapter was carried out a number of years ago, and some of the methods that were used at that time may now be considered to be outdated. The discussion is, of course, limited to those methods used for conserving the objects recovered from the *Mary Rose*. Also, some of the chemicals and processes are potentially hazardous. It is therefore most important that this chapter should not be regarded as a practical conservation manual. The conservation of any object should only be undertaken with due regard to current practice relating to the type of material and its condition, also the range of methods available, and in accordance with the relevant health and safety requirements; these topics are not covered in this chapter.

The topics covered here are as follows:

i)   the nature of the ceramic, glass and stone objects in relation to their long term exposure to the marine environment,
ii) the basis of the conservation methods that were used, and
iii) examples of specific treatments.

The types of object recovered from the *Mary Rose* are listed in Table 8.1. Generally, the stone objects had suffered very little deterioration while most of the glass was fragmentary and in very poor condition. The ceramic objects were certainly the most interesting from the conservation point of view.

The Materials

Ceramics

Ceramic objects are made by forming them from clay, followed by firing at high temperature. The number of parameters involved is enormous. First, the clay itself is a highly variable material, depending on its origins. Furthermore, it may need to be subjected to a variety of physical processes, such as milling and sieving, before it can be used – and it may be necessary to add various other materials such as fillers and fluxes. After forming, the clay is dried to remove most of the water in order to avoid damage caused by the excessive release of steam

Table 8.1 Types of ceramic, glass and stone objects from the *Mary Rose*

Category	Object
Ceramic	
Domestic	Cooking pot
	Bowl
	Flask/bottle
	Jar/flagon
	Jug
	Tankard
Medical	Canister
	Jar/jug
Glass	
Domestic	Flask/bottle
Medical	Bottle
Navigation	Compass part
Personal	Bead (ornament)
	Mirror
	Sandglass part
	Sundial part
Ship's fittings	Window
Tools/equipment	Balance case part
Stone	
Ordnance	Shot, flint for canister shot
	Shot, inset (lead covered)
	Shot, stone
	Shot mould
Personal	Bead (ornament)
Stowage	Pebble (in staved container)
	Grindstone
	Whetstone

during the firing process. Firing introduces more parameters, especially those which determine the temperature-time cycle. Indeed there may be more than one firing if the ceramic is to be glazed – generally a 'biscuit firing' then another, after the glaze has been applied to the surface, possibly followed by others.

The changes that occur during firing are complex, nevertheless it is helpful to consider the process very briefly. The 'ceramic change' is generally regarded as occurring around 550–600°C (Gibson and Woods 1997) where the clay undergoes a change to ceramic which will prevent it from recovering its original plasticity with water. Vitrification begins at about 800°C (Buys and Oakley 1998). As the temperature is raised further, glassy phases form and the porosity decreases and the end-product becomes harder and more impermeable. There are many factors determining porosity, which may vary from less than 1% for high-fired porcelain to more than 15% for underfired earthenware (Cronyn 1996).

Glazes tend to make a ceramic surface impermeable as well as strengthening it and providing a decorative finish (Buys and Oakley 1998). They are generally applied to the surface of biscuit-fired ware as a suspension in water. Salt glaze is an exception and is obtained by throwing common salt into the kiln at high temperature; the salt reacts with the hot surface of the clay body to form an orange-peel textured glaze which may be coloured by the presence of other minerals.

Ceramics are relatively inert and resistant to chemical deterioration. However, they are brittle and easily broken. Furthermore, their porosity introduces a particular problem in a marine environment since sea water contains dissolved salts which it can carry into the fabric of a porous ceramic.

If a ceramic object is allowed to dry out without first removing the salts, they tend to crystallise within the pores. This can cause internal pressure which, depending on the type and condition of the object, is sometimes high enough to force surface layers (including glazes) to flake away from the clay body and can even damage the clay body itself. Further problems can arise where the salts are hygroscopic or deliquescent and the object experiences varying humidity conditions (Cronyn 1996; Buys and Oakley 1998; Pearson 1987). (NB hygroscopic salts absorb water from the atmosphere; deliquescent salts do this to such an extent that they actually dissolve in the water which they absorb.)

Certain salts absorb 'water of crystallisation' into their crystal structures at higher humidity, causing their volume to expand which, in turn, creates high internal pressures within the pore structure. If the humidity falls sufficiently, the salt releases the water and contracts, allowing the internal pressure to fall. Continual repetition of this pressure cycle, as the humidity fluctuates, can cause serious damage to the internal structure of the ceramic. Some salts deliquesce when the humidity rises to a certain point, then recrystallise when it falls. Again, this provides a mechanism for humidity fluctuations to cause pressure cycling, and it may result in concentration of the salt at the ceramic surface where the water evaporates, sometimes damaging the surface layers – including glazes. Lower fired wares tend to be more susceptible to deterioration both due to the marine environment generally and to the recrystallisation of dissolved salts (Pearson 1987).

Finally, the surface of ceramic objects can be affected by immersion in the sea: concretions of insoluble salts such as calcium carbonate are often formed, and staining can occur for a variety of reasons.

Glass

Ordinary glass is made from silica (SiO_2), usually in the form of sand. The silica is crystalline, that is to say, its constituent silicon (Si) and oxygen (O) atoms are arranged in a regular three-dimensional network structure, as suggested by the simplified two dimensional model in Figure 8.1(A). The chemical bonds are so strong that, when the silica is melted, its viscosity is very high; on cooling, the high viscosity prevents the silicon and oxygen atoms from recrystallising to reproduce their previous regular arrangement. Instead, they retain an irregular amorphous structure that is characteristic of the molten state, as in Figure 8.1(B). This is why glass is sometimes referred to as a supercooled liquid.

Silica melts at such a high temperature (c. 1700°C) that it is necessary to add a flux to partially disrupt the three-dimensional network and make the glass workable at lower temperatures. Soda or potash, which provide positively charged sodium ions (Na^+) and potassium ions (K^+) respectively, can be used as fluxes. (NB ions are charged atoms, for example sodium and potassium atoms (Na and K respectively) become positively charged ions by the loss of an electron; similarly, calcium and magnesium atoms (Ca and Mg) become double-charged ions (Ca^{2+} and Mg^{2+}) by losing two electrons.) The sodium and potassium ions work by forming breaks in the silica network and, in effect, seal off the broken ends, which consist of negatively charged oxygen atoms that hold the positive ions in place because of their opposite charge – as suggested by the two dimensional model of 'soda glass' in Figure 8.1(C). In fact, the sodium and potassium ions are not very tightly held because they only have a single positive charge so, given the necessary stimulus, they do have a certain amount of freedom to move around. Ultimately, this can affect the durability of the glass, particularly in the presence of water. Stabilisers such as lime or magnesia, which provide calcium ions (Ca^{2+}) and magnesium ions (Mg^{2+}) respectively, are therefore added; their double charge holds them more firmly in place, making them much less mobile and stabilising the glass generally. Nevertheless, depending on the relative proportions of the various components, the sodium and potassium ions can still cause problems resulting from long term immersion in water.

108

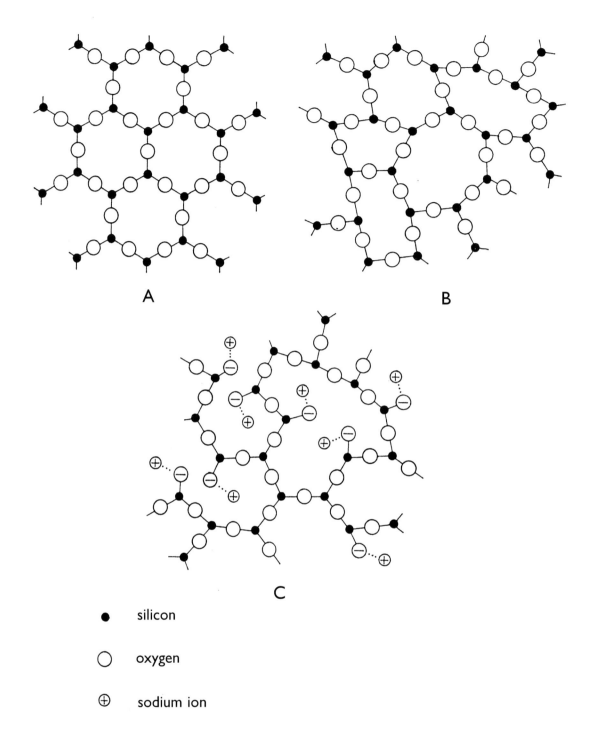

• silicon

○ oxygen

⊕ sodium ion

Figure 8.1 Simplified two-dimensional models of A) crystalline silica; B) silica glass; C) 'soda glass' (redrawn from Watson (1998) by courtesy of the publisher)

Under some conditions, the sodium and potassium ions may be sufficiently mobile to diffuse out of the glass into the water and may be replaced by hydrogen ions (H^+) from the dissociation of water molecules:

$$H_2O \longrightarrow H^+ + OH^- \qquad (1)$$

This ultimately leads to the breakage of Si-O bonds. The chemical reactions involved are beyond the scope of this discussion and can be found elsewhere (Pollard and Heron 1996) but the net effect can be represented by:

$$Si\text{-}O\text{-}Si + H_2O \longrightarrow Si\text{-}OH + HO\text{-}Si \qquad (2)$$

The overall result of these processes is that the surface of the glass deteriorates, tending to laminate into thin layers (lamellae) which often cause a characteristic iridescence and which may eventually exfoliate (Pearson 1987). The iridescence, which is rather like that on soap bubbles and oil films on water, is due to optical interference between the lamellae and tends to become visible when the surface is dry and the lamellae are separated by layers of air (Newton and Davison 1997).

It follows that wet glass, with no apparent iridescence, may actually be in a worse condition than it appears. Furthermore, surface tension effects due to the water may help to hold a deteriorated glass surface together. Also, if the glass is allowed to dry, the crystallisation of dissolved salts in the water between the lamellae is liable to cause damage by similar mechanisms to those that operate in ceramics. It is therefore important to prevent deteriorated glass objects from drying out before treatment begins.

Stone

The various types of stone recovered from the *Mary Rose* are shown in Table 8.2. As noted earlier, these objects generally had suffered very little deterioration. However, some of these stone types have significant porosity, with the concomitant possibility of damage due to the recrystallisation of soluble salts on drying. (N. Duncan (1969) gives porosity values – not necessarily typical – for millstone grit and Kentish Rag, in the dry state, as 8.7% and 11.7% respectively.)

Conservation Methods

Removal of soluble salts and other soluble materials

As the previous section indicates, it is generally very important to remove any soluble salts from an object before it is dried. This is usually done by washing the object in water. The washing process relies on diffusion, which occurs where the dissolved salts form a concentration gradient. There is a natural tendency for the salts in a region of higher concentration to diffuse into a region of lower concentration; this continues until an equilibrium is reached where the concentration is uniform throughout. In practice this means that, if a ceramic vessel that is saturated with sea water is placed into clean water, the dissolved salts in the pore structure will diffuse out of the fabric.

However, there are two problems. First, as the salts diffuse out of the surface pores they tend to form a more or less stationary layer around the object which reduces the concentration gradient so that the process slows down. This can be overcome by washing the object in running water or, less wastefully, by stirring the water so that the stationary layer cannot form; in the latter case, of course, the process will still slow down as the salt concentration builds up in the wash water.

The second problem is the danger that osmotic pressure may develop between the sea water within the pore structure and the clean water outside (Pearson 1987). Osmosis occurs where two solutions of different concentration are separated by a semi-permeable barrier through which the solvent can pass but the dissolved substance cannot; solvent (water in this case) tends to

Table 8.2 Types of stone recovered from the *Mary Rose*

Object	Stone
Grindstone	Millstone grit
Shot	Flint (canister shot), Kentish ragstone
Shot mould	Malmstone
Whetstone	Sandstones, metasandstones, chert, clay ironstone, limestone, micaceous phyllite
Unidentified	Flint, limestone, slate

pass through the barrier from the weaker solution to the stronger until the concentration is the same on both sides. The precise nature of the barrier is not fully understood in the case of ceramics, nevertheless osmosis can lead to internal pressure which is capable of damaging the object if it is in poor condition.

These problems were avoided with the *Mary Rose* materials by using a water cascade in which the objects were washed in progressively dilute salt solutions, eventually finishing in clean water. The cascade consists of a series of water tanks arranged at different height levels (Fig. 8.2). Clean water slowly flows into the top tank and circulates around any objects that it contains. The water then overflows into the second tank, which is at a lower level, and circulates around any objects there. It then overflows into a third tank, at a still lower level, and so on down the entire cascade. As the water passes downwards through the successive tanks it progressively accumulates an increasing concentration of dissolved salts which reaches a maximum at the bottom. Any object placed in the bottom tank will therefore be less liable to osmotic 'shock' and, when sufficient salts have been removed to bring it to equilibrium with the wash water, it is lifted into the tank at the next highest level. There it encounters a wash water with a lower concentration of dissolved salts. When it has come to equilibrium at that concentration it is lifted to the next highest level, and so on. When it is removed from the top tank most of the soluble salts should have been removed. This can be tested by placing the object in a container of clean water and, after allowing time for any diffusion to occur, checking the salt content of the water either by chemical analysis or by measuring its electrical conductivity; the electrical conductivity is increased by the presence of ions due to the dissolved salts.

It was sometimes necessary to use organic solvents to remove modern materials such as marking ink and adhesives. Also, acetone was used to remove residues from some of the ceramic vessels after their contents had been removed for analysis.

Washing proved to be insufficient to remove the residues in a few cases, and efflorescence (ie, the appearance of dry, powdery material that had come to the surface) appeared some time after the initial treatment. Electroendosmosis was therefore employed.

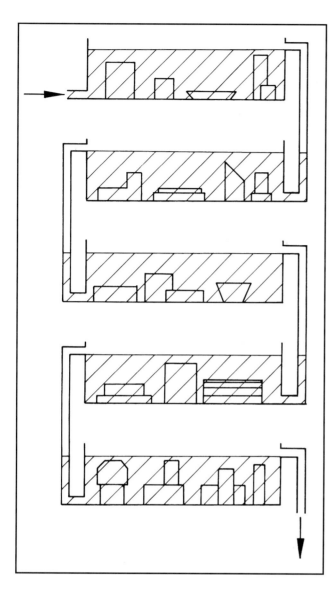

Figure 8.2 Diagrammatic representation of the water cascade system

This is a technique that can be useful where the soluble salts are particularly resistant to removal from a ceramic object by washing, for example because the pore structure of the clay body is too fine, and where fugitive pigments are present (Buys and Oakley 1998). The dissolved salts exist as ions; for instance, sodium chloride (NaCl, common salt) exists as positively charged sodium ions (Na^+) and negatively charged chloride ions (Cl^-). If a small current is passed through a salt solution between two oppositely charged electrodes, positively charged ions will tend to move towards the negative electrode and negatively charged ions will tend to move towards the positive electrode. If a ceramic object is placed between the electrodes and the current is switched on, any ions in solution within the pore structure tend to migrate outwards into the surrounding water towards their respective oppositely charged electrode. In the case of a hollow vessel, a convenient arrangement is to use a cylindrical electrode round the outside of the object with the second

electrode inside; the choice of polarity (positive or negative) of the internal electrode is determined by the nature of any pigments present (*ibid.*).

Unfortunately, electroendosmosis did not cure the problem with some of the vessels from the *Mary Rose*, probably because not all the contaminants were water soluble; chemical treatment (described below) was therefore used.

Solvent drying

Deteriorated glass surfaces can be very fragile and special methods may be needed to remove any water before they can be consolidated safely. Solvent drying is a simple but effective technique which removes the water by displacing it from the object in stages by successive immersion in progressively more concentrated baths of an appropriate solvent. After the initial wash, many of the glass objects from the *Mary Rose* were solvent dried using industrial methylated spirits (IMS) in water – typically 25%, 50%, 75% and finally 100% IMS. Depending on the condition of the glass, the total immersion time ranged from a day to several weeks. Consolidation of the glass objects is discussed below.

Removal of concretion

Problems involved in removing concretion and other surface deposits were largely confined to the ceramics out of the group of materials discussed in this chapter. Concretion on a ceramic surface can often be removed mechanically, using a tool such as a scalpel, but chemical methods are sometimes necessary.

Depending on the type of ceramic, treatment with ordinary acids can cause damage, for example by reacting with iron compounds present in the clay bodies and glazes. In some instances ethylenediamine-tetraacetic acid (EDTA) can be used, with caution, as a sodium salt in alkaline solution which may dissolve calcium from calcareous concretions without damaging the object itself (Buys and Oakley 1998; Pearson 1987). EDTA solutions of this kind were used to treat several of the ceramic vessels from the *Mary Rose*.

Removal of organic staining

Buys and Oakley (1998) point out that chlorine-based bleaches should not be used for removing organic stains from ceramics since they tend to leave chloride residues behind which may lead to serious damage later. Hydrogen peroxide (H_2O_2) is recommended (*ibid.*; Pearson 1987); this is a strong oxidising agent which breaks down to give oxygen and water – the oxygen does the bleaching and the water remains as a harmless residue. However, hydrogen peroxide should be used with care since its strong oxidising action can have a variety of adverse effects (Buys and Oakley 1998).

Reconstruction and repair

There is a variety of adhesives used in the reconstruction of archaeological ceramics. The type used in reconstructing many of the ceramics from the *Mary Rose* is based on cellulose nitrate, which is dissolved in solvent to give a clear, viscous and fairly rapidly setting adhesive. Setting depends on evaporation of the solvent, and this type of adhesive is particularly suitable for joining rough, porous surfaces together.

Cellulose nitrate adhesives have been widely used by conservators for many years, and they continue to be, despite some potential drawbacks, because they have some very helpful working properties (Pearson 1987; Buys and Oakley 1998). Their viscosity helps to hold the joint together while setting occurs, and their relatively short setting times enable the work to proceed without long delays between successive stages in the reconstruction process. But they have an especially important advantage in being readily reversible, that is to say artefacts can be readily dismantled by dissolving the cellulose nitrate from the joints using an appropriate solvent either applied directly as a liquid or, less drastically, in vapour form in a sealed container.

Figure 8.3 Stoneware jar after reconstruction

This assumes, of course, that the solvent does not harm the artefact in any way and preliminary tests may be necessary to confirm that this is the case. There is also the danger that the solvent may soak into a porous ceramic and deposit dissolved adhesive within the pore structure as it evaporates. In some cases it is possible to minimise this problem by first blocking the pores with water by pre-soaking the artefact, as long as this causes no damage. When the joint has been dismantled the remaining adhesive can then be removed. This may be done by swabbing the exposed edges with solvent which, of course, may introduce the sort of problems discussed above. Alternatively it may be removed mechanically, using a scalpel or similar tool, taking great care to avoid scratching the ceramic surface.

Reversibility is desirable from an ethical point of view since conservation should disturb an artefact as little as possible. It is also desirable from a practical point of view since a difficult reconstruction may require joints to be dismantled and rejoined a number of times. Furthermore, the subsequent excavation or discovery of sherds from a vessel that has already been partially rebuilt may require the reconstruction to be dismantled in order to fit the new pieces into position.

Cellulose nitrate adhesives do have their drawbacks but these tend to be offset by the benefit gained from their working properties (Pearson 1987; Buys and Oakley 1998). Some have a tendency to deteriorate with time. Furthermore, they may react quite rapidly with some epoxy resins to produce a strong yellow colouration. This can occur where epoxy resins are used to join surfaces that have previously been joined with cellulose nitrate, since it is often very difficult to remove the old adhesive completely.

Adhesive tapes such as masking tape are often used to support joints while setting occurs. These need to be used with a certain amount of caution since they can cause problems. They may react with the adhesive used to make the joint, sometimes causing discolouration. Also, when they are removed they may cause mechanical damage to the artefact, particularly at the surface, and they may leave sticky residues which attract dirt.

Consolidation

A once popular treatment for consolidating friable ceramics was soluble nylon. It was very easy to apply and had the great advantage of allowing an object in poor condition to be consolidated before it was washed. However, a number of problems developed with ageing – including shrinkage, increasing insolubility and a tendency to attract dirt – and it is no longer recommended for consolidating ceramics (Cronyn 1996; Buys and Oakley 1998; Pearson 1987). Several ceramic vessels from the *Mary Rose* were consolidated with soluble nylon and have shown no signs of deterioration.

112

Table 8.3 Treatment of selected ceramic objects

Object	Comments	Treatment
C1 Domestic container 80A1867	Sherd	Cascade washed; dried
C2 Cooking pot/bowl 78A0311	Unglazed; high fired. 2nd reconstruction needed; dirt collected between joints	Cascade washed; dried. Reconstructed with cellulose nitrate adhesive. *2nd recon.:* previous bonds dismantled with acetone vapour; edges swabbed with acetone; mechanically cleaned. Reconstructed with cellulose nitrate adhesive
C3 Cooking pot 79A0439	Residual masking tape adhesive apparent later	Cascade washed; dried. Reconstructed with cellulose nitrate adhesive. Masking tape adhesive removed with trichloroethylene; repaired with cellulose nitrate adhesive
C4 Jar/flagon 78A0133	Unglazed; soft, fine paste; very low fired. 2nd reconstruction needed; dirt collected between joints	As for C2
C5 Cooking pot 80A1225	Orange stain inside; few hairline cracks in body	Cascade washed; dried; reconstructed with cellulose nitrate adhesive
C6 Medicine jar 80A1459	6 weeks after initial treatment salts crystallising on & just under surface threatened stability	Contents removed & sampled. Cascade washed; dried. *After 6 weeks (efflorescence):* electroendosmosis unsatisfactory (not all contaminants water soluble). Treated with EDTA solution at 60°C for 2 hrs; 3% H_2O_2 for 12 hrs; intensive washing; dried; 5% soluble nylon in IMS brushed on to consolidate surface
C7, C10, C12–13 Medicine jars (eg. 80A1534)		Contents removed & sampled. Cascade washed; dried
C8 Medicine jar 80A1559	Corked; contained yellow compound	Contents removed & sampled. Acetone washed; dried
C9 Medicine jar 80A1573	Corked; contained waxy whitish solid smelling of eucalyptus	Contents removed & sampled. Acetone washed; dried. *After 9 months (efflorescence):* electroendosmosis; water washed; dried. *After 7 weeks (further efflorescence):* treated with EDTA solution at 50°C for 6 hours. water washed; dried
C11 Medicine jar 80A1575		Contents removed & sampled. Cascade washed; dried; reconstructed with cellulose nitrate adhesive
C14 Tin-glazed jug 80A1483	Corked with contents; fragile surface	Contents removed & sampled. Cascade washed; dried; surface consolidated with 5% soluble nylon in IMS
C15 Flask/bottle 81A3880	Earthenware with iron concretion	Initial cascade wash; dried. Mechanically cleaned. Local application of EDTA solution. Cascade washed; treated with EDTA solution at 90°C for 15 mins; cascade washed. Mechanically cleaned with hammer & chisel
C16 Bottle 81A0697	Wicker bound; corked. Hairline crack; dark stain lines under wicker	Cascade washed; wicker discarded (unconservable). Treated with 7% H_2O_2; water washed; dried
C17 Bottle 80A1660	Wicker bound; dangerous hairline crack; powdery surface. Initial storage in 5% borax solution	Cascade washed for 2 weeks. Wicker removed for separate conservation. Cascade washed for 2 weeks; dried; crack repaired with cellulose nitrate adhesive applied with syringe. Surface consolidated with 5% soluble nylon
C18 Bottle 81A3288	Wicker bound; neck broken into 10 frags. Initial storage in 5% borax solution	Cascade washed then washed in distilled water. Surface dried. Wicker treated *in situ*. Neck reconstructed with cellulose nitrate adhesive
C19 Jar 82A1687	10 frags; poor quality clay with v. fine inclusions	As for C5
C20 Jar/pot 82A4724	Concretion with some staining. Hairline cracks in glaze. Green glaze revealed	Cascade washed for 15 weeks; dried; chloride test; dried; mechanically cleaned

A commonly used consolidant for the glass objects from the *Mary Rose* was poly(methyl acrylate)/poly(ethyl methacrylate) copolymer (PMA/PEM) in toluene. Silica matting agent was sometimes added to the last coat or two to adjust the surface to the correct degree of glossiness.

Other consolidants included poly(vinyl acetate) (PVAC), poly(butyl methacrylate) and an unspecified polymethacrylate resin.

Specific Treatments

Ceramics

Twenty examples are given in Table 8.3. Seven vessels (C2–C5, C11, C18 and C19 in Table 8.3) were reconstructed using cellulose nitrate adhesive. Subsequently, two of these (C2 and C4) needed to be rebuilt. In both cases there had been sufficient sherds to make the original reconstructions about 50% complete. However, dirt had collected between the joints and cleaning would have been impossible without dismantling them. This was effected by enclosing the vessels in polythene bags with acetone swabs. The broken edges were then cleaned with acetone and the remains of the original adhesive were removed mechanically with a scalpel. Finally the vessels were rebuilt using cellulose nitrate adhesive. A third vessel (C3) showed evidence of residual masking tape adhesive, which was removed with trichloroethylene and, at the same time, repair work was carried out using cellulose nitrate adhesive.

The eight medicine jars and jug (C6–C14), with their contents, were found in the Barber-surgeon's chest and cabin. Apart from one earthenware jar (C6) and the tin-glazed stoneware jug (C14), they are all imported German salt-glazed stoneware (Fig. 8.3; see *AMR* vol. 4, chapters 4 and 11 for details). Following removal of their contents, the general method of treatment was desalination in the water cascade or, in two cases (C8 and C9), washing in acetone to remove other residues. One of the jars (C11) was reconstructed with cellulose nitrate adhesive.

Two jars (C6 and C9) suffered from efflorescence some time after initial cleaning and were treated by electroendosmosis. This did not cure the problem so further treatment was carried out with EDTA solution, followed by washing in water. Soluble nylon was used to consolidate C6 since salts had recrystallised upon and beneath the surface, threatening the stability of the vessel. In the case of C9, efflorescence reappeared some five years later, after the vessel had been on tour in the USA.

The tin-glazed stoneware medicine jug (C14), probably imported from Antwerp, is decorated with a yellow criss-cross pattern and white decoration on a grey background. After removal of the contents of the jug, and desalination in the water cascade, the fragile surface was consolidated using 5% soluble nylon in industrial methylated spirits.

The condition of the wicker around three wicker-bound Martincamp bottles (C16–C18) varied considerably. In two cases the wicker was conservable and they were stored initially in 5% borax, which acted as a fungicide. In the worst case (C16) the wicker was discarded and the flask itself was treated with 7% hydrogen peroxide to remove dark stain lines that remained underneath (Fig. 8.4). In the worse of the remaining two cases (C17), the wicker was removed after two weeks washing in the water cascade and conserved separately. The flask itself was returned to the water cascade for a further two weeks and then dried. A hairline crack, which threatened the integrity of the flask, was repaired with cellulose nitrate adhesive diluted with acetone and applied with a hypodermic syringe. The surface, which was slightly powdery, was consolidated with 5% soluble nylon brushed on. In the best case (C18), the conservation strategy was aimed at conserving the wicker *in situ*; the neck of the flask was reconstructed from broken fragments with cellulose nitrate adhesive.

Concretion was not a major problem. In one case (C20), mechanical cleaning with a scalpel was sufficient to remove a loose area of iron stained concretion. The

Figure 8.4 Ceramic flask

Table 8.4 Treatment of selected glass objects
(all objects had initial water wash)

Object	Comments	Treatment
G1 Compass 81A0071	Glass cover	Solvent dried in successive baths of acetone followed by IMS prior to consolidation
G2 Flask/ bottle 81A0561	Neck only; v. fragile. Glass flaking badly within 2 years of consolidation	Solvent dried in successive IMS baths; solvent evaporated over 2 days. Consolidated with 5 coats of 5% PMA/ PEM in toluene, with silica matting agent added to last coat. *Remedial treatment:* loose flakes restored with cellulose nitrate adhesive; consolidated with 2 coats 5% PMA/PEM in toluene, then 2 coats at 10% in toluene containing silica matting agent
G3 Sundial 80A1669	Mirror frags	Glass removed & dried; re-paired with cellulose nitrate adhesive
G4 Balance case 81A4107	Mirror frags	Solvent dried in successive IMS baths; consolidated with 3 coats of PMA/PEM
G5. Medical bottle 80A1540	Frags, v. fragile. Outer surface laminating within 2 years of initial treatment	As for G2. *Remedial treatment:* consolidated with 1 coat 5% PMA/PEM in toluene, then 1 coat at 10% containing silica matting agent
G6 Medical bottle 80A1565	Complete; fair condition. Weathering crust flaking off surface within 2 yrs of initial treatment	As for G2. *Remedial treatment:* as for G5 but 3 coats of 5% PMA/PEM rather than 1
G7 Medical bottle 80A1631	Base & neck only; v. fragile. Surface deteriorating within 2 years of initial treatment	As for G2. *Remedial treatment:* consolidated with 2 coats 10% PMA/PEM in toluene containing silica matting agent
G8 Sandglass 81A1172	Frags of bulb. Frags flaking badly within 5 yrs of initial treatment	Solvent dried in successive IMS baths; consolidated with 6 coats PMA/PEM. *Remedial treatment:* consolidated with 2 coats 5% PMA/PEM in toluene
G9 Mirror 81A4139	Frags	Solvent dried in successive IMS baths; consolidated with poly(butyl methacrylate)
G10 Sundial 82A5076	Mirror frags	Consolidated with PVAC emulsion; mechanically cleaned; coated with 5%PMA/PEM in toluene containing 1% silica matting agent
G11 Window frag. 82A5161	Poor condition with concretion over large areas	Mechanically cleaned; consolidated with PVAC emulsion

other case (C15), also with iron stained concretion, was more intractable. Initial mechanical cleaning was ineffective so EDTA solution was applied locally, followed by washing to remove any traces. This did not fully soften the concretion, so the vessel was immersed for 15 minutes in EDTA solution at 90°C, again followed by washing. However this had no further effect, and the concretion was finally removed by tapping very gently with a hammer and chisel.

Glass

Table 8.4 gives some examples of treatments used for the glass objects after their initial wash. Some were components of larger artefacts made from several different materials. Four glass vessels were represented (G2, G5–G7), only one of which (G6) was in sufficiently good condition for display.

Treatment of most of the objects involved solvent drying followed by consolidation. The four vessels had begun to deteriorate within two years of their initial treatment (solvent drying with IMS followed by

Figutre 8.5 Canister shot: a particularly nasty kind of shrapnel mortar consisting of a wooden canister filled with lethally sharp, smashed up flint fragments

Figure 8.6 Shot mould, indicating that some of the lead shot was made on on board the ship

consolidation with PMA/PEM) and the sandglass fragments (G8) were flaking badly within five years; consolidation was therefore repeated, although the technique was varied depending on the condition in each case.

Stone

Table 8.5 shows some examples of treatments used for the stone objects. Generally very little was required other than washing in water to remove the soluble salts. With most of the canister shot (Fig. 8.5) this was done *in situ*. In two cases (S4 and S7), it was necessary to remove felt-tip pen markings with solvent. Also the shot mould (S7) needed consolidation (Fig. 8.6), and loose flint contents of three of the shot canisters (S2, S5 and S8) required fixing *in situ* with consolidants.

Table 8.5 Treatment of selected stone objects

Object	Comments	Treatment
S1 Canister shot 81A0101	Flint contents of canister	Cascade washed; dried
S2 Canister shot 81A1905	Flint contents of canister	Left *in situ* during treatment of canister. Fixed in position using PVAC in acetone containing 5% silica matting agent
S3 Stone shot including 79A0370; 80A0415; 80A0623	27 items 150-200mm diam; 5–10kg mass	As for S1
S4 Whetstone 80A1569	Micaceous phyllite. Felt-tip pen markings	Markings removed with solvent. Water washed; dried
S5 Canister shot 82A2298	Flint contents of canister	Left *in situ* during treatment of canister. Loose flints removed; mechanically cleaned, washed and replaced. Fixed in position with 10% polymethacrylate resin in toluene; gloss on visible surfaces removed by brushing
S6 Canister shot 81A2859	Flint contents of canister	Left *in situ* during treatment of canister
S7 Shot mould 80A1847	Felt-tip pen markings; consolidation required	Markings removed with solvent. Cascade washed; dried. Consolidated with poly(butyl methacrylate) containing 5% silica matting agent
S8 Canister shot 82A2696	Flint contents of canister	Left *in situ* during treatment of canister; fixed in position with 5% polymethacrylate resin in toluene

9. Exhibition and Storage of The *Mary Rose* Collection

Bringing almost 19,000 objects to a stabilised state is only part of the conservation process. Even in a dry and conserved state, archaeological objects can be very susceptible to the forces of display or storage environments.

Environmental factors such as light, relative humidity, heat and atmospheric pollution are the major forces that can cause serious irreversible damage to conserved objects. Therefore, the continued existence of an artefact displayed within a museum or kept in storage will depend upon the creation of an artificial environment that eliminates or significantly reduces deterioration. Without this degree of intervention, all objects recovered from the wreck of the *Mary Rose* are liable to deteriorate.

Here lies the paradox. Vast amounts of money were needed in the recovery and preparation for display and study of the *Mary Rose* hull and objects. The desire for display of a large quantity of objects made from a variety of materials, however, introduces a set of concerns for the conservator in that public display of the treated object can, itself, lead to further degradation. Conservation staff had to address this delicate balance between the visitors' needs and conservation considerations. The Mary Rose Trust has achieved this by the introduction of a stable display and storage environment in which temperature, light, relative humidity, biological pests and atmospheric pollution are carefully controlled, while still remaining true to the educational function of a museum. Deterioration can affect all forms of objects, inorganic and organic, small or large during display. Of the two main material types, organic materials are the ones most susceptible to deterioration by environmental forces.

This chapter addresses environmental considerations for the storage and display of *Mary Rose* artefacts. The approach taken by the Mary Rose Trust to improve the chances of long-term artefact survival was based upon both experiment and on theory of the interaction between an object and the various environmental factors. While general guidelines are offered here, Thompson (1978) should also be consulted.

The Mary Rose Museum

The Mary Rose Museum contains what is undoubtedly one of the most important Tudor collections in the country and suitable long-term accommodation for the treated artefacts was required to maintain and display this important resource. The decision by the Trustees of the Mary Rose to create a museum in the heart of Portsmouth was an exiting development involving a unique maritime resource.

The initial study for a Tudor Ship Museum focused on a new build development on a site of nearly 5 hectares at Eastney. In parallel with this study, Trustees were asked to explore other options involving listed buildings at the Royal Naval Base, Portsmouth. In 1981, the Trustees gave due consideration to the findings of the study and preferred the option to bring the hull into Dry Dock No. 3 and to develop Boathouse No. 5 as a museum within the Naval Base. The architectural simplicity and elegance of Boathouse No. 5 was considered appropriate for the exhibition and interpretation of objects recovered from the *Mary Rose* (further details of the creation of the museum are given in *AMR* Vol. 1, chapter 6).

Boathouse No. 5 is prominently situated in the Naval Base conservation area, which is made up of a large number of distinguished Listed Buildings. The Royal Naval Museum and the Ministry of Defence occupy the majority of the heritage site of 23 hectares. The Boathouse was constructed in 1822 to build and service small boats and was in use until the late 1970s. It is a particularly distinguished example of its kind. The building itself is timber-framed and clad, supported over sea water by metal piers, with a corrugated iron roof. Overall it is a fine piece of military architecture. The boathouse is listed Grade II, and this has been a major deterrent to the redevelopment of the existing building. The development proposal put forward by the Trust went to great pains to preserve both internal and external features and structures (Fig. 9.1).

To provide displays and information which will excite, stimulate and educate people of all nationalities, ages, educational and socio-economic backgrounds, a museum must be alive, providing an experience which will be remembered with pleasure for a long time. The Mary Rose Museum aims to provide a wide range of visitors with the opportunity to learn; to be entertained; to be motivated to extend their knowledge; to have all senses stimulated; and to understand the significance of the *Mary Rose* and the military and social material found within the ship within the context of history and development of Britain as a seafaring nation and of the Tudor period in general. It is important that the specifically Tudor elements are represented in the context of pre- and post-Tudor developments in ship-building and maritime history.

In terms of presentation, there were obvious and inescapable story lines, which include the following:

- Henry VIII, the nation state and the Henrician Navy.
- Life in Tudor England.
- The revolutionary design of the *Mary Rose*.
- The art of ordnance.
- The sinking of the *Mary Rose*.
- The search for and discovery of the wreck.
- The excavation and raising of the *Mary Rose*.
- Navigation in the sixteenth century.
- Life on board a Tudor warship.
- Maritime archaeology.
- Marine archaeological conservation.

Following the decision by the Trustees to proceed with the development of Boathouse No. 5, conservators and conservation scientists were charged with the task of writing a design brief to safeguard treated objects on display to the public. Particular attention was paid to the following:

- Providing stable environmental conditions within the building.
- Constructing showcases to display objects.
- Constructing floors to high loading capacity.
- Installing of adequate specialised services such as air-conditioning and monitoring equip-ment.
- Incorporating technologies and features that are highly energy efficient.

These recommendations were accepted by Trustees and incorporated into the Trust's proposals and design. The sections that follow consider the principal destructive factors that can affect museum display materials and the measures that have been adopted by the Mary Rose Trust to control them.

Destructive Environmental Factors

Light

Light, whether natural or artificial, can cause significant and irreversible damage to museum collections. Damage can occur even at low levels of lighting and the effects are cumulative. Particularly susceptible are objects made from organic materials such as wood, textiles and leather. Although light is generally considered not harmful to inorganic materials (stone, ceramics, glass, metals, etc), it should be remembered that treatment of these materials involve adhesives, consolidants and surface coatings that are all organic in nature. Deterioration of these organic treatment systems will be accelerated by exposure to excessively high light levels. As discussed in the relevant preceeding chapters, organic objects such as wood, textiles and leather are composed of long-chain natural polymers (Pearson

Figure 9.1 The Mary Rose Museum

1987), which are susceptible to photo-oxidation by Ultra-Violet (UV) radiation and light. Organic objects subjected to high light levels will eventually decay, a process which often involves a range of chemical reactions. This form of decay usually takes place in the presence of oxygen and can be accelerated by air pollutants. To ensure the objects' longevity during display and long-term storage it is necessary to store objects in the dark and to display them at low light levels using ultra-violet filtered artificial light. All UV radiation within the museum is removed by the use of UV filters and low UV-emitting fluorescent lights.

The minimum amount of light needed to exhibit an object adequately is 50 lux and this was recommended for the display of organic objects. For less sensitive objects (such as stone and metal objects), levels of up to a recommended maximum of 100 lux were considered acceptable. For visitor movement within the museum, health and safety advisors recommended a lighting level of 10–30 lux.

Since the effects of light are cumulative, it is important to control the length of time *Mary Rose* objects are exposed. Annual exposure levels for organic objects are never exceeded. These objects are often retired to dark storage or, if kept on permanent display, are not exposed to light sources when the gallery is closed.

Temperature and relative humidity

Stable temperature and relative humidity within the Mary Rose Museum are among the most important factors in the preservation of the collection. Increases in temperature can accelerate rates of chemical reactions and encourage the activity of micro-organisms and insects. Temperature fluctuations can also cause expansion and contraction in most organic and inorganic materials which, in turn, leads to irreversible damage to the artefact. A temperature of 18–20°C is recommended for the display of all *Mary Rose* artefacts within the museum complex. Higher temperature levels should also be avoided because the various impregnants used to treat artefacts may soften and migrate. Lowering the temperature will cause a corresponding increase in relative humidity and vice versa. Objects made from proteinaceous and cellulosic material are very sensitive to changes in relative humidity (RH). Maintaining constant RH levels is the goal of all conservators involved in the long-term stability of treated archaeological artefacts. At constant RH, hygroscopic material present in all organic artefacts will neither expand nor contract. Relative humidity is usually expressed as a percentage and it can be defined as follows:

$$RH = \frac{\text{amount of water in a given quantity of air}}{\text{amount of water which the air can hold at that temperature}} \times 100\%$$

Relative humidity levels above 70% will increase swelling of an organic object and encourage biological growth. Inorganic objects are also susceptible to high humidity levels: ceramics and glass suffer from salt efflorescence; metals from corrosion; dyes and pigments are also affected. Relative humidity levels below 40% encourage shrinkage, warping and embrittlement to organic artefacts. Within this range of RH (40–70%), a stable and constant level should be found and maintained, varying at maximum over a ±2% range. Marine archaeological artefacts require more precisely controlled levels of RH: 55–58% for organic artefacts and 40% for metals.

Biological control

Current best practice of insect, rodent and microbial activity control in museums is based on preventing infestation, monitoring museum buildings and collections and using safe methods of control. Keeping the RH below 70% is a simple and practicable method of preventing fungal and bacterial activity. Insects, on the other hand, can flourish over a wide humidity range (20–90%). Maintaining a level below 20% would be preventative but unsuitable for the artefacts. Preventing insect infestations requires good housekeeping, checking incoming materials for infestation, ensuring that display cases are well sealed and kept under positive pressure, and not allowing food or drink to be consumed within the museum complex. An insect monitoring programme is an effective and economic weapon against infestation.

The control of insects in the Mary Rose Museum involves a thorough daily cleaning regime of all areas that are accessible. Inaccessible high-level areas are inspected regularly by conservation staff and cleaned twice yearly by outside contractors. Carpets within the museum are cleaned daily and sprayed twice yearly with a low toxicity insecticide (permethrin based). Rodents are seldom seen within the museum (only two recorded instances over the past 15 years). These were swiftly

Table 9.1 Typical levels of gaseous pollutants within the museum

Sample location	Nitrogen dioxide (ppb v/v)	Sulphur dioxide (ppb v/v)
Pewter case	16	5
Gallery	14	3
Barber-surgeon's case	11	2
Swivel gun case	13	2
External	18	4
Air-conditioning supply	26	1
Air return	25	1

controlled by the use of conventional poisons placed well away from both public and the collection.

Atmospheric pollution

Although invisible to the naked eye, airborne and gaseous pollutants are present within the Mary Rose Museum. Since it is situated within a busy naval base, the museum collection can be subjected to a range of pollutants that originates from sources both outside and inside the museum. Outside air entering the museum contains a number of harmful airborne chemicals that can damage an object on display. Externally produced pollutants detected within HM Naval Base Portsmouth include salt particles from sea water, carbon particles from fires, sulphur dioxide from naval and commercial ships operating in the harbour complex, hydrogen sulphide from rotting seaweeds, nitrogen dioxide and ozone.

Scientists at BP National Physical Laboratory carry out examinations of air quality within the Mary Rose Museum on a regular basis. The sampling method uses a diffusion tube which absorbs air pollutants onto a disc. After deployment, typically for a four-week period, the tube is recapped and returned to the laboratory for analysis by gas chromatography-mass spectroscopy (Table 9.1).

Levels of air pollutants detected within the museum display cases are quoted to the nearest parts per billion (v/v) with a limit of detection of 1ppb v/v. Analysis of the data indicates low levels of atmospheric pollutants in the display cases. Sulphur dioxide levels are typical of a clean rural coastal environment. The higher nitrogen dioxide values are typical of a suburban residential area.

Analysis of solid particles within the museum shows that it varies from 1–20μ in size and is removed effectively by the use of in-line filters, which are an integral part of the display case air-conditioning system. These filters are replaced monthly during the servicing of the museum and display case air-conditioning system.

Although sea salts (chlorides) were removed from all treated *Mary Rose* artefacts, these still pose a threat to objects displayed within the museum because it is situated in a coastal area. Levels of up to 20mg/m³ of chloride have been detected in the museum environment. Metals (large bronze and iron guns) on open display are constantly under threat and require regular monitoring to prevent further corrosion by airborne chlorides. The surfaces of these artefacts are heavily impregnated by micro-crystalline wax.

Air pollution from sources inside the museum is caused primarily by emissions from construction materials used in case construction. The suitability of the materials proposed for use in displays needs to be tested since their composition may emit chemicals that are harmful to the artefacts. For instance, the greatest internal pollution offender is timber, by virtue of its prominent use in display situations (Harvey and Freedland 1987). In its natural state, timber can release organic acids and formaldehyde vapours. The exact amount of gaseous pollutants emitted by timber varies with species, tree age and the season in which the tree was cut. In the presence of moisture, these vapours will corrode metal artefacts. Other construction materials, such as rubber seals, contain sulphur compounds which can tarnish metals such as silver and pewter. All materials chosen for the construction of display cases should, if finances permit, be inert. Trust conservators carried out tests on all materials (wood, display textiles, paint, sealants, seals, and adhesives) that were to be in the environment of the exhibited object. Sources of pollutants are summarised in Table 9.2.

People control

To avoid accidental damage to the collection, *Mary Rose* artefacts are displayed within glazed display cases. Large objects kept on open display are clearly labelled with 'do not touch' signs. When objects are handled, the use of cotton gloves is essential and helps reduce surface contamination and damage.

Table 9.2 Sources of internal pollutants

Pollutant	Source	Affects
Sulphur compounds (H_2S and SO_2)	Rubber adhesives & seals	Tarnishes metals (silver & pewter)
Organic acids (CHOOH and CH_3COOH)	Timber, plywood, MDF, paints, adhesives, sealants	Corrosion of metals & stone
Formaldehyde (CH_2O)	Adhesives, timber, MDF, plywood, fabrics, paint	High levels can attack most metals & organic artefacts
Chlorides (Cl)	Fire retardants, plastics	Corrode copper alloys & iron artefacts
Nitrogen dioxide (NO_2)	Plastics, adhesives	Corrodes copper & iron artefacts

Providing a Stable Environment

The most destructive forces faced by the Mary Rose collections are, therefore:

- Fluctuating and inappropriate relative humidity levels.
- Fluctuating and inappropriate temperature levels.
- Exposure to light and UV.
- Atmospheric pollution.
- Materials used in the construction of display cases.

It is often the failure to control these environmental factors that gives rise to the need for remedial conservation.

Boathouse No. 5 is situated in the heart of the Naval Base, where atmospheric pollution is high, partly as a result of the movement of naval shipping and surrounding vehicle traffic activities. Noise levels are also high, again primarily because of Ministry of Defence activities. Environmental conditions within the boathouse fluctuate constantly, primarily due to the nature of the building material, which is predominantly wood. Several commissioned reports identified problems associated with the use of Boathouse No. 5 and proposed environmental solutions that would not only preserve the appearance and external fabric of this historic building, but also provide an opportunity to maximise the interior space to the requirements of the Mary Rose Trust. The main conclusion of the report dictated the use of air-conditioned showcases for the display of all treated objects. Light levels and close environmental control could all be met by this scheme. The environmental conditions required for the storage and display of *Mary Rose* objects to the public were defined as follows:

- The temperature of the galleries within which the display cases were to be exhibited would be conditioned to a temperature of 18–20°C.
- Within each display case the air would also be controlled to a temperature of 18–20°C.
- Light levels in areas where original organic material were to be exhibited would be maintained below 50 lux.
- A relative humidity of 55% was recommended for the display and storage of organic material (wood, textiles, leather, etc.).
- A relative humidity of 40% was recommended for the display of inorganic material (metals).
- Gaseous pollutants would be removed by chemical filtration (sulphur dioxide and nitrogen dioxide to levels not more than 10mg/m³ and ozone reduced to trace levels).

These requirements were to be achieved 24 hours a day, every day of the year. The story line within the museum would be developed to encourage grouping of material requiring similar environmental conditions. All display environments would be continuously monitored by a computerised system. The design team, led by R.Wade, interpreted these requirements in the museum layout in an imaginative and efficient manner.

Artefacts displayed in showcases

The preferred design solution for the display of treated artefacts was to build air-tight showcases which would protect objects from physical damage and meet the defined requirements for providing suitable environmental conditions for long-term preservation, which could not be achieved in an open gallery. A display case also provides good security and enables visitors to get as close as possible to the artefacts. The design team fully assessed the specialised requirements of the artefacts and incorporated them into the design brief (Fig. 9.2).

Three basic types of showcase were recommended, each with numerous variations in shape and size, and all connected to an air conditioning system. Display showcases are solidly constructed of wood with a hollow wooden base, which acts as a supply air plenum. Each case is provided with a number of glazed areas, enabling close viewing of the artefacts by the public. Air is introduced into the case via perforations in the top of the plenum base. The roof of each case is also wood and contains a light source. Air is extracted via an air path situated within the structural framework at high level. All cases are kept under positive pressure. Access into each is usually through gasketed doors or access panels, tightly fitted to maintain a high degree of air-tightness.

Materials used in the construction of display cases

Conservators are fully aware of the damage caused to objects from chemicals released by the range of material used in the construction of display cases. Wood for example, as stated above, is a common material of construction. It is also an extremely corrosive substance and can be made more corrosive by any additional treatment it has received. The corrosive agent is acetic acid emitted in the vapour form, causing corrosion to nearby metal artefacts –the degree of possible corrosion being commensurate with the susceptibility of the specific metal to attack by the acid. The degree of susceptibility of different metals to attack is given below:

Group 1 – Severe attack
Wrought iron, cast iron and lead

Group 2 – Moderate attack
Copper and its alloys

Group 3 – Very slight attack
Aluminium

Group 4 – Insignificant attack
Gold, silver, tin and pewter

Figure 9.2 Example of one of the museum display cases containing organic materials

In order to minimise damage, all materials used in the construction of display cases were subjected to testing under strict and controlled laboratory conditions. Only those materials that did not release damaging vapours were used. Acid-free Sundeala boards were used as internal lining to each case and painted with a pH neutral vapour barrier to minimise the risk of emissions of formaldehyde and acetic acid. Whenever a paint or adhesive system was used, ample curing time was allowed before artefacts were placed within the case. For aesthetic reasons, the boards were then lined with a pH neutral fabric. The cases have glass panels to front and, in some cases, to the sides for viewing.

Support materials
Some materials need to be provided with physical supports. Great care is needed in selecting the correct material. Custom-built perspex supports lined with 'moleskin' fabric were used to support most *Mary Rose* objects. Materials that should never be used include pins, rubber foam and adhesive tapes. All support materials were tested before use.

Glass
Laminated glass, typically 6mm in thickness, has been used for showcase glazing. This type of glass provides adequate security as laminates hold pieces in position in the event of accidental or deliberate breakage. The glass used is non-reflective and panels are held in position by wooden battens screwed into the showcase framework.

Each batten is sealed with a pH neutral silicon sealant to prevent ingress of untreated air.

Access

Access panels are incorporated into a number of showcases, providing sufficient area of opening to enable objects to be put inside or taken out without risk of accidental damage during handling and routine cleaning. Larger showcases were designed without doors or panels and access into these units is achieved by removal of the glass panels. Personnel are required to wear safety boots and safety glasses during this activity. Glass panel suckers are used to lift glass panels safely in and out of the showcase unit.

Lighting

The method of lighting the interior of the museum display case is by low-voltage fluorescent lighting to achieve an overall illuminance of approximately 50 lux for all material on display. These tubular lamps are mounted in integral boxes on top of the cases, separated from the display by clear Perspex panels. The light boxes are screened from the exhibits by ultraviolet resisting film positioned between the perspex panel and light source. The museum also uses layers of drafting film placed between the light source and perspex panel to reduce lux levels. Provision of visual hierarchies within the museum helps the visitor to focus upon objects on display. Museum galleries are lit at lower levels making objects on display more conspicuous. Control of daylight in the gallery is achieved by use of light-reduction filters on the windows.

Current practice (January 2003)
Light and UV measurements are used to record Lux and UV levels within the boat display case (Fig. 9.3). These show that UV is negligible, both in the case and within the surrounding gallery (typically<15mW/ Lumen). The light levels vary between 50–100 lux. At present light and UV levels are monitored on a one-hourly basis.

Temperature and relative humidity

A constant temperature of 18–20°C is recommended for the display of all artefacts within display cases. Wood is very sensitive to changes in relative humidity; therefore, it is important to maintain constant levels of relative humidity so that organic artefacts will neither expand nor contract. Higher temperature levels are also avoided because polyethylene glycol used to treat the hull timbers may soften and migrate.

Relative humidity levels are maintained at a level of of 55–58% for organic objects and 40% for metals. Air within the case is recirculated and system losses replaced with filtered fresh air.

Current practice (January 2003)
Each museum showcase unit is designed as a sealed system and temperature and humidity levels have been

Figure 9.3 A Light and UV meter (arrowed) recording levels within one of the museum display cases

maintained at the recommended levels. Problems have been encountered with the case humidification equipment during extreme external conditions (high and low external temperatures) and concerns have been expressed about the reliability of this system during these periods.

Each case is sealed and under positive pressure. Food or drink is not allowed in the gallery. The carpets and glass are cleaned daily. Inspection of ducting is part of a monthly service of the air-conditioning equipment.

Atmospheric pollution

Solid particles from externally produced pollutants (see above)are removed by the use of in-line filters which are an integral part of a display case air-conditioning system. Staff change these filters when the pressure across the filter has risen by 100pa. As stated above, pollution from sources inside the museum is caused primarily by emissions from materials used in case construction. These are minimised by the use of appropriately inert materials as described above.

Current practice (January 2003)
Scientaire Thermal Systems Ltd supplies air filters. The main air supply filter is an AB95G bag filter with airflow of 7.6m³/s. The display case air-conditioning units have one 50mm panel (IC50 EU5 CP413) bag filter on each air handling unit plus a PPS600 EU3 primary panel filter and a Grade 209M carbon filter. This filter reduces NO_2, SO_2 and O_3 levels to values less than 10mg/m³.

People control

To avoid accidental damage to the displayed objects, both organic and inorganic material are displayed within a glazed display case. When artefacts are examined,

Figure 9.4 Temperature and relative humidity sensor (arrowed) used to monitor conditions within display case

trained personnel use gloves which helps to reduce surface contamination.

Current practice (January 2003)
No one is allowed into the case apart from curatorial staff and, then, only when necessary. Cotton gloves are worn if any part of the display needs to be handled or touched.

Monitoring strategy

This checklist is intended as a framework for prolonging the life of artefacts from the *Mary Rose*. The interaction of these delicate artefacts with the museum environment requires a high level of monitoring. The monitoring strategy of the Mary Rose Trust is designed to:

- monitor and advise on the physical effects of displaying the *Mary Rose* artefacts,
- monitor the environment and other damage prevention measures, and take or initiate appropriate mitigation action;
- monitor the preservation of artefacts by periodic audits of condition; and
- take appropriate action to clean artefacts on display.

Environmental monitoring
As stated above, the museum's environment policy for the display of organic and inorganic artefacts specifies 'ideal' environmental conditions of 18–20°C and a 55% RH for organic and 40% RH for inorganic artefacts. In order to minimise deterioration while ensuring public display of artefacts, tight environmental control is important. To control something to a certain level, however, we must first be able to measure it. Continuous monitoring of environmental variables will therefore ensure that ideal display conditions are maintained.

Temperature and humidity levels are monitored by means of an electronic and computer-based data logging system (Fig. 9.4) accompanied by written monthly reports with graphic presentation. RH fluctuations must be avoided since these are usually the symptoms of a poorly operated HVAC system. Proper operation and regular maintenance (monthly) is necessary to keep the system efficient and effective. Any problems encountered with the display case HVAC system are addressed immediately.

Insect control
A small cardboard trap lined with a sticky surface is a safe and effective method for detecting insects within the display case. These are distributed judiciously within the museum and examined every month. Insects trapped are identified and infestations dealt with promptly by means of a non-toxic process that will not damage the objects. Advice is sought as necessary from a conservator with experience in insect taxonomy.

Artefact condition
In order to diagnose any changes to objects on display, a condition survey is undertaken on a yearly basis (Table 9.3). Such audits are designed to take as little valuable conservation time as possible, and the results are analysed immediately. Comparisons are then made with previous audits. This sort of assessment is clearly essential when setting priorities for action to be taken as a result of condition surveys. Conservators with appropriate skills are required to carry out this work.

Data concerning the condition of artefacts that should be collected include the following:

Damage
Major structural damage: large cracks likely to open, major splitting to organic artefacts
Minor structural damage: small splits to organic material
Surface damage: small hairline cracks to organic material
Dimensional changes: shrinkage, warping, cupping, twisting to organic material
Chemical deterioration: exudations, salts, tarnishes on organic and inorganic objects
Biological attack: insect, mould
Previous treatment failures: adhesion, misalignment
Accretions: dirt.

Table 9.3 Objectives of monitoring and data required

Survey objective	Data required
Condition of individual artefact	Condition audit Damage types and severity
Identify causes of deterioration	Environmental records; past & present, damage type & severity
Diagnose trend	Condition past, condition present, condition predicted future
Affect trend	Display conditions, handling procedures Change environment Re-treat

Condition

Condition Good: artefacts are in a good condition, or are stable.

Condition Fair: fair condition but stable, needs no immediate action.

Condition Poor: poor condition and unstable, action desirable.

Condition Unacceptable: severely unstable and actively deteriorating; immediate action should be taken.

The data collected on display environment and artefact condition are presented yearly to a committee of advisors. The advisory panel includes conservators, an environmental engineer, museum curators and trustees. The information collected enables staff at the Mary Rose Trust to manage the ongoing preservation of artefacts on display to the general public.

Cleaning objects

Trained conservators clean the surface of artefacts when necessary. Externally produced pollutants, such as dust or sometimes grit, will often settle on surfaces. It is particularly important to remove such contaminants from objects that are usually acidic in nature and often contain traces of metals such as iron, which can catalyse cellulose deterioration in artefacts made from plant fibres.

Current practice (January 2003)

Each case is fitted with an electronic data-logging system that records temperature and relative humidity over a weekly period. The data is analysed by museum staff and a short report is produced for the weekly conservation meetings. There is also a hair hygrometer on a number of showcases and museum custodians inspect both these and real time environmental data throughout the day. They do not record the readings but inform conservation staff of any sudden changes of readings outside the recommended range. The hair hygrometers are calibrated every three months using a Novatron Novasina ms 1 hygro measuring system (accurate to ± 1% and ±°0.3C). This is calibrated annually using a sensor-check apparatus. The air conditioning system is maintained on a monthly service with call-outs as necessary. *Mary Rose* technical staff currently carry out any minor, day-to-day maintenance.

Reserve Collection

This storage area contains several thousand artefacts that are maintained in secure, insulated rooms wherein temperature (18–20°C) and humidity (55% for organic material and 40% for inorganic artefacts) are controlled within closely defined parameters. Light levels are maintained at 0 lux, except for occasional access during which they are maintained at approximately 50 lux. Reserve collections environments are monitored continuously by means of a thermohydrograph.

10. Future Directions and Concerns

In the field of archaeological conservation, one thing that has become abundantly clear is that the excavation of any major underwater wreck site presents considerable problems for the recovery team. The decision to proceed with lifting and recovery has to be taken with the full knowledge and understanding of the implications that flow from it – the high costs that will have to be faced for storage and conservation of all the materials recovered. If adequate assurances cannot be obtained that there are reserves of finance and space adequate to cover those needs, then it is difficult to justify the disturbance of any wreck site. Unless there is an external threat the archaeological evidence buried undisturbed on the seabed will be better protected there until a more supportive climate is met.

Adequate funding needs to be put in place from the outset to cover the high cost of excavation, recovery, passive and active conservation, post-excavation analysis and publication and, finally, display; but in the real world this is rarely possible. Most maritime projects tend to be extremely long term – even as long as 30 years – to complete all stages to the final conservation of recovered artefacts. During those years there are inevitably going to be periods of uncertainty, particularly if public funding is being relied on to cover the major proportion of the costs.

The Mary Rose Trust, like any other heritage trust established to preserve facets of our history for future generations, has been obliged to rely on support from many sources. Visitor income alone could never produce enough to cover the costs involved in preserving and displaying 19,000 or so artefacts from the *Mary Rose*, not to mention the hull itself. It has been a mammoth undertaking. Of course, it was never expected that the turnstile would cover more than a small percentage of the enormous costs that had to be faced and that appeals would have to be made to public and private sources of funding over such a long period of time.

There is still much to be done, and not only to complete the final phases of the hull conservation programme which itself will take at least another 12 years from the time this book goes to press. Alongside that work there are ambitious plans to provide a purpose-built museum in which the ship and collection will be displayed together. This is going to present a formidable challenge for the Mary Rose Trust. No one would deny that the high cost of the hull conservation programme has put a strain on the Trust's resources and tested its commitment to that final objective of establishing the Mary Rose Trust as a centre of excellence for maritime archaeology and conservation. But then, these are challenging times and, to help meet that challenge, the Trust has had the most consistent support from the Heritage Lottery Fund, not only in funding the *Archaeology of the Mary Rose*, of which this volume is a part, but also in covering the far greater costs of the hull conservation as we approach that final phase. We are grateful to them for that support.

Over the past 25 years of painstaking work by conservators dealing with the *Mary Rose* collection one thing has been clear, the public interest has grown considerably both in the recovery of these precious items and the conservation processes that followed. Not only that, but the work has also attracted considerable international recognition, reaching well beyond the world of archaeology. In itself that surely is a tribute to the skill of the conservation team and importance of their work.

Over the next decade or so the final treatment of the hull must be funded and completed. Then a new museum and shiphall will rise over the *Mary Rose*, displaying the Tudor warship and her contents in a much more exciting and imaginative way than has ever been possible before. Only then will the true importance of the Mary Rose project be realised for the benefit of future generations.

Figure 10.1 The hull of the Mary Rose *on display in the present shiphall*

Bibliography

Albright, A.B. 1966. The preservation of small waterlogged wood specimens with polyethylene glycol. *The Curator*, 9, 3.

Ambrose, W.R. 1975. Stabilising degraded swamp wood by freeze drying. *ICOM Committee for Conservation, 4th Triennial Meeting, Venice 1975*, 1–14.

Amoignon, J. and Larrat, P. 1985. Traitement des bois gorges d'eau par lyophilisation a la pression atmospherique – application aux objets de grandes dimensions. In Ramiere and Colardelle (eds), 1985, 181–6.

Anon. 1952. *Marine Fouling and its Preservation*, Prepared for Buteau of Ships, Navy Dept by Woods HOLE oceanographic Inst., Annapolis, Maryland.

Anon. 1980. *Breox polyethylene glycols*. Data sheet PEGSDS 1, Belgium: BP Chemicals.

Anon. 1994. *A Guide to Designing for Irradiation Sterilization*. Swindon: Isotron plc.

Archer, J. 1991. *Conservation of Archaeological Artefacts by Thermal Methods*. Unpublished PhD Thesis, Portsmouth Polytechnic.

Archer, P.J. and Barker, B.D. 1987. Phase changes associated with the hydrogen reduction conservation process for ferrous artefacts. *Journal of the Historical Metallurgy Society* 21.3, 86–91.

Arrhenius, O., Barkman, L. and Jostrand, E.S. 1973. *Conservation of Old Rusty Iron Objects*. Swedish Corrosion Institute Bulletin 61E.

Ashley Smith, J. 1982. The ethics of conservation. *The Conservator* 6, 5–7

Astrup, E.E. 1994. A medieval log house in Oslo – conservation of waterlogged softwoods with polyethylene glycol (PEG). In Hoffmann *et al.* (eds), 1994, 41–50.

Atlas, M. and Bartha, R. 1987. *Microbial Biology*. Benjamin/Cummins.

Barker, B.D. 1985. Conservation of ferrous archaeological artefacts. *Industrial Corrosion* 3.2.

Barker, B.D., Kendall, K. and O'Shea, C. 1982. The hydrogen reduction process for the conservation of ferrous objects. In: R.W Clarke and S.M. Blackshaw (eds), *Conservation of Iron*, 23–7. London: National Maritime Museum, Maritime Monographs and Reports 53.

Barker, D., Clos, P. Crean, C., Lomer, R., Waterton, K. and Wlash, F. 1992. *Case Studies in Marine Corrosion: copper, lead and tin alloy artefacts*. Manchester: Proceedings of UK Corrosion 1992.

Barkman, L. 1975. The preservation of the Warship Vasa. In W.A. Oddy (ed.), *Problems of the Conservation of Waterlogged Wood*, 65–105, Greenwich: National Maritime Museum, Maritime Monographs and Reports 16.

Barkman, L. 1977. Conservation of rusty iron objects by hydrogen reduction. In: B. Brown, B. Floyd, H.C. Burnett, W.T. Chase, M. Goodway, J. Kruger, and M. Pourbaix (eds), *Corrosion of Metal Artefacts – a Dialogue between Conservators and Archaeologists and Corrosion Scientists*, 155–66. Washington DC: National Bureau of Standards Special Publication 479.

Barbour, R.J. 1990. Treatments for waterlogged and dry archaeological wood. In Rowell and Barbour (eds), 1990, 177–92.

Barbour, R.J. and Leney, L. 1982. Shrinkage and collapse in waterlogged wood. In Grattan and McCawley (eds), 1982, 209–25.

Battersby, N.S. and Brown, C.M. 1982. Microbial activity in organically enriched marine sediments. In D.B Nedwell and C.M. Brown (eds), *Sediment Microbiology*, 147–70. London: Academic Press.

Becker, G. 1971. On the biology, physiology and ecology of marine wood-boring crustaceans. In E.B.G. Jones and S.K. Eltringham (eds), *Marine Borers, Fungi and Fouling Organisms of Wood*, 303–26. Paris: O.E.C.D.

Boyd, A. 1968. Comparitive histology of mammalian teeth. In A.A. Dahlberg (ed.), *Dental Morphology and Evolution*, 81–94. Chicago: University Press.

Bravery, A.F. 1971. The application of scanning electron microscopy on the study of timber decay. *Journal of the Institute of Wood Science* 5, 13–19

Bravery, A.F. 1976. Interactions between organic solvent preservatives, wood and decay. *Mat. Org. Beihft* 3, 331–44.

Burgess, R. 1934. Experiments on the preservation of wool against harmful microbes. *Journal of the Society of Dyers Colourists* 51.3, 138–42.

Buys, S. and Oakley, V. 1998. *The Conservation and Restoration of Ceramics*. Oxford: Butterworth-Heinemann.

Cartwright, K. St G. and Findley, W.P.K. 1958. *Decay of Timber and its Preservation*. London: HMSO.

Christensen, B. 1970. *The Conservation of Waterlogged Wood in the National Museum of Denmark*. Copenhagen: National Museum of Denmark.

Clarke, R.W. 1987. Waterlogged wood. In C. Pearson (ed.), *Conservation of Marine Archaeological Objects*, 200–206. London: Butterworths.

Cohen, O. 1991. The recovery of the Kinneret boat. In: P. Hoffmann (ed.), *Proceedings of the 4th ICOM group*

126

on wet organic materials conference, 9–16. Bremerhaven: Deutsches Schiffahrtsmuseum.

Collier, A.M. 1970. *A Handbook of Textiles*. Oxford: Pergamon Press.

Collins, K. and Mallinson, J. 1983. *Biology of the Wreck Site*. Unpublished internal report for the Mary Rose Trust.

Corbett, N.H. 1965. Micro-morphological studies on the degradation of lignified cell walls by Ascomycetes and Fungi Imperfecti. *Journal of the Institute of Wood Science* 14, 18–21.

Corfield, M. 1994. The Dover Bronze Age boat. In Hoffmann *et al.* (eds), 1994, 391–400.

Crawford, D. L. and Sutherland, J.B. 1980. Isolation and characterization of lignocellulose-decomposing actinomycetes. In T. K. Kirk, T. Higuchi and H. Chang (eds), *Lignin biodegradation: microbiology, chemistry, and potential applications, vol. II*, 95–101. CRC Press.

Cronyn, J.M. 1996. *The Elements of Archaeological Conservation*. London: Routledge.

Dawson, J.E., Rawindra, R. and Lafontaine, R.H. 1982. A review of storage methods for waterlogged wood. In Grattan and McCawley (eds) 1982, 227–35.

Dean, L.R., Jones, E.B.G. and Jones, A.M. 1994. The stabilisation of ancient waterlogged oak with polyalkylene glycols. In Hoffman *et al.* (eds), 1994, 213–27.

Delaporta, K. and Bound, M. (1993). *A wreck beside the signalo reef outside the main port of Zakynthos, Greece, Preliminary report of 1991–1993*. Tropis.

Droucourt, D. and Morel–Deledalle, M. 1985. Marseille, lyophilisation a la pression atmospherique d'une epave de bateau romain. In Ramiere and Colardelle (eds), 1985, 169–74.

Duncan, G.C. 1961. Relative Aeration Requirements by Soft Rot Basidiomycete Wood Destroying Fungi. U.S. Forestry Service Laboratory Report 2218.

Duncan, G.S. 1969. *Bibliography of Glass*. London: Dawsons.

Duncan, N. 1969. *Engineering Geology and Rock Mechanics Volume 1*. London: Leonard Hill.

Eaton, R.A. and Hale, M.H. (eds). 1993. *Wood. Decay, Pests and Protection*. London: Chapman and Hall.

English Heritage, 1995. *Waterlogged Wood. Guidelines on the Recording, Sampling, Conservation, and Curation of Waterlogged Wood*.

Esau, K. 1953. *Anatomy of Seed Plants*. New York: Wiley International.

Finney, R.W. and Jones, A.M. 1993. Direct analysis of wood preservatives in ancient oak from the *Mary Rose* by laser microprobe mass spectrometry. *Studies in Conservation* 38, 36–44.

Florian, M-L.E. 1987. The underwater environment. In C. Pearson (ed.), *Conservation of Marine Archaeological Objects*, 3–32. London: Butterworth.

Florian, M-L.E., Seccombe-Hett, C.E. and McCawley, J.C. 1978. The physical, chemical, and morphological condition of marine archaeological wood

should dictate the conservation process. In *Papers from the First Southern Hemisphere Conference on Maritime Archaeology, Perth, Western Australia 1977*, 128–44. Melbourne: Ocean's Society of Australia Any editors??

Gambrell, R.P. And Patrick, W.H. Jr. 1978. Chemical and microbiological properties of anaerobic soils and sediments. In D.D. Hook and R.M.M. Crawford (eds), *Plant Life in Anaerobic Environments*, 20–35. Michigan: Science.

Gibson, A. and Woods, A. 1997. *Prehistoric Pottery for the Archaeologist*. London: Leicester University Press.

Goddio, F. 1994. The tale of San Diego. *National Geographic* 186, 35–57.

Grattan, D.W. 1987. Waterlogged wood. In: C. Pearson (ed.), *Conservation of Marine Archaeological Objects*, 55–67. London: Butterworth

Grattan, D.W. and Clarke, R.W. 1987. Conservation of waterlogged wood. In C. Pearson (ed.) 1987, 164–206.

Grattan, D.W. and McCawley, J.C. 1978. The potential of the Canadian winter climate for the freeze drying of degraded waterlogged wood. *Studies in Conservation* 23, 157–67.

Grattan, D.W. and McCawley, J.C. (eds), 1982. *Proceedings of the ICOM Waterlogged Wood Working Group Conference, Ottawa 1981*. Bremerhaven: ICOM.

Grattan, D.W., McCawley, J.C. and Cook, C. 1980. The potential of the Canadian winter climate for the freeze-drying of degraded waterlogged wood. *Studies in Conservation* 25, 118–36.

Gray, J. 1981. *The Ecology of Marine Sediments*. Cambridge: University Press.

Green, J.N. 1975. The VOC ship Batavia wrecked in 1629 on the Houtman Abrolhos, Western Australia. *International Journal of Nautical Archaeology* 4, 43-63.

Gregson, C.W. 1975. Progress on the conservation of the Graveney Boat. In W.A. Oddy (ed.), *Problems of the Conservation of Waterlogged Wood*, 113–14. Greenwich: National Maritime Museum, Maritime Monographs and Reports16.

Gregson, C.W. 1977. Aspects of waterlogged wood conservation. In S. McGrail (ed.), *Sources and Techniques in Boat Archaeology*, 45–53. Oxford: British Archaeological Report S29.

Griffiths, C.J. 1967. *Scientific Method in Analysis of Sediments*. New York: McGraw-Hill.

Hafors, B. 1985. The drying pattern of the outer planking of the Wasa hull. In Ramiere and Colardelle (eds), 1985, 313–26.

Hafors, B. 1990 The role of the Vasa in the development of the Polyethylene Glycol preservation method. In Rowell and Barbour (eds), 1990, 95–216.

Hamilton, D.L. 1996. *Basic Methods of Conserving Underwater Archaeological Material Culture*. Washington DC: Department of Defence.

Harada and Cote, W. 1985. *Exhibition and Storage of Archaeological Wood*.

Harvey and Friedland 1990. In Rowell and Barbour (eds), 399–418.

Hedges, J.I. 1990. The chemistry of archaeological wood. In Rowell and Barbour (eds), 1990, 111–40.

Hickin, N.E. 1968. *The Insect Factor in Wood Decay*. London: Hutchinson.

Higgins, R.A. 1993. *Engineering Metallurgy. Part 1, Applied Physical Mettallurgy* (6th edn). London: Edward Arnold.

Hodges, H. 1968. *Artefacts: an introduction to early materials and technology*. London: John Baker.

Hoffman, P. 1981. Short note on the conservation programme for the Bremen Cog. In L.H. de Vries-Zuiderbaan (ed.), Conservation of Waterlogged Wood. *International Symposium on the Conservation of Large Objects of Waterlogged Wood*, 41–4. The Hague: UNESCO.

Hoffmann, P. 1985. On the stabilisation of waterlogged oakwood with PEG. Molecular size versus degree of degradation. In Ramiere and Colardelle, (eds), 1985, 95–115.

Hoffman, P. and Jones, A.M. 1990. Structure and degradation Process for waterlogged archaeological wood. In Rowell and Barbour (eds), 1990, 35–67.

Hoffmann, P., Daley, T. and Grant, T. (eds), *Proceedings of the 5th ICOM Group on Wet Organic Materials Conference, Portland, Maine, 1993*. Bremerhaven: ICOM.

Holt, D.M. 1981. *Bacterial Breakdown of Timber in Aquatic Habitats and their Relationship with Wood Degrading Fungi*. Ph.D. Thesis, University of Portsmouth.

Horie, C.V. 1983. Reversibility of polymer treatments. In Tate et. al. (eds) chapter 3. Tate et al not in bibliography- what is it

Horie, C.V. 1998. *Materials for Conservation*. London: Architectural Press.

Jenssen, V. and Murdock, L. 1982. Review of the conservation of Machault ships timbers. In Grattan and McCawley (eds), 1982, 42–50.

Jenssen V. and Pearson, C. 1987. Environmental considerations for storage and display of marine finds. In Pearson (ed.), 1987, 268–71.

Jones, A.M. and Rule, M.H. 1991. Preserving the wreck of the *Mary Rose*. In P. Hoffmann (ed.), *Proceedings of the 4th ICOM Group on Wet Organic Archaeological Materials Conference, Bremerhaven 1990*, 25–47. Bremerhaven: ICOM

Jones, A.M., Rule, M.H. and Jones, E.G.B. 1986. Conservation of the timbers of the Tudor warship *Mary Rose*. In Houghton, D.S., Lewellyn, G.G. and O'Rea, C. (eds), *Biodeterioration* 6, 354–62. London: Biodeterioration Society.

Jong, J. de. 1977. Conservation techniques for old archaeological wood from shipwrecks found in the Netherlands. In: A.H. Walters (ed.), *Biodeterioration Investigation Techniques*, 295–338.

Jong, J. de. 1978. The conservation of shipwrecks. *ICOM Committe for Conservation, 5th Triennial Meeting, Zagreb 1978* 78/7/1, 1–10.

Jong, J. de, Eenkhoorn, W. and Wevers, A.J.M. 1981. Controlled drying as an approach to the conservation of shipwrecks. *Proceedings of the ICOM Committee for Conservation 6th Triennial Meeting, Ottawa 1981* 81/7/2, 1–10.

Kaye, B. and Cole-Hamilton, D. 1994. Novel approaches to the conservation of wet wood. In J.A. Spriggs (ed.), *A Celebration of Wood: Proceedings of a Conference held by York Archaeological Wood Centre, York 1993*. York: York Archaeological Wood Centre.

Keene, S. 1982. Waterlogged wood from the City of London. In Grattan and McCawley (eds), 1982, 177–80.

Kendall, K. 1982. *The Gaseous reduction of Archaeological Ironwork. Unpublished PhD Thesis*, Portsmouth Polytechnic.

Kenward, H.K. Hall, A.R. and Jones A.K.G. 1980. A tested set of techniques for the extraction of plant and animal macrofossils from waterlogged archaeological deposits. *Science and Archaeology* 22, 3–15.

Kirk, T.K. 1973. The chemistry and biochemistry of decay. In D.D. Nicholas (ed.), *Wood Deterioration and its Prevention by Preservative Treatments, volume 1: degradation and protection of wood*, 149–81. New York: Syracuse University Press.

Kohlmeyer, J. and Kohlmeyer, E. 1970. *Marine Mycology; The Higher Fungi*. New York: Academic Press.

Kollmann, F.F.P. and Cote, W.A.J. 1968. *Principles of Wood Science and Technology I. Solid Wood*. Berlin: Springer-Verlag.

Kuhne, H. 1966. Uber Beziehungen zwischen *Teredo, Limnoria* and *Chelura. Mat. Org. Beiheft* 1, Holz und Organismen, 447–56.

Kuhne, H. 1971. The identification of wood-boring crusteans. In E.B.G. Jones and S.K. Eltrinham (eds), *Marine Borers, Fungi, and Fouling Organisms of Wood*, 65–88. Paris: O.E.C.D.

Leary, G.J., Morgan, K.R. and Newman, R.H. 1987. Solid-state carbon nuclear magnetic resonance study of *Pinus radiata* wood. *Appita* 40, 181–4.

Levi, M.P. and Preston, R.D. 1965. A chemical and microscopic examination of the action of the soft rot fungus *Chaetonium globossum* on beechwood (*Fagus sylvatica*). *Holzforschung* 19, 183–90.

Levy, J.F. 1982. The place of basidiomycetes in the decay of wood in contact with the ground. In J.C. Frankland, J.N. Hedger and M.J.Swift (eds), *Decomposer Basidiomycetes, their Biology and Ecology*, 161–78. Cambridge: University Press.

Libes, S.M. 1992. *An Introduction to Marine Biogeochemistry*. New York: Wiley

Macfarlane, G.T. and Gibson, G.R. 1991. Sulphate reducing bacteria. In P.N. Levett (ed.), *Anaerobic Microbiology: a practical approach*, 201–22. Oxford: IRL Press.

128

MaCleod, I.D. and North, N.A. 1980. 350 years of marine corrosion in Western Australia. *Corrosion Australasia* 5, 11–15.

Madden, R.H., Bryder, M.J. and Poole, N.J. 1980. The cellulolytic community of an anaerobic estuarine sediment. In W. Palt, P.Chartier and D.O. Hall (eds), *Energy from Biomass, 1st EC conference*, 366–71. London: Applied Science.

McCawley, J.C., Grattan, D.W. and Cook, C. 1982. Some experiments in freeze drying: designing and testing a non-vacuum freeze dryer. In Grattan and McCawley, (eds), 1982, 253–62.

Mouzouras. R. 1990. *Investigation of Microbial Decay of Waterlogged Archaeological Wood*. Final report to SERC. University of Portsmouth.

Mouzouras, R. 1991. *Microbial aspects of strored timbers from the Mary Rose and the decay of wood by marine fungi*. Ph.D Thesis, University of Portsmouth.

Mouzouras, R., Jones, A.M., Jones, E.G.B. and Rule, M.H. 1990. Non destructive evaluation of hull and stored timbers from the Tudor ship *Mary Rose*. *Studies in Conservation* 35, 175–88.

Mouzouras, R., Jones, E.B.G., Venkatasamy, R. and Moss, S.T. 1986. Decay of wood by microorganisms in marine environments. *Rec. Ann. Con. B.W.P.A.*

Muckelroy, K. 1992. *Maritime Archaeology*. Cambridge: University Press.

Muhlethaler, B. (ed). 1973. *Conservation of Waterlogged Wood and Wet Leather*. Paris: Eurolles.

Newton, R. and Davison, S. 1997. *Conservation of Glass*. Oxford: Butterworth-Heinemann.

Nielson, H.O. 1985. The treatment of waterlogged wood from the excavation of the Haithalsu Viking ship. In Ramiere and Colardelle (eds), 1985, 299–312.

Noack, D. 1965. Der gehenwartige Stand der Dimensiosstabilisierung von Holz und Schluss-folgerungen fur die Konservierung der Bremer Kogge. *Bremishes Jahrbuck* 50, 43–72.

North, N.A. and MaCleod, I.D. 1987. Corrosion of metals. In C. Pearson, (ed.), *Conservation of Marine Archaeological Objects*, 68–99. London: Butterworths.

Oddy, W.A. 1972. On the Toxicity of Benzotriazole. *Studies in Conservation* 17.3, 135.

Oddy W.A. 1974. International research on the possible health hazards in the use of Benzotriazole. *Studies in Conservation* 19.3, 188-9.

O'Shea, C., Davies, B., Kendall, K. and Aked, S. 1982. The use of hydrogen reduction in stabilising large iron objects from the sea. In: N.S. Bromelle and G. Thomson (eds), *Science and Technology in the Service of Conservation, Preprints of the Contributions to the Washington Congress, 3-9 September 1982*, 126–9. London: International Institute for Conservation.

Panshin, A.J. and Zeeuw, C. de. 1980. *Textbook of Wood Technology. Structure, Identification, Properties and Uses of the Commercial Woods of the United States and Canada*. London: McGraw-Hill.

Pearson, C. 1979. The use of polyethylene glycol for the treatment of waterlogged wood – its past and future.

In L.H. de Vries-Zuiderbaan, (ed.), *Conservation of Waterlogged Wood. International Symposium on the Conservation of Large Objects of Waterlogged Wood*. The Hague: UNESCO

Pearson, C. 1987. *Conservation of Marine Archaeological Objects*. London: Butterworths

Pitman, A.J. 1994. *The Biology of the Wharf-borer Beetle* Nacerdes melanura *in Waterlogged Timber*. Unpublished Ph.D. Thesis, University of Portsmouth.

Plendelith, H.J. and Werner, A.E.A. 1971. *The Conservation of Antiquities and Works of Art*, 2nd edn. Oxford: University Press.

Pointing, S.B. 1995. *Gamma Irradiation and Reburial as Potential Novel Passive Conservation Treatments for Waterlogged Archaeological Timbers of the* Mary Rose. Unpublished PhD thesis, University of Portsmouth.

Pointing, S.B., Jones, A.M.and Jones, E.G.B. 1997. The wood decay potential of anaerobic marine sediments at the *Mary Rose* excavation site, In P. Hoffmann, T.Grant and T. Daley (eds), *Proceedings of the 6th ICOM Group on Wet Organic Archaeological Materials Conference, York*, 73–91. Bremerhaven: ICOM.

Pollard, A.M. and Heron, C. 1996. *Archaeological Chemistry*. Cambridge: The Royal Society of Chemistry.

Pournou, A.P. 1999. *In-situ Protection and Conservation of the Zakynthos Wreck*. Unpublished PhD thesis, University of Portsmouth.

Ramiere, R and Colardelle, M. (eds) 1985. *Waterlogged Wood: Study and Conservation. Proceedings of the 2nd ICOM Waterlogged Wood Working Group Conference, Grenoble 1984*. Bremerhaven: CETBGE–CENG ORIS.

Robinson, W. 1981. The wreck laws, *The Conservator* 5

Robinson, W. 1998. *First Aid for Underwater Finds*. London: Archetype.

Robertson. M.E. 1957. *Hides, Skins and Leather under the Microscope*. British Leather Manufacturers Research Association.

Rowell, R.M. and Barbour, R.J. (eds). 1990. *Archaeological Wood. Properties, Chemistry and Preservation*. Washington DC: American Chemical Society.

Rule, M.H. 1983. *The* Mary Rose, *the Excavation and Raising of Henry VIII's Flagship*. Leicester: Windward.

Sangstrom, M., Jaliliehvand, F., Persson, I., Gelius, U. and Frank P. 2002. Acidity and salt precipitation on the *Vasa*: the sulfur problem. In P. Hoffmann, J. Spriggs, T. Grant, C. Cook and A. Recht (eds), *Proceedings of the 8th OICOM Group on Wet Organic Archaeological Materials Conference*. Bremerhaven: ICOM

Savory, J.G. 1954. Breakdown of timbers by ascomyces and Fungi imperfecti. *Annals of Applied Biology* 41, 336–47.

Sawada, M. 1985. Some problems of setting PEG 4000 impregnated wood. In Ramiere and Colardelle (eds), 1985, 117–24.

Scheffer, T.C. 1973. Microbiological degradation and the causal orgamisms, In D.D. Nicholas (ed.), *Wood*

Deterioration and its Prevention by Preservative Treatments, Volume 1: degradation and protection of wood, 31–106. New York: Syracuse University Press.

Schniewind, P.A. 1990. Physical and mechanical properties of archaeological wood. In Rowell and Barbour (eds), 1990, 87–110.

Schweingruber, S.H. 1978. *Microscopic Wood Anatomy.* Birmensdorf: Swiss Federal Institute of Forestry Research.

Schweizer, F. 1994. Bronze objects from lake sites: from patina to 'biography'. In D.A. Scott, J. Podany and B.B. Considine (eds), *Ancient and Historic Metals: conservation scientific research,* 31–50. New York: Getty Conservation Institute.

Schweizer, F., Houriet, C. and Mas, M. 1985 Controlled air drying of large Roman timber from Geneva. In Ramiere and Colardelle (eds), 1985, 327–38.

Seifert, B. and Jagels, R. 1985. Conservation of the Ronson ship's bow. In Ramiere and Colardelle (eds), 1985, 269–97.

Shrew, L.L., Jarman, R.A. and Burstein, G.T. 1994. *Corrosion* (3rd edn). Oxford: Butterworth-Heinemann.

Siau, J.F. 1971. *Flow in Wood.* New York: Syracuse University Press.

Singh, A.P. and Kim, Y.S. 1997. Biodegradation of Wood in Wet Environments: a review. International Research Group on Wood Preservation, Document IRG/WP 97-1021.

Singley, K.R. 1982. The recovery and conservation of the Brown's ferry vessel. In Grattan and McCawley (eds), 1982, 57–66.

Skaar, C. 1988. *Wood – Water Relations.* Berlin: Springer-Verlag.

Stamm, A.J. 1956. Dimensional stabilization of wood with carbowaxes. *Forest Products Journal* 6, 201–4.

Stamm, A.J. 1964. Factors affecting the bulking and dimensional stabilization of wood with polyethylene glycol. *Forest Products Journal* 14, 403–8.

Squirrel, J.P. and Clarke, R.W. 1987 An investigation into the condition and conservation of the hull of the *Mary Rose.* Part 1: assessment of the hull timbers. *Studies in Conservation* 32, 153–62.

Siu, R.G.H. 1951. *Microbial degradation of Cellulose.* Rheinhold, New York.

Thompson, G. 1978. *The Museum Environment.* Boston: Butterworth.

Titus, L. 1982. Conservation of wooden artifacts. In Grattan and McCawley (eds), 1982, 153–8.

Tran, Q.K., Hiron, X. and Damery, E. 1997. Treatment of a neolithic dugout canoe from Paris – Bercy: Controlled drying after PEG impregnation and attempt at modelling of the drying process. In: P. Hoffmann, T. Grant, J.A. Spriggs and T. Daley (eds), *Proceedings of the 6th ICOM Group on Wet Organic Archaeological Materials Conference, York, 1996,* 569–82. Bremerhaven: ICOM.

Tretheway, K.R. and Chmberlain, J. 1995. *Corrosion for Science and Engineering* (2nd edn). Harlow: Longman.

Turner, R.D. 1966. *A Survey and Illustrated Catalogue of Teredinidae (Mollusca:Bivalvia).* Harvard University Museum of Comparative Zoology.

Turgoose, S. 1982. The nature of surviving iron objects. In: R.W. Clarke and S.M. Blackshaw (eds), *Conservation of Iron,* 8–12. London: National Maritime Museum Maritime Monographs and Reports 53.

Tylecote, R.F. 1962. *Metallurgy in Archaeology.* London: Edward Arnold

United Kingdon Institute for Conservation. 1986. *Guidance for Conservation Practice.* London: UKIC

United Kingdon Institute for Conservation. 1999. Code of Ethics and Rules of Practice. In: *UKIC Members Handbook.* London: UKIC

Van der Heide, G.D. 1972. Wrecks, as ancient monuments. In *Underwater Archaeology; a Nascent Discipline,* 161–74. Paris UNESCO.

Van der Heide, G.D. 1981. Considerations regarding the Amsterdam as an historic monument. In L.H. de Vries-Zuiderbaan (ed.), *Conservation of Waterlogged Wood. International Symposium on the Conservation of Large Objects of Waterlogged Wood,* 376–80. The Hague: UNESCO.

Waddell, P. 1986. The disassembly of a 16th century galleon. *International Journal of Nautical Archaeology* 15, 137–48.

Walker, R., Dunham, R.. Hildred, A. and Rule, M. 1989. Analytical study of composite shot from the *Mary Rose. Journal of the Historical Metallurgy Society* 23.2, 84-9.

Watson, K.L. 1998. *Foundation Science for Engineers.* Basingstoke: Macmillan.

Wheeler, E.A., Baas, P. and Gasson P.E. (eds) 1989. *IAWA List of Microscopic Features for Hardwood Identification.* Leiden: International Association of Wood Anatomists, reprint from *IAWA Bulletin* ns 10. 3, 219–332.

Witte, de, Tervfe, E. and Vynche, J. 1984. The consolidation of the waterlogged wood from the Gallo-Roman boats of Pommeroeul. *Studies in Conservation* 29, 77–83.

Appendix 1: Details of *Mary Rose* Conservation Facilities

Equipment for a Conservation laboratory

Basic laboratory furniture

The laboratory needs to have wet and dry areas to allow wet finds to be kept away from dry objects and documentation areas. Benches should be free standing to allow flexibility in layout when required.

- Light duty work bench, vinyl covering, 1200 x 700mm.
- Similar bench containing cupboard and drawers
- Chairs: polypropylene swivel type.
- Cupboards etc. for storage of materials and equipment.
  cupboards, 800 x 1000 x 300mm.
  five-drawer unit 1m wide.
- Large sinks for washing objects.
- Fume extraction cupboard, and possibly also local extraction hoods at work benches.
- Lockable, fireproof cupboard for solvent storage, 710 x910 x480 mm.

Security and emergency planning

Security
- Security system with locks, bars on windows, burglar alarms and security lighting as appropriate

Fire alarm system
- control system
- smoke detectors
- break glass alarm
- fire extinguishers, CO_2 type

- Backup electricity generators in case electricity fails, to maintain freezers and refrigerated stores - THIS IS VITAL IF ELECTRICAL SUPPLY IS UNRELIABLE.

Materials and equipment for lifting artefacts from the sea bed

- Chloridometer (see equipment list) for measuring salinity.
- Polyethylene garden plant tags for labelling.
- Pentel N50 permanent markers for labelling.
- Polypropylene twine for attaching labels.

- Non ferrous nails for labelling timbers, eg brass panel pins.
- Water resistant bags or boxes for raising several small items at once eg. perforated 36litre plastic stacking boxes.
- Netlon Mini Mesh 10 tubing (Netlon Ltd) two reels of 2000m.
- Grip seal polythene bags.
- Scaffolding poles, angle irons and planks suitable for supporting large objects/timbers.
- Hoists or winches (could be supplied by a contractor).
- Water absorbent padding materials for objects, eg synthetic foam, and other padding, eg polystyrene foam, expanded polyurethane foam, bubble pak (depending on the type of support required).
- Strapping material for securing objects to supports eg. 200m polyester strapping, dispenser and 80 buckles in kit.
- Adequate tanks and lidded plastic containers, or sealed waterproof polythene bags (see equipment list) must be provided at the surface because all finds MUST be kept wet until they can be conserved.

Preliminary storage facilities for wet finds

Preliminary storage could either be in wet tanks or in a refrigerated store. Biological deterioration could be a major problem for stored wet finds awaiting treatment. Although this can be controlled by adding biocides to storage solutions in tanks, biocides contaminate the objects and reduce the possibilities for analysis. Refrigerated storage will reduce the need for biocides, though some biocides may still be needed.

- Refrigerated containers, perhaps from a cargo ship, which could stand outdoors. Otherwise a cool dark building to keep the finds.
- Large tanks for large finds, preferably with lids to exclude light, made from plastic or mild steel to resist alkaline storage solutions.
- A range of smaller plastic lidded tanks and containers for small finds. Lidded plastic containers 10–30litre capacity.
- For large timbers if tanks are not available, waterproof barrier foil, eg 70 Nylon/125I, Surlyn; T1-19v; T1-25x; Camvac or 20 Nylon/60

Polyethylene. The type of foil is very important to prevent insects such as wharf borer from penetrating the wrappings of stored material.

- Cryovac 570Y perforated polyolefin film for fragile objects, which allows objects to remain visible, yet in the same packaging throughout storage and treatment, reducing damage from handling.
- Water absorbent foam or similar to provide wet padding if required.
- Heat sealer, portable with 300mm seal length
- Appropriate metal shelving
  shelving angle iron packs (5x3m irons)
  nuts and bolts for shelving
  corner plates
  metal shelves.
- Hosepipes, 30m including tap connector and nozzle.
- Fungicides, eg borax and boric acid; bactericides, eg quaternary ammonium salts, and insecticides in case of infestation by wharf borer etc, eg primethrin. If possible use alternatives like fresh water perch or pond snails for killing bacterial growth.
- Sodium sesquicarbonate to add to iron and copper object storage solutions (see chemicals list).
- Weighing scales, measuring jugs and scoops for making up solutions (see equipment list).
- Freezer for storing organic samples, or very fragile non-wood organic items (see equipment list).
- Crane and/or forklift truck and cradles for moving large timbers and cannons etc around (see equipment list; could also be supplied by contractors).

Conservation equipment

- Freezers for use before freeze-drying.
- Vacuum freeze dryers.
- Heatable PEG treatment tanks. Must be made from mild or stainless steel to resist corrosion by PEG. The tanks can also be used for alkaline sulphite reduction of less corroded iron. Pumps to allow circulation and filtration of PEG are good if reliable ones can be found, but are optional.
- Humidifier with humidistat for controlled air drying of objects, + electric fan to ensure good air mixing during drying. Humidifier with humidistat: Consult supplier for appropriate model.
- Electric fan with 360° tilt
- Equipment for electrolysis of iron, ie mild steel tank; rectifier-transformer working from normal a.c. mains supply, with controllable output of up to 150amps at 6V; insulated electric cable for connections; supply of mild steel sheet to make connectors and anodes.

- Acid resistant tank for chemical stripping of copper alloys, eg concrete or mild steel lined with plastic.
- Still for distilling water, Merit W4000.
- Tanks for desalinating objects, eg household water tanks.
- Balance for weighing samples etc to within 0.01g
- Balance for weighing larger objects (up to 6.1kg) to within 0.1g.
- Scoop for measuring powders for solutions.
- Lifting equipment for large objects (see preliminary storage list).
- Trolleys for transporting small objects, eg three shelf trolley
- Chloridometer for analysis of chloride levels during treatment of iron, Cu alloy, etc. Must be accurate at least to within 2ppm.
- Conductivity meter for measuring salt levels during desalination of ceramics.
- pH meter, eg Hanna Checker.
- Tools for removing concretions
  lump hammers
  dental picks
  vibro tools.
- Oven for moisture content analysis.
- Hot plate, ceramic.
- Hot air blower, Finesse MK4.
- Heat gun, Bosch.
- Magnetic stirrer.
- Glassware
  pyrex beakers in various sizes
  test tubes, 75mm borosilicate glass.
- Watch glasses.
- Measuring cylinders.
- Squeezey plastic bottles for washing fragile objects.
- General conservation tools, eg
  assorted paintbrushes (see preservation equipment)
  scalpels
  scalpel blades
  tweezers
  disposable pipettes
  disposable syringes
  syringe needles
  clamps (can also use pegs, etc).
- Fibre bristle brushes for scrubbing metals during chemical treatments .
- Rotary saw for sawing wood samples or concretions
  fine toothed blades.
- Reference books, articles and other sources.
- Workshop floor crane.
- Flatbed trolley, 1530 x 760mm, 500kg capacity.
- Mechanical plastic pump for removing PEG from barrels.

Support materials for conservation

- Volara polyethylene foam 25 foot roll.
- Ethafoam polythene foam 100 x 300 x 600mm (4in x 12in x 24in) planks.
- Melinex polyester film 20m roll.
- Coroplast 1520 x 1010mm.
- Acid free tissue.
- Mesh in different grades for supporting objects before and after treatment. Mesh to be used during treatment must be resistant to treatment solutions, eg. Terram Geotextile. Conservation fly mesh netting.
- Polyethylene sheeting.
- Plastic trays for supporting during washing.

Chemicals for conservation

- Polyethylene glycol in low and high grades
  PEG200
  PEG400
  PEG4000
  PEG6000.
- Glycerol for leather treatment.
- Sodium hydroxide for electrolysis of metals, especially iron.
- Citric acid and thiourea for chemical stripping of bronzes.
- Sodium sulphite to make alkaline sulphite for washing iron after electrolysis.
- Sodium sesquicarbonate for storage, washing bronzes after stripping, etc.
- Microcrystalline wax for coating iron and lead.
- Paraloid B72 resin.
- Paraloid B67
  PVAC emulsion
- HMG cellulose nitrate adhesive.
- Corrosion inhibitors for metals
  eg. Benzotriazole for copper alloy
  Incralac coating lacquer
  fumed silica matting agent.
- Synperonic N non-ionic detergent for cleaning artefacts.
- Acetone.
- IMS.
- Toluene.
- Materials for removing concretions on different types of artefacts
  Hydrochloric acid
  Nitric acid
  Disodium EDTA (for lead).

Monitoring equipment during treatment

- Incremental corer for taking core samples of waterlogged wood.

- HPLC for measuring PEG concentrations in core samples (this is only really necessary if a large hull is being conserved). Alternatively timbers can be weighed periodically.
- Two refractometers for measuring concentrations of PEG in impregnating solutions
  Leica Brix 0–50% RFA600-030S
  Leica Brix 50–90% RFA600-041N.
- Thermometers, range 1–105°C.
- Agar biological slides for measuring microbial activity in storage and treatment solutions.

Health and safety equipment for personnel

- Overalls.
- Disposable gloves.
- Heavy duty plastic gauntlets.
- Goggles to protect against splashes, etc.
- Disposable dust masks.
- Organic vapour respirator.
- Steelcapped rubber safety boots.
- First aid kit.
- Eye wash station.

Storage facilities for conserved objects

These are very important. If conserved artefacts cannot be kept in controlled humidity conditions, damage will ensue. PEG treatments for wood are not suitable if objects are to be exposed to high humidities after conservation.

- Secure, weatherproof building required, with separate areas for organic artefacts and metals if possible.
- Shelves/racking/drawers for objects. These should be made of metal NOT wood, eg metal shelving, etc (see preliminary storage list).
- Climate control equipment for storage area. Organic objects treated with PEG should be maintained around 55% RH, metals should be maintained at as low an RH as possible, at least below 40%. Composite objects should be kept between 45–50%. Temperature should be kept to around 20°C or less if possible (see Chapter 9). Dehumidifiers and humidifiers will be needed in the storage areas. The storage area should be well insulated and have no windows to prevent solar heating, and could be underground. All these measures would keep temperature in the stores low. Alternatively if running costs can be met, full air conditioning could be provided.
- If metals cannot be stored separately from organic objects, a supply of airtight polypropylene containers and desiccating silica gel are needed. Large objects can be encased in sealed polythene containers with silica gel. Humidity in the

surrounding area should then be maintained to
suit the organic artefacts.

- Stewart polypropylene boxes.
- Blue indicating silica gel.
- Humidity indicator strips for containers.
- Climate monitoring equipment. If computerised:
  temperature and humidity monitors
  calibration salts
  software and computer.
  Alternatively traditional monitoring equipment
  can be used:
  thermohygrograph
  calibration kit
  year supply of replacement charts
  two replacement pens
  sling hygrometer
  wicks for sling hygrometer.
- Materials to make coverings for objects to keep
  them dust free:
  Tyvek sheet, 25m roll
  polyethylene tubing.
- Insect traps for monitoring pests.

Equipment for analysis

- X-ray cabinet for examining concretions, metals,
  etc. X-ray film and facilities for developing X-rays,
  namely darkroom, tanks, developer, fixer and stop
  bath, special clips for X-ray film, or an X-ray
  cabinet where images are displayed on a screen.
- Microscopes: low powered with reflecting light for
  examining finds and to help some conservation
  work
  Leica GZ6 with swing arm stand, x10-22.
- Microscopes: transmitted light up to x100
  magnification for identifying wood and fibres, etc.
  A useful extra would be to have an attachment
  allowing photos to be taken through the
  microscope
  Leica Galen III
  camera attachment (camera not included).
- Microscope slides.
- Cover slips.
- Digital calipers.
- Glass sample vials.

Documentation

- Computerised or failing this a paper based system
  for recording all conservation treatments. The
  system should be cross-referenced with other
  documentation of the site.
- Cameras, tripods, lights, etc for photographing
  objects (alternatively a digital camera which is
  compatible with computers in the laboratory).

Appendix 2: Processing and Storage of Environmental Samples and Materials

by Julie Gardiner

This appendix gives a very brief outline of the processing and storage methods employed for environmental samples and materials excavated from the *Mary Rose*. It is based on archive information provided by Peter Boyd, Ian Oxley, R.G. Stewart and A. Naylor, and on more recent information provided by Frank Green and Michael J. Allen. A full discussion will appear in *AMR* volume 4.

No targeted sampling strategy for the recovery of environmental data was implemented during the early seasons of excavation of the *Mary Rose*. Although it is an integral part of any archaeological research design for excavation on land or underwater today, a detailed sampling programme was a rare thing in the 1970s, and virtually unheard of for an underwater site. From 1980, however, a set of general aims and objectives was established with sampling focused towards 1) elucidating the economic and social background of the ship and 2) understanding the past and present micro-environments within and around the wreck site. An outline strategy and set of procedures was drawn up.

Some 3533 samples were taken. These included bulk samples of sediments, of concentrations of animal and fish bones, of material associated with a variety of ships fittings, such as rigging elements and ropes, and with cultural material such as shoes, baskets, 'straw' and barrels. The decision to sample underwater was largely based on the observation of the diver that there was an unusual deposit or one of specific interest or association that might contribute to one or both of the two themes mentioned above. General samples to enable characterisation of the sedimentary layers within and over the wreck were also taken, including several sample columns. Once excavated, objects raised complete were emptied of their contents and many more samples for analysis were thus obtained, for instance from the Barber-surgeon's medical containers and from personal chests.

The primary/bulk samples obtained underwater were generally taken in rigid plastic containers, ranging from 1 litre 'ice cream' cartons to 10 litre tubs with clip top lids. The samples were not subject to chemical preservation treatments and relied on being kept wet and stored in cool conditions to minimise decay. Some samples were subsequently transferred for storage to a wide range of plastic and glass sample tubes, plastic clip top and other containers. Many of these containers required regular inspection to top up their water content.

The intended programme of processing and analysis of the environmental material suffered severely from lack of funds and staff. Specialist staff were not available 'in house' and little funding was available to employ external specialists. Nevertheless, some analyses were undertaken as part of research projects, usually through University or Polytechnic departments. The work was, however, conducted piecemeal as and when personnel, funding and/or an appropriate research topic were available and by no means all of the samples have yet been processed or analysed.

Processing and storage methods for various classes of material recovered from the samples are outlined below.

Inorganic remains (sediment, stone, etc)

These samples were wet sieved at various mesh sizes and the resulting residues air dried and stored in sealed polythene bags.

Fish/animal/human bone

Small bones, especially of fish, are easily missed in hand excavation and samples were taken where human or probable food remains were encountered in order to recover the smaller elements. Material was wet sieved with a minimum mesh size of 1mm and hand sorted. Bone was air dried and stored in cardboard boxes (see Chapter 6).

Textiles

Samples associated with items of clothing were expected to contain hair, fibres and textile fragments. The samples were gently washed through to remove sediment (see Chapter 7 above) and fragments stored in 50–100% IMS. Solutions above 50% were found to cause leaching of any surviving colours.

Leather

Many small fragments of leather were recovered from samples. These samples were treated as for texile samples and the leather stored in IMS (see Chapter 6).

Plant remains

Plant remains were recovered largely by flotation with material collected in a 250 micron sieve and transferred to sample tubes containing 50–100% IMS. Solutions below 50% resulted in the expansion of a black, slimy organic product and hydrogen sulphide. Solutions much above 50% caused leaching of colour surviving in, for instance, 'grass', that was still quite green in colour when recovered. The residues were also water-sieved using a 250 micron sieve and then the archaeobotanical and other material was transferred to plastic boxes. From 1984 some botanical material was stored in an alcohol-glycerine formalin solution (AGF) (cf. Kenward *et al.* 1980). However, the AGF solution had to be removed before analysis could take place. Botanical material extracted for analysis since 1996–7 has been stored in IMS. Oak leaves were recovered from the Hold and these were found to remain in a flexible condition stored in distilled water. Some seed pods (eg peppercorns) and fruit stones were successfully air or freeze dried for display purposes.

Insects

Insects extracted from floated samples were stored in 100% IMS. A few were successfully air dried for display purposes.

Pollen and other scientific analyses

Some samples were processed for the extraction of pollen, the examination of animal fats, and for various forms of chemical analysis. These involved specialised processing procedures that were carried out by the relevant analysts.

Index

by Barbara Hird

THE MARY ROSE TRUST

Formed in 1979, the Mary Rose Trust has responsibility for the unique and most remarkable historical collection, which is of national and international importance. The Trust set itself the following objectives and Mission Statement:-

Objectives

- To find, record, excavate, raise, bring ashore, preserve, publish, report on and display for all time in Portsmouth the *Mary Rose*.
- To establish, equip and maintain a museum or museums in Portsmouth to house the *Mary Rose* and related or associated material.
- To promote and develop interest, research and knowledge relating to the *Mary Rose* and all matters relating to the underwater cultural heritage.
- All for the education and benefit of the nation.

Mission Statement

- An international museum of Tudor life and a recognised centre of excellence for maritime archaeology and the conservation of material recovered from underwater.
- Recognised nationally and internationally as a centre for innovation in education and life-long learning.
- Recognised as a major contributor to the economic and cultural well-being of the region.

Since its opening to the public in 1983, over six million visitors have come to enjoy and learn from the *Mary Rose* and its museum.

The excavation and raising of the *Mary Rose* has provided us with a wealth of information of enormous value to specialists, students of all ages, and the general visitor alike. The Trust has, since its very beginnings, embraced the responsibility this implies for making the hull, artefacts and archive physically and intellectually accessible to all. Every year graduate and undergraduate students benefit from the knowledge and expertise of the Trust's archaeologists and conservation team. Many thousands of school pupils visit the museum and the ship and more than half of them take part in special additional activities led by museum staff and volunteers. Nor is the general visitor forgotten. Full use is made of interactive displays, costumed interpreters, replicas, re-enactors and experimental archaeology in order to make sure that the *Mary Rose* offers all visitors a positive learning experience – accessible, enjoyable and memorable. The Trust takes pride in the success and popularity of its website and delivers a programme of outreach designed to given the local community in Portsmouth a greater sense of their involvement in the history of this remarkable ship. Further afield the Mary Rose Information Group is a national network of volunteers who lecture on the subject.

The knowledge of the science of conservation continues to expand and the Trust is at the forefront of new and exciting techniques. Institutions and organisations, both national and international, approach the Trust for help through the Mary Rose Archaeological Services Company. Additionally, the Trust is supported in its aims by the Mary Rose Trading Company, which provides a first class shopping experience founded on the unique *Mary Rose* brand. All profits are returned to further the work of the Trust.

There is much more information on the Trust to be found on the award winning website:-

www.maryrose.org

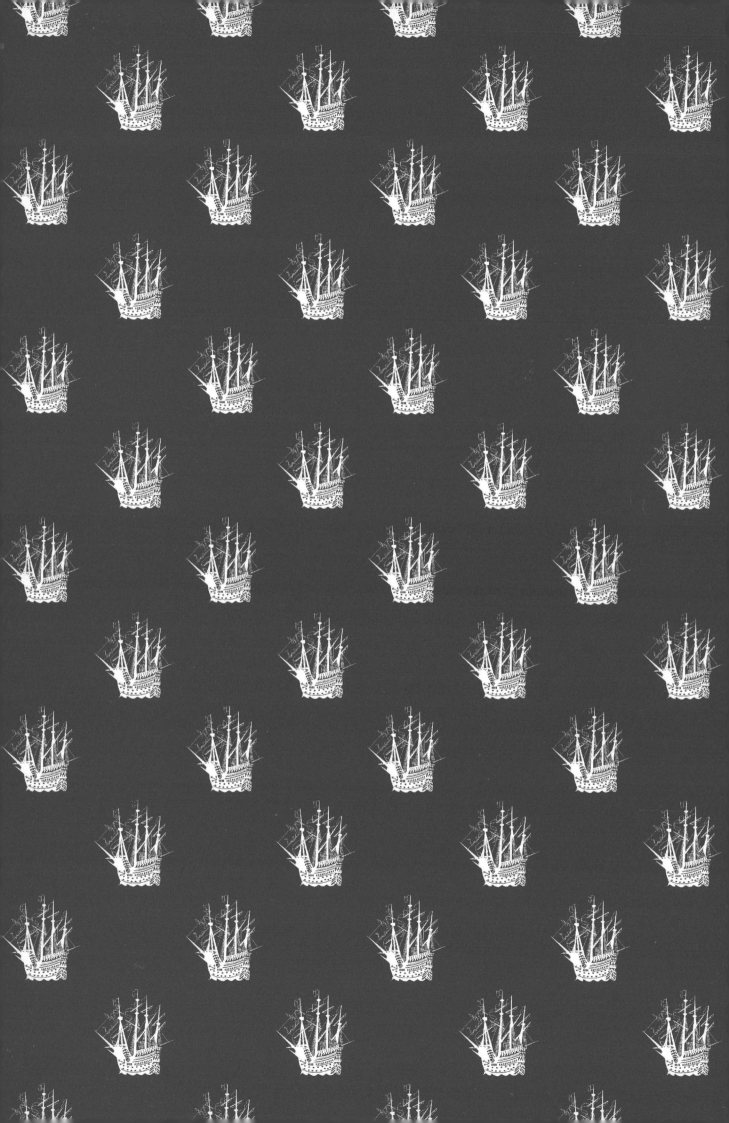